a new genealogical atlas of ireland

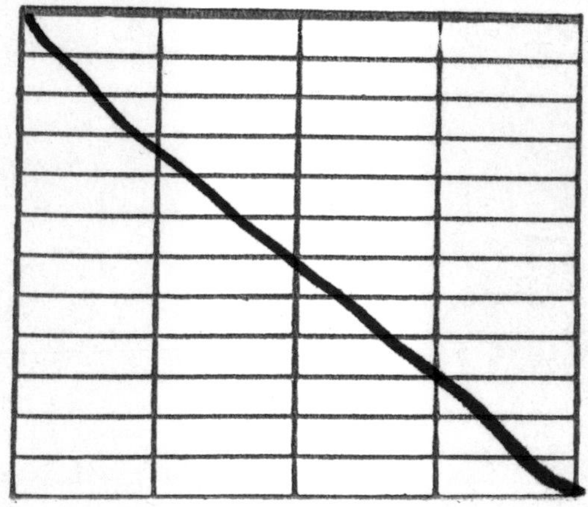

a new genealogical atlas of ireland

Brian Mitchell

GENEALOGICAL PUBLISHING CO., INC.

Baltimore *1988*

Second Printing 1988
Library of Congress Catalogue Card Number 85-82530
International Standard Book Number 0-8063-1152-5
Made in the United States of America

INTRODUCTION

Ancestral research in Ireland requires familiarity with historical records and an understanding of how these records are organized. The geographical dimension in Irish genealogy is of the utmost importance, as historical records were gathered by various administrative divisions. Books such as *Irish and Scotch-Irish Ancestral Research,* by Margaret Dickson Falley (1962; repr. by Genealogical Publishing Company, Baltimore, 1981) and *Irish Genealogy—A Record Finder,* edited by Donal Begley (Heraldic Artists Ltd., Dublin, 1981) have described in great detail both the nature of the records available and the administrative divisions.

It is intended that this volume of maps be used in conjunction with the *General Alphabetical Index to the Townlands and Towns, Parishes and Baronies of Ireland* (Alexander Thom, Dublin, 1861; repr. by Genealogical Publishing Company, Baltimore, 1984). This book will identify the county, barony, parish and poor law union of every townland in Ireland. The townland is the smallest and most ancient of Irish land divisions, and its identification is essential to researchers who wish to pinpoint the precise origin of their ancestors. The townland was named at an early period, and it usually referred to a very identifiable landmark in the local area such as a mountain, a bog, an oak forest, a village, a fort or a church. The townland became standardized as a basic division in the seventeenth-century surveys by people with little knowledge of the Irish language. As a consequence many place names were either lost or had their meaning or construction altered. A record of townland names, shapes and sizes for all Ireland exists in the Maps of the Ordnance Survey completed in 1846 at the scale of six inches to one mile. There are 60,462 townlands in Ireland. It is not within the scope of this volume to map townlands.

It is, however, the intention of this atlas to locate six major administrative divisions; namely, counties, baronies, civil parishes, dioceses, poor law unions and probate districts. All main record sources are organized by at least one of these divisions.

Major Administrative Divisions of Ireland

County

This division reflects the imposition of the English system of local government in Ireland. Begun in the twelfth century, the thirty-two county framework was completed with the creation of Wicklow in 1606. County boundaries usually reflected the lordships of major Gaelic families. The four provinces of Ireland—Ulster, Connaught, Munster and Leinster—owe their origin to the pre-eminence of the families O'Neill (Ulster), O'Connor (Connaught), O'Brien (Munster) and Mac Murrough (Leinster). It was these families that strived for the High Kingship of all Ireland in the centuries before the Norman invasion of the twelfth century. The Irish families reflected in the county divisions owed allegiance to these provincial kings.

Barony

This is now an obsolete division, but in the nineteenth century it was widely used. There were 331 baronies and they also tended to reflect the holdings of Irish clans. Baronies and counties became established in the government land surveys of the seventeenth century.

Poor Law Union

Under the Poor Relief Act, 1838, Ireland was divided into districts or "unions" in which the local rateable inhabitants were to be financially responsible for the care of all paupers in their areas. These unions, which didn't respect county boundaries, were usually centered on a large market town. By 1850, 163 unions had been created. The Local Government (Ireland) Act, 1898, adopted the poor law union as the basic administrative division in place of the civil parish and barony. The poor law unions of Ireland were subdivided into 829 registration districts and 3,751 district electoral divisions. Townlands were now arranged according to these divisions, with parishes and baronies being retained only as a means to make comparisons with records gathered before 1898.

Civil Parish

From the seventeenth century the so-called civil parish, based on the early Christian and medieval monastic and church settlements, was used extensively in various surveys. By the mid-nineteenth century the pattern of civil parishes was well established. By 1841 the population of Ireland had risen to 8,175,124 and this was reflected in changing parish boundaries. New parishes were created by either subdividing larger ones or by withdrawing townlands from adjoining parishes. For example, in 1765 Montiaghs Parish in County Armagh was separated from Seagoe Parish, while in County Londonderry Carrick Parish was created in 1846 by withdrawing eleven townlands from the adjoining parishes—three from Balteagh, three from Bovevagh and five from Tamlaght Finlagan. The civil parish essentially covered the same area as the established Church of Ireland. The Roman Catholic Church, owing to the Reformation of the sixteenth century, had to adapt itself to a new structure centered on towns and villages. The parishes depicted in this volume, 2,508 in all, are civil parishes. Civil Parishes frequently break both barony and county boundaries, indicating they were drawn up at an earlier period.

Dioceses

Three ecclesiastical synods—Cashel in 1101, Rathbreasail in 1111 and Kells in 1152—imposed a diocesan organization of four provinces: Armagh, Cashel, Dublin and Tuam, each headed by an archbishop and under them twenty-two bishops in charge of as many dioceses. These diocesan boundaries have remained virtually constant to the present day and are in use by both the Catholic and Anglican Churches. The number of dioceses has, however, varied with consolidation through time by both the Catholic and Anglican Churches. Dioceses have little or no relation to the boundaries of the counties, the latter having been created long after the dioceses. It is the Church of Ireland dioceses, as existing in the mid-nineteenth century, that are mapped here. Until 1834 the dioceses of the Church of Ireland were grouped into four provinces. The number of provinces was then reduced to two, Armagh and Dublin.

Probate Districts

In 1858 a principal registry and eleven district registries were established for the purpose of proving wills and granting administrations.

The Griffith's Valuation, undertaken between 1848 and 1864, is a record of extreme importance as no census material of the nineteenth century survives for many parishes in Ireland. As this survey was carried out to determine the amount of tax each person should pay towards the support of the poor within their poor law union, it was organized by poor law union, civil parish, barony and county.

Tithe Books were compiled by civil parish in the period from 1823 to 1837 and they list all tenants who paid tithe—a tax based on the size and quality of a tenant's farm—to the Established Church. Again owing to the patchy survival of census records, this record gives a very valuable insight into rural Ireland before the famine.

Early Nineteenth-Century Census Records. The few census records that survive for the years 1821, 1831, 1841 and 1851 were organized by barony and civil parish. Remnants of the 1821 census survive for County Cavan, while the returns for nearly all parishes in County Londonderry in 1831 still exist. Hardly any returns for 1841 survive, while a few parish returns in County Antrim for 1851 are intact.

Eighteenth-Century Census Returns, such as that of 1766 carried out by the Church of Ireland clergy, were compiled by parishes. These Church of Ireland parishes virtually match the boundaries of the civil parishes.

Seventeenth-Century Surveys, such as the Civil Survey of Ireland carried out between 1654 and 1656, were arranged by county, barony and parish. Perhaps the most useful seventeenth-century record is the Hearth Money Roll, which exists in full for the Ulster counties of Antrim, Armagh, Donegal, Fermanagh, Londonderry, Monaghan and Tyrone. Compiled by parish, these rolls were drawn up between 1663 and 1666 to list all householders who had a fireplace, which was liable to a tax of two shillings.

Wills with their tendency to list surviving relatives—brothers, sisters, children and even grandchildren—are very important documents. The limitation of wills is that before the twentieth century few people—usually the better off, such as farmers and merchants—made wills. From the time of the Reformation in 1536 until 1858 ecclesiastical courts of the Church of Ireland based in each diocese were responsible for all matters of probate. To identify a will, therefore, it is necessary to determine in which Church of Ireland diocese the family lived. If the deceased had property valued at more than £5 in a second diocese the will had to be proved or the administration granted in the Prerogative Court presided over by the Archbishop of Armagh. Only the indexes to these wills, not the wills themselves, have survived.

The Court of Probate and Letters of Administration Act (Ireland), 1857, transferred testamentary jurisdiction to a principal registry in Dublin and eleven district registries covering the remainder of the country. Those wills or administrations concerned with property in more than one district were proved in the principal registry. With printed volumes, called calendars, existing for every year from 1858 it is an easy matter to identify wills proven and administrations granted.

Parish Registers are the records people tend to associate with genealogy. Which register to search depends on the residence and religion of the ancestor. The record of parishes in this volume is of civil parishes and not ecclesiastical. However, by use of *A Topographical Dictionary of Ireland,* by Samuel Lewis (London, 1837; repr. by Genealogical Publishing Company, Baltimore, 1984), it is possible to locate all churches within their civil parishes. The civil parish or parishes covered by each Catholic parish is likewise listed. It is therefore possible, by using the civil parish maps produced in this volume in conjunction with the *Topographical Dictionary,* to identify the area covered by Catholic parishes. In addition, Lewis' *Dictionary* gives a brief description of the geography, history, agriculture and industry of every civil parish in Ireland.

In the absence of parish registers Marriage License Bonds are a useful tool in identifying marriages. Marriage bonds were under the jurisdiction of the Church of Ireland, and before the Bishop would grant a license for a proposed marriage he required a guarantee or bond that there was no impediment to the marriage. The indexes to these bonds are compiled by diocese and arranged alphabetically by the name of the groom.

With the introduction of Civil Registration for Protestant marriages from April 1845, and births, deaths and Roman Catholic marriages from January 1864, the identification of a birth, marriage or death becomes very feasible. Access to these records is through indexes arranged by year in which the only information given is the name of the person and the poor law union in which the event was registered. To use these indexes effectively a knowledge of the areas served by each union is essential.

★ ★ ★ ★

The sources used in compiling this volume include *Irish County Maps Showing the Location of Churches* for the four provinces of Ireland (Church of Jesus Christ of Latter-day Saints, 1977) and the county maps accompanying the *Index of Surnames of Householders in Griffith's Primary Valuation and Tithe Applotment Books* by the National Library of Ireland, together with the *General Alphabetical Index to the Townlands and Towns, Parishes and Baronies of Ireland,* based on the census of 1851 and printed in 1861 by Alexander Thom, Dublin (repr. by Genealogical Publishing Company, Baltimore, 1984). In addition, the dioceses are based on Table 147 accompanying *The General Report to the Census of Ireland* for the year 1901 (H.M.S.O., Dublin, 1902). The diocesan boundaries tabled in the 1901 census were those as legally recognized prior to the Irish Church Act, 1869. The "Ecclesiastical Directory" of *Thom's Irish Almanac* of 1854, which lists the established Church of Ireland dioceses, was also consulted. The probate districts are those shown on the map and table of district registries in Appendix 11 to the *Third Report of the Deputy Keeper of the Public Records in Ireland* (Alexander Thom, Dublin, 1871).

Three maps for every county, or part of a county in the case of Cork, Dublin and Tipperary, are included in this volume. The first county map shows the civil parishes, which are numbered and listed in alphabetical order. The second shows the boundaries and names of the baronies and, as a footnote, the dioceses of that county and the parishes included within them. The third and final county map illustrates the boundaries and names of the poor law unions and, as a footnote, the parishes included within the probate districts serving that county.

By way of introduction, three maps of Ireland are also included to show the area covered by each county, diocese and probate district. The intention of these maps is to enable the reader to see at a glance the geographical position and the relationship of these divisions to each other.

The administrative divisions mapped here are those that existed in the mid-nineteenth century when all Ireland was being surveyed in the so-called Griffith's Valuation. This period, and the decades following it, was one of great change. From 1841 to 1901 the population of Ireland fell from 8,175,124 to 4,458,775. (By 1981 the population of Ireland stood at 5,005,605.) In the fifty years from 1851 to 1901 3,846,393 people emigrated from Ireland. In seven of those years, namely 1851, 1852, 1853, 1854, 1863, 1864 and 1883, over 100,000 people left Ireland each year to a new and different way of life. Figures for the years 1891 to 1900 show that 90% of these emigrants settled in the United States.

a new genealogical atlas of íreland

THE COUNTIES OF IRELAND

THE DIOCESES OF IRELAND

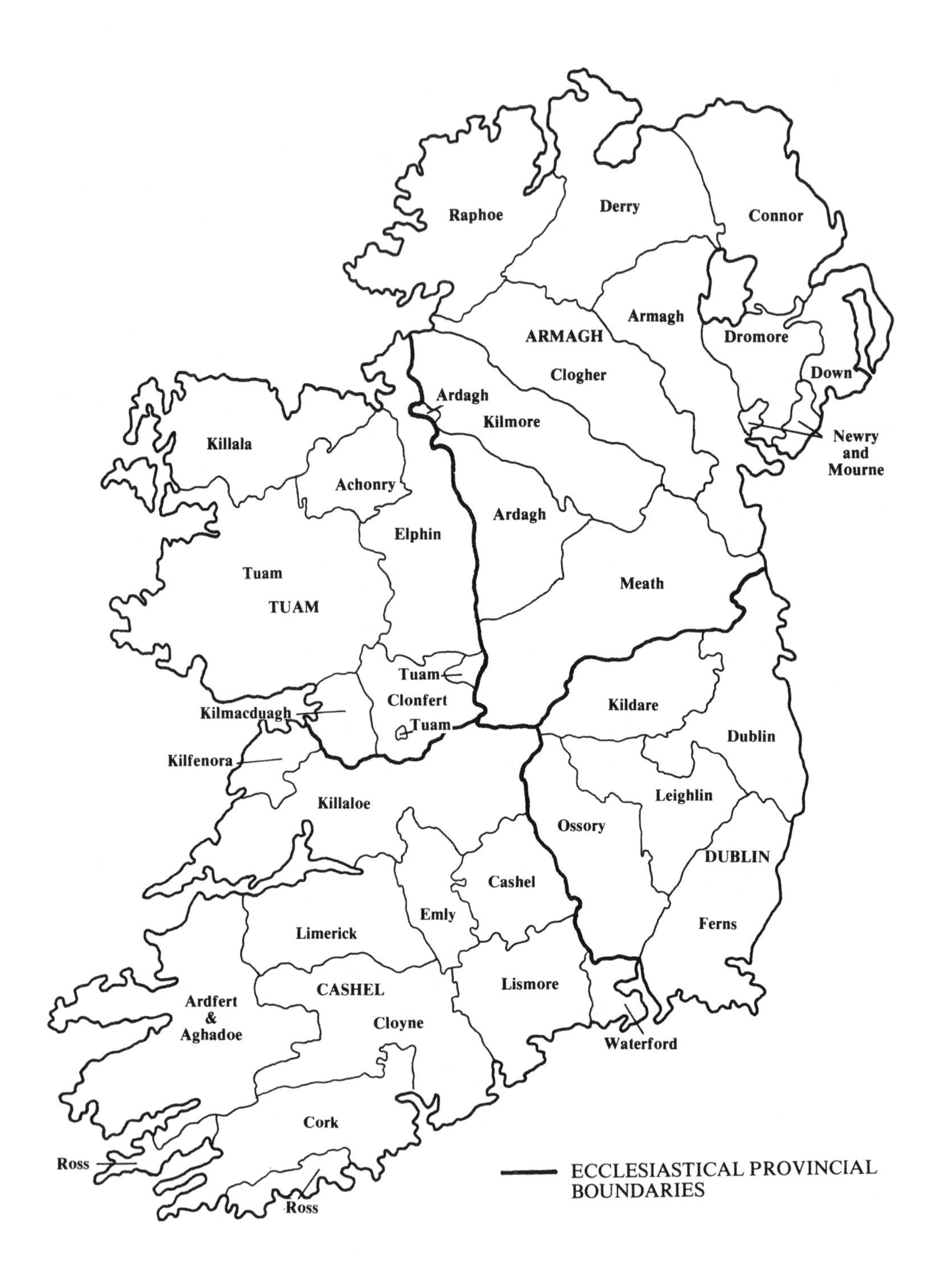

THE PROBATE DISTRICTS OF IRELAND

THE PARISHES OF COUNTY ANTRIM

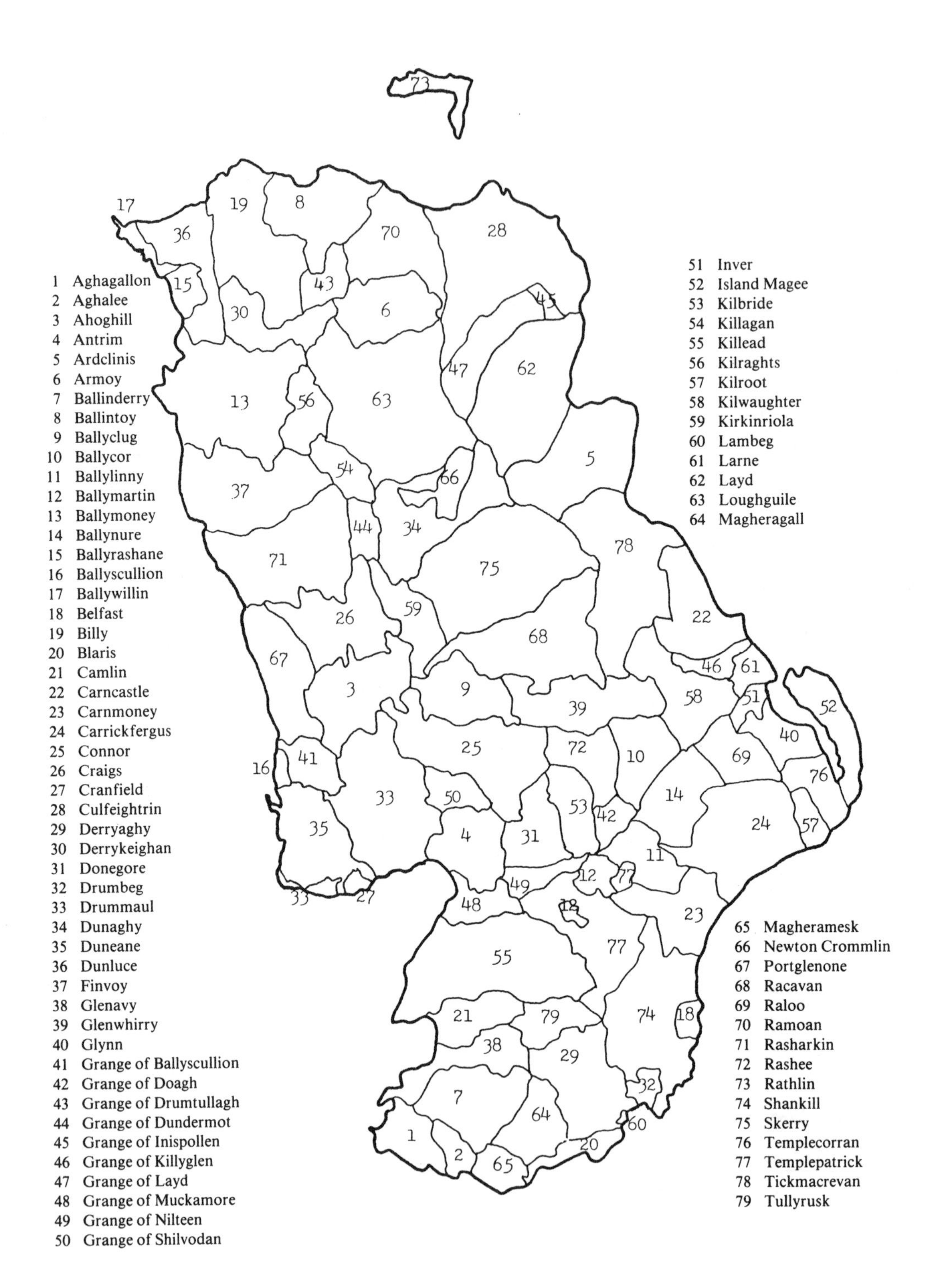

THE BARONIES OF COUNTY ANTRIM

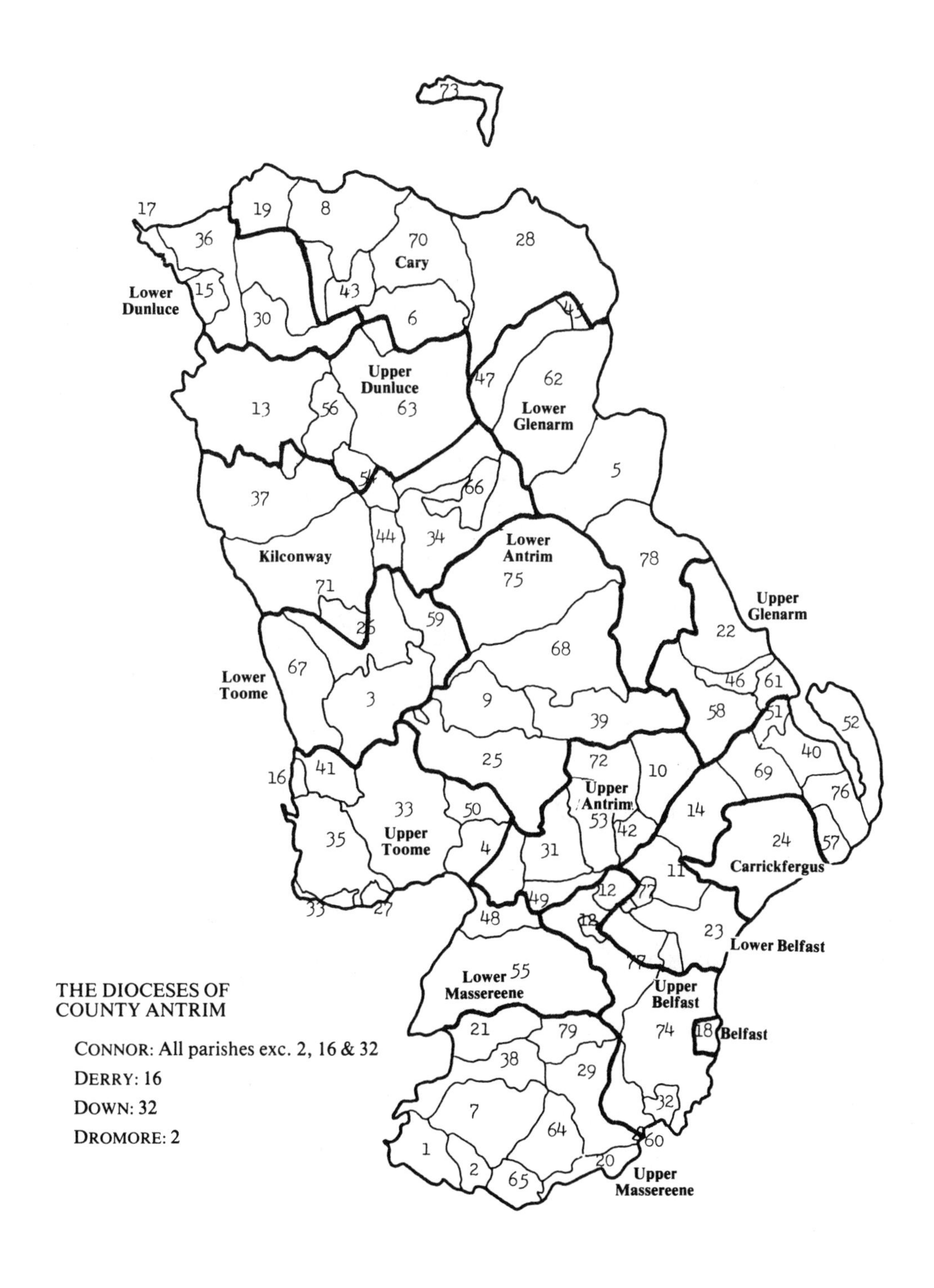

THE POOR LAW UNIONS OF COUNTY ANTRIM

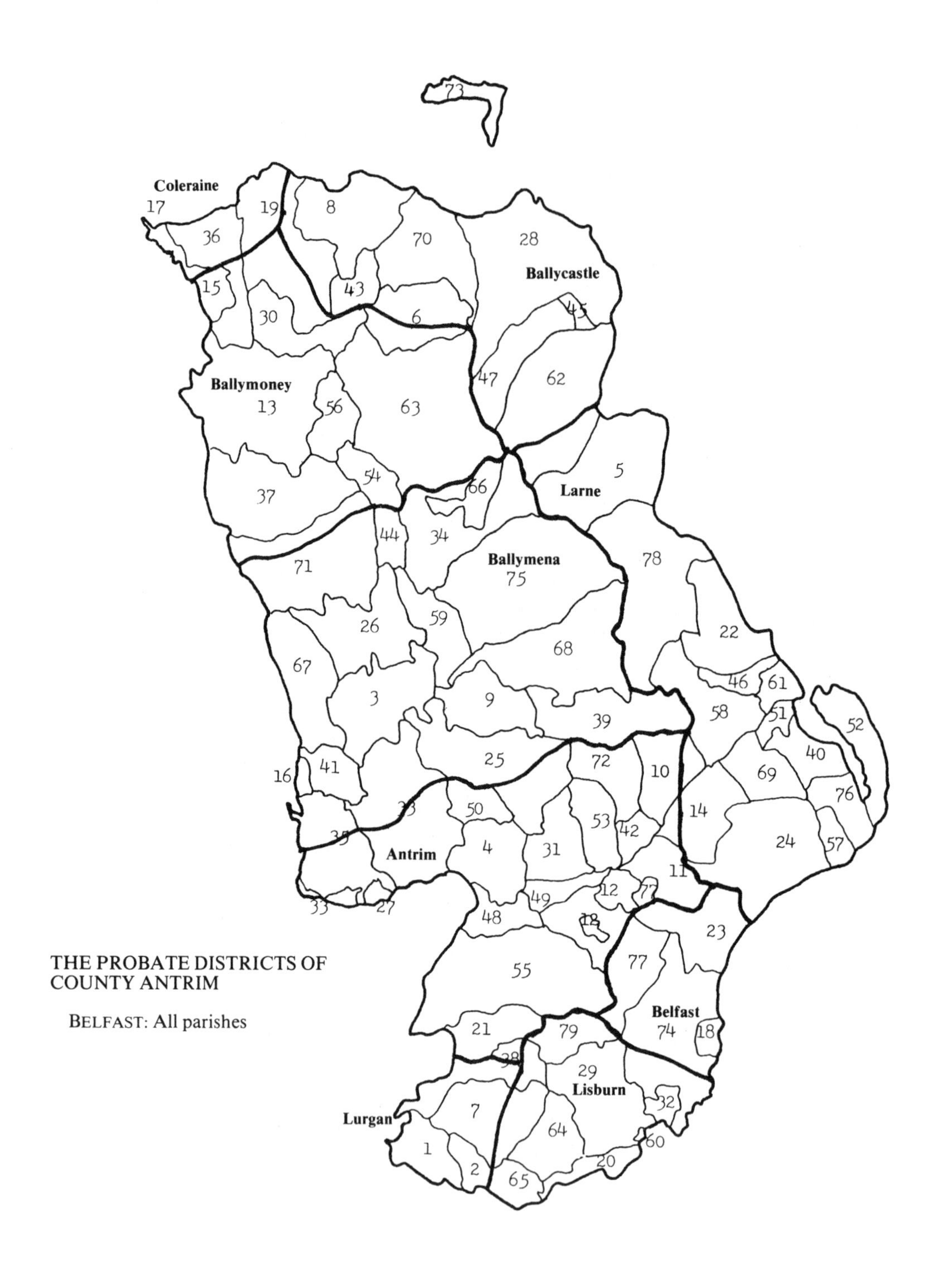

THE PROBATE DISTRICTS OF COUNTY ANTRIM

BELFAST: All parishes

THE PARISHES OF COUNTY ARMAGH

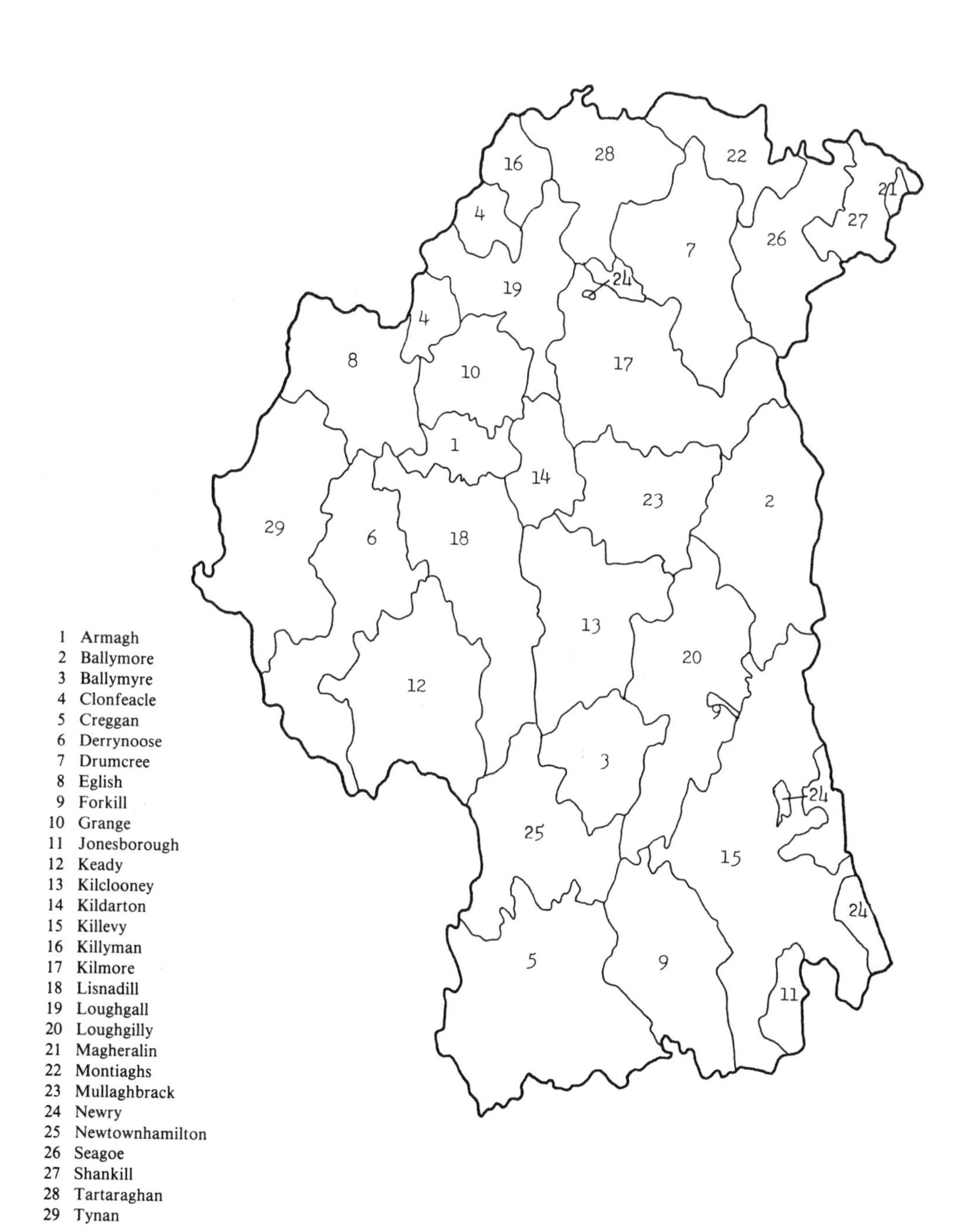

1 Armagh
2 Ballymore
3 Ballymyre
4 Clonfeacle
5 Creggan
6 Derrynoose
7 Drumcree
8 Eglish
9 Forkill
10 Grange
11 Jonesborough
12 Keady
13 Kilclooney
14 Kildarton
15 Killevy
16 Killyman
17 Kilmore
18 Lisnadill
19 Loughgall
20 Loughgilly
21 Magheralin
22 Montiaghs
23 Mullaghbrack
24 Newry
25 Newtownhamilton
26 Seagoe
27 Shankill
28 Tartaraghan
29 Tynan

THE BARONIES OF COUNTY ARMAGH

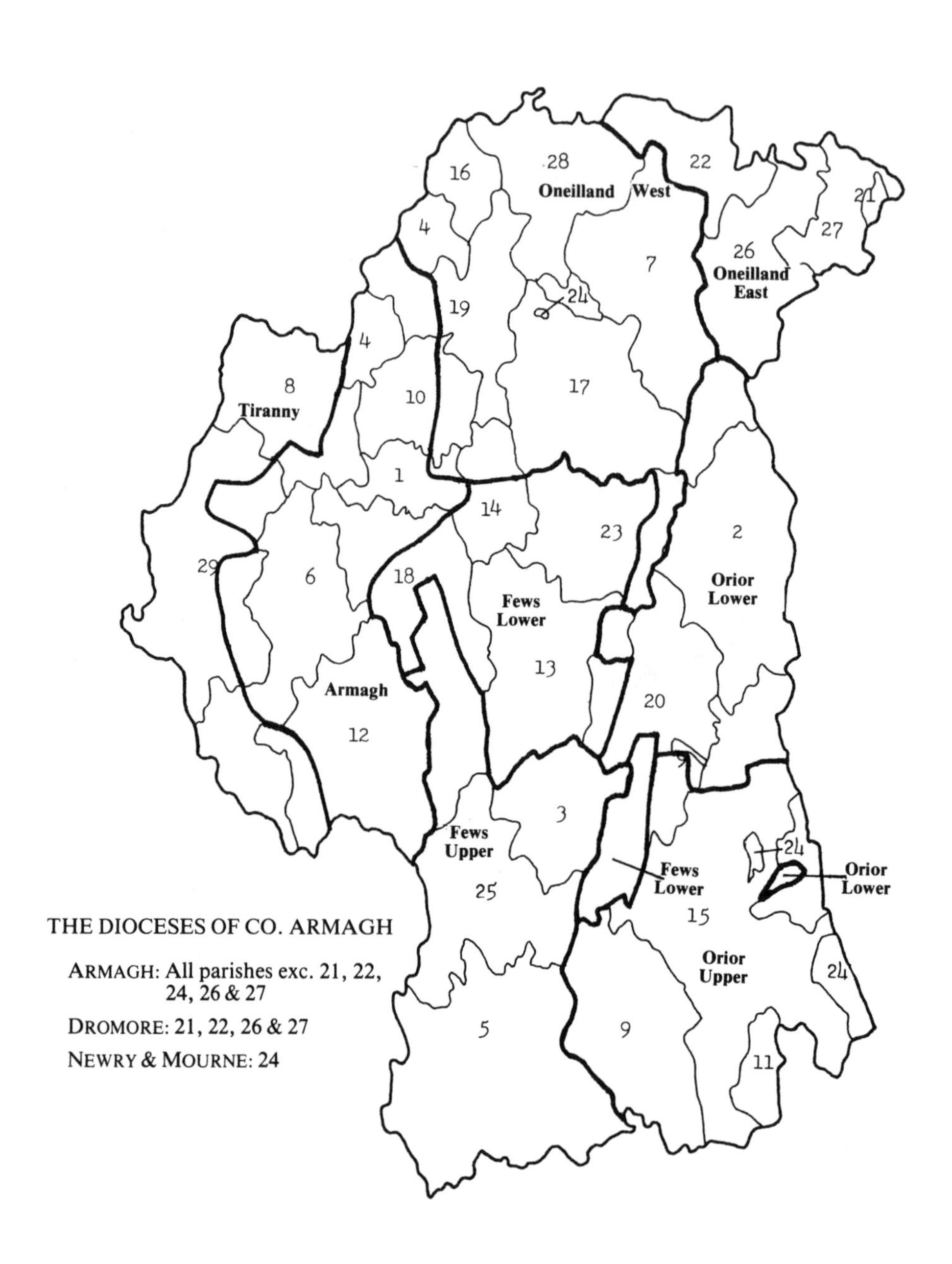

THE POOR LAW UNIONS OF COUNTY ARMAGH

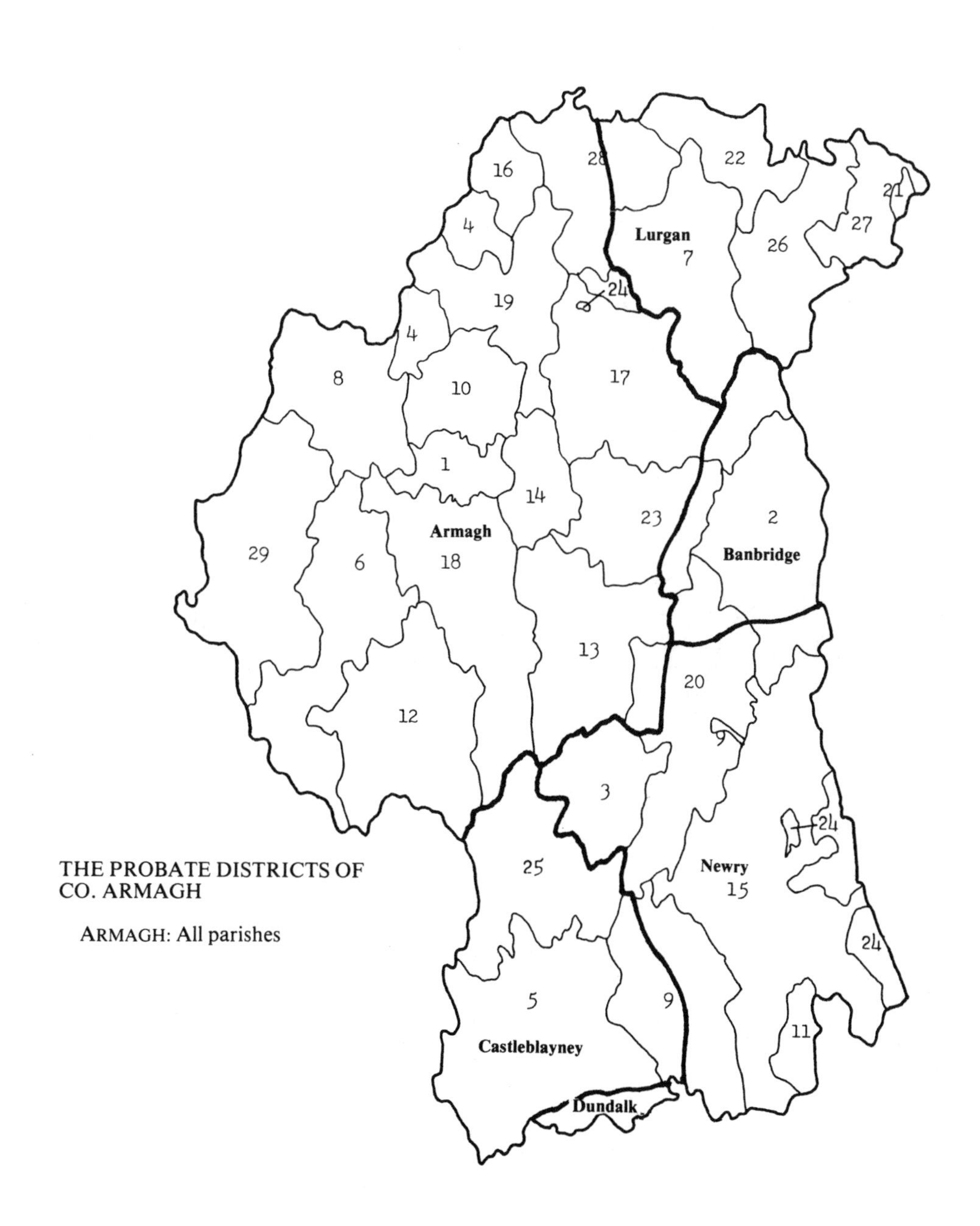

THE PROBATE DISTRICTS OF CO. ARMAGH

ARMAGH: All parishes

THE PARISHES OF COUNTY CARLOW

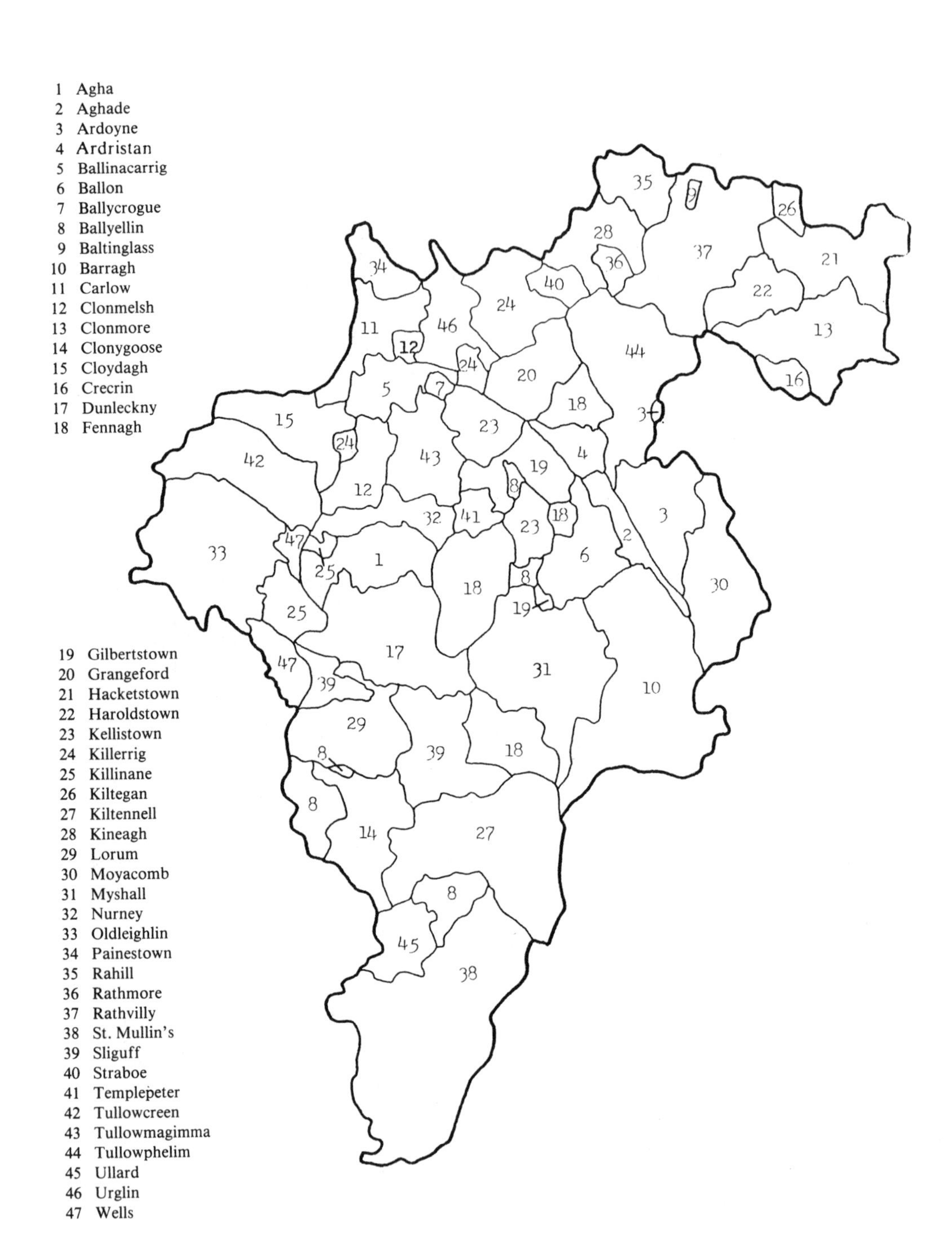

THE BARONIES OF COUNTY CARLOW

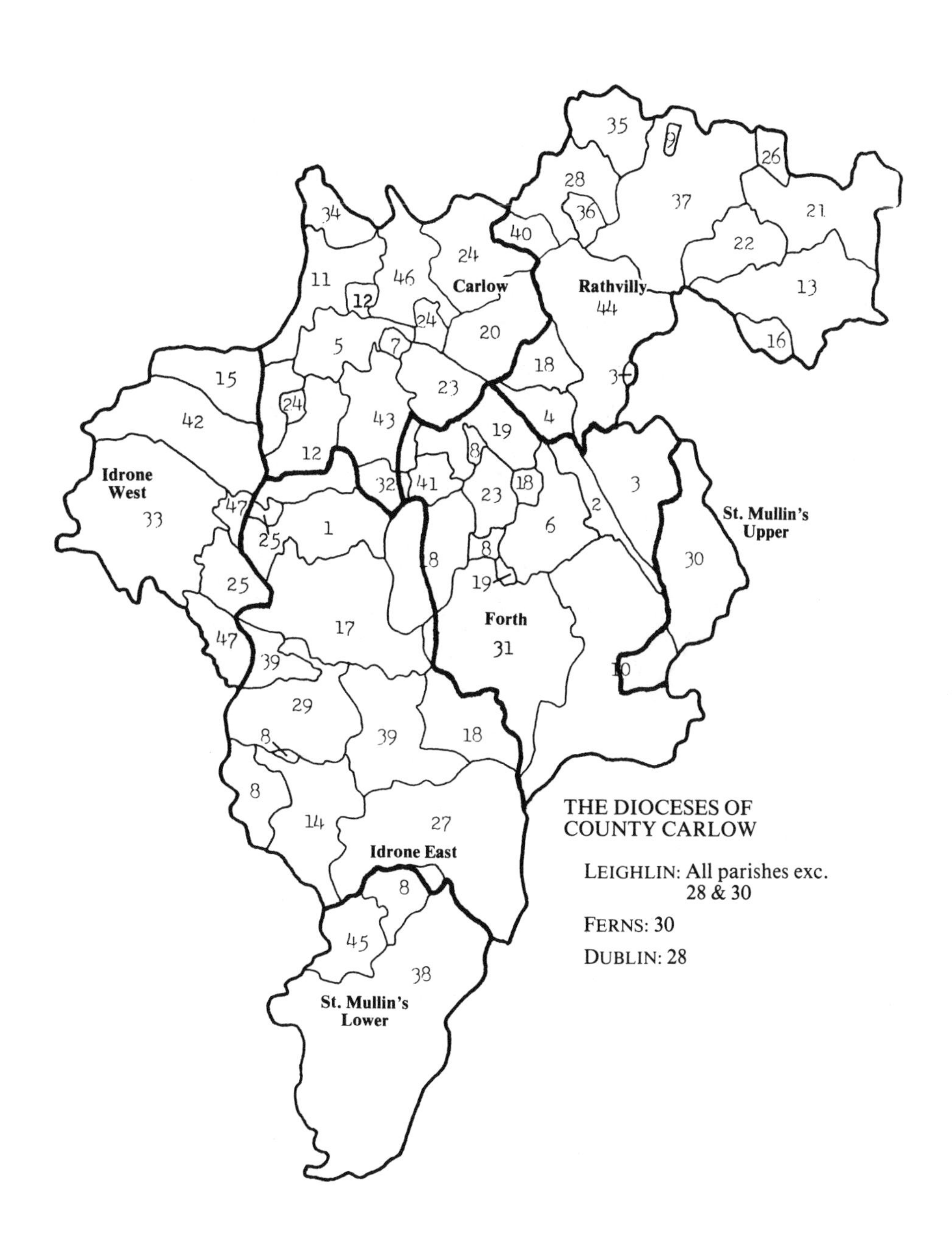

THE POOR LAW UNIONS OF COUNTY CARLOW

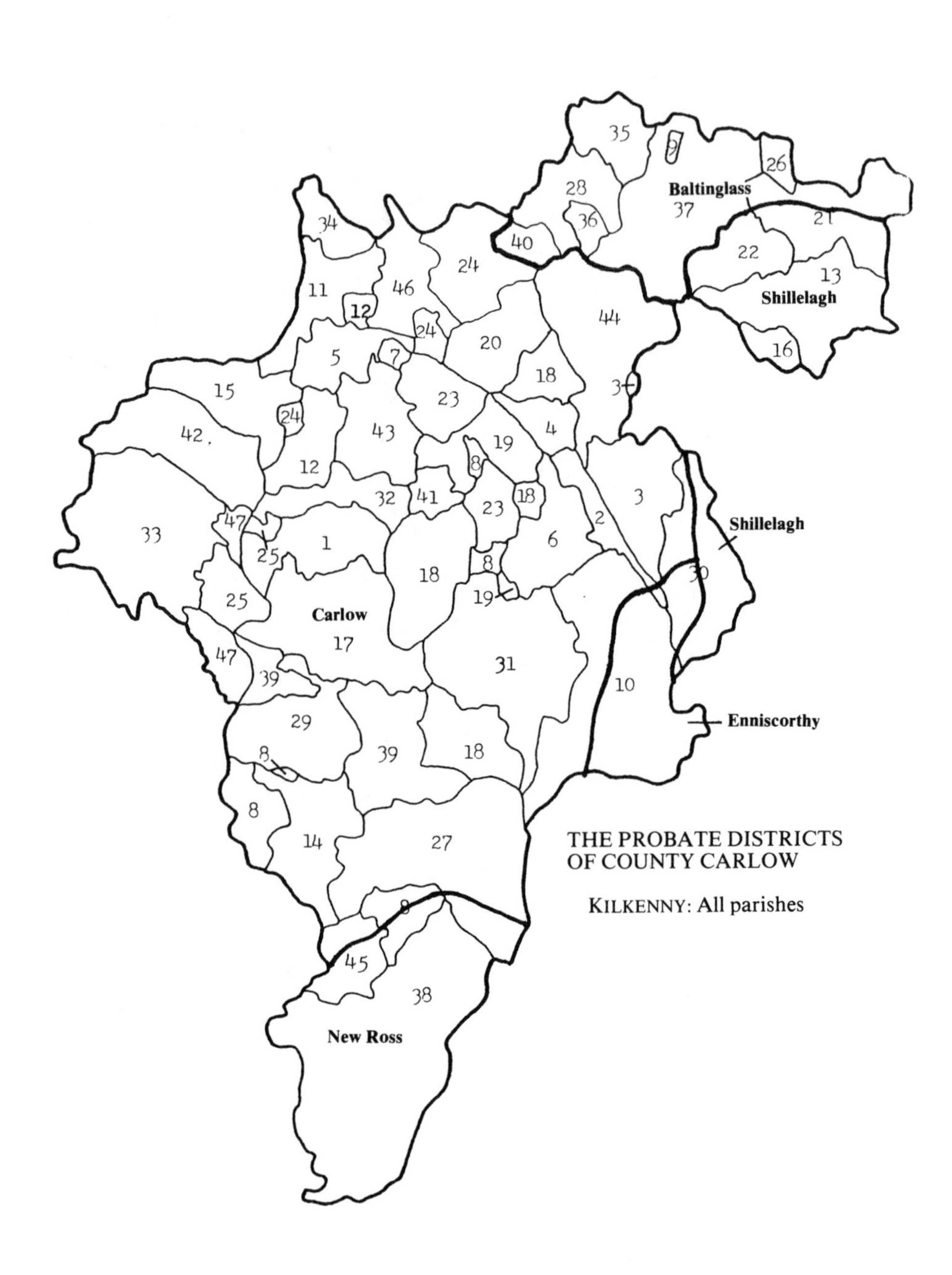

The Parishes Of County Cavan

1 Annagelliff
2 Annagh
3 Bailieborough
4 Ballintemple
5 Ballymachugh
6 Castlerahan
7 Castleterra
8 Crosserlough
9 Denn
10 Drumgoon
11 Drumlane
12 Drumlumman
13 Drumreilly
14 Drung
15 Enniskeen
16 Kilbride
17 Kildallan
18 Kildrumsherdan
19 Killashandra
20 Killinagh
21 Killinkere
22 Kilmore
23 Kinawley
24 Knockbride
25 Larah
26 Lavey
27 Loughan or Castlekeeran
28 Lurgan
29 Moybolgue
30 Mullagh
31 Munterconnaught
32 Scrabby
33 Shercock
34 Templeport
35 Tomregan
36 Urney

THE BARONIES OF COUNTY CAVAN

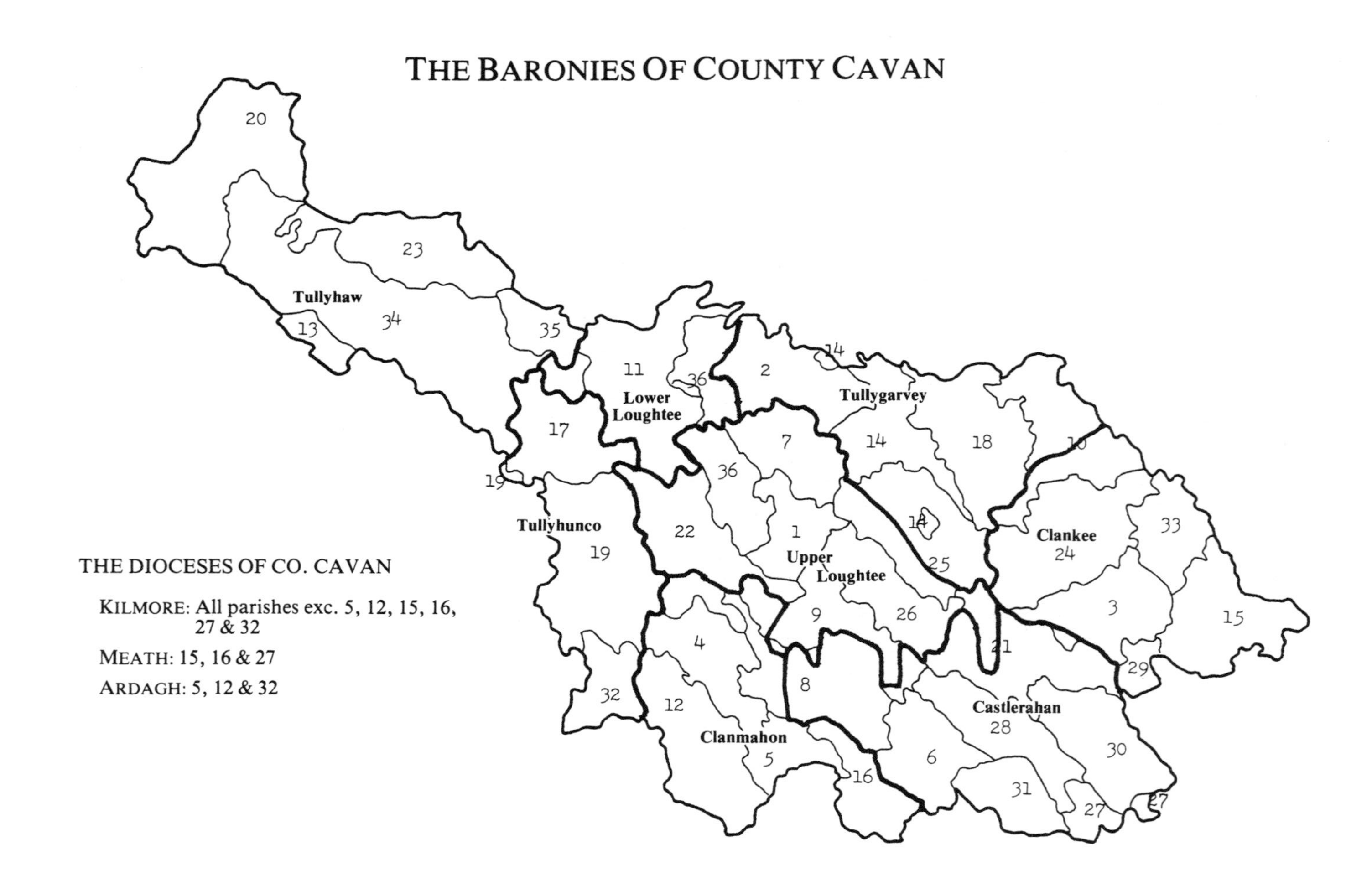

THE DIOCESES OF CO. CAVAN

KILMORE: All parishes exc. 5, 12, 15, 16, 27 & 32

MEATH: 15, 16 & 27

ARDAGH: 5, 12 & 32

THE POOR LAW UNIONS OF COUNTY CAVAN

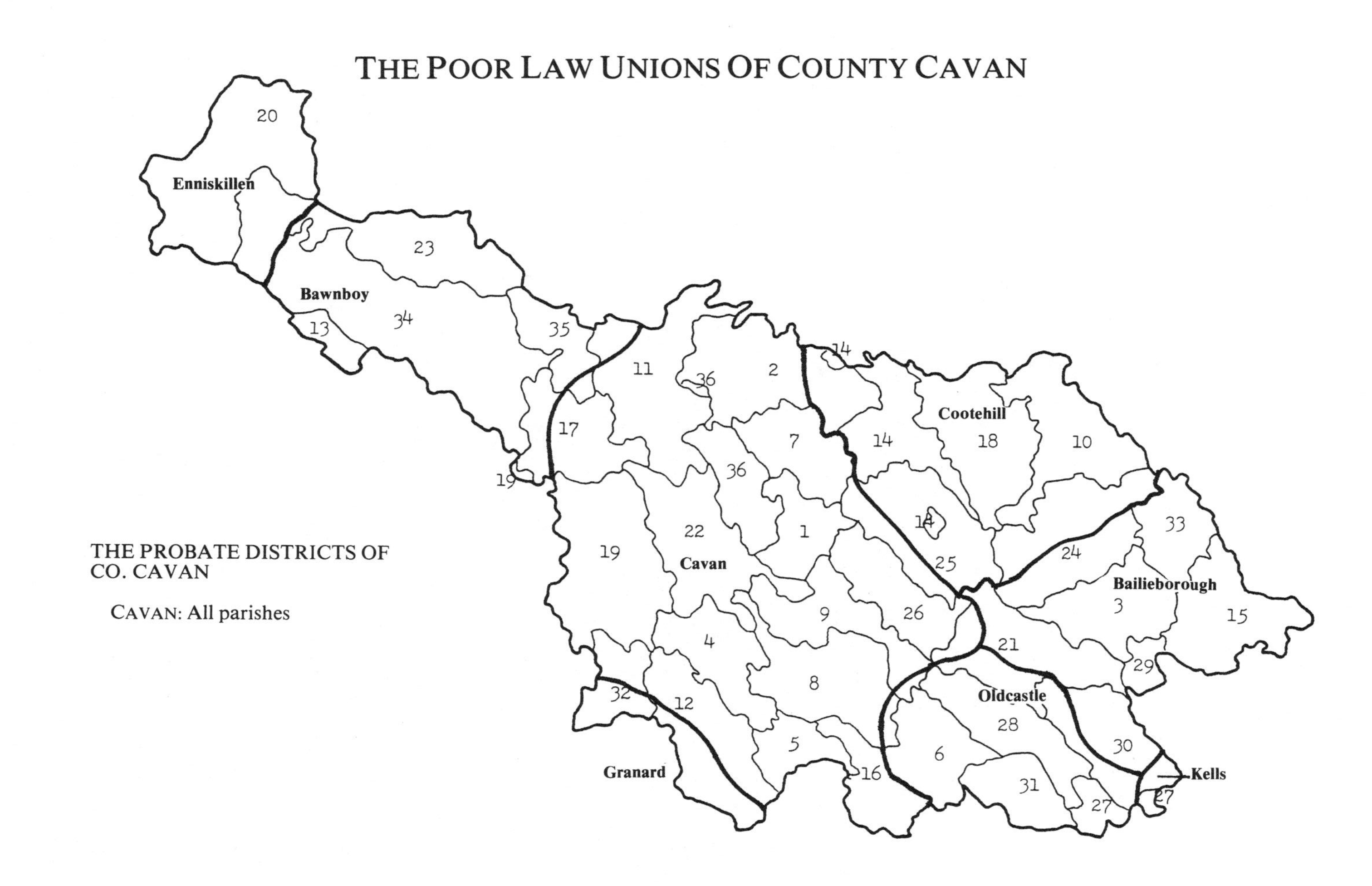

THE PROBATE DISTRICTS OF
CO. CAVAN

CAVAN: All parishes

THE PARISHES OF COUNTY CLARE

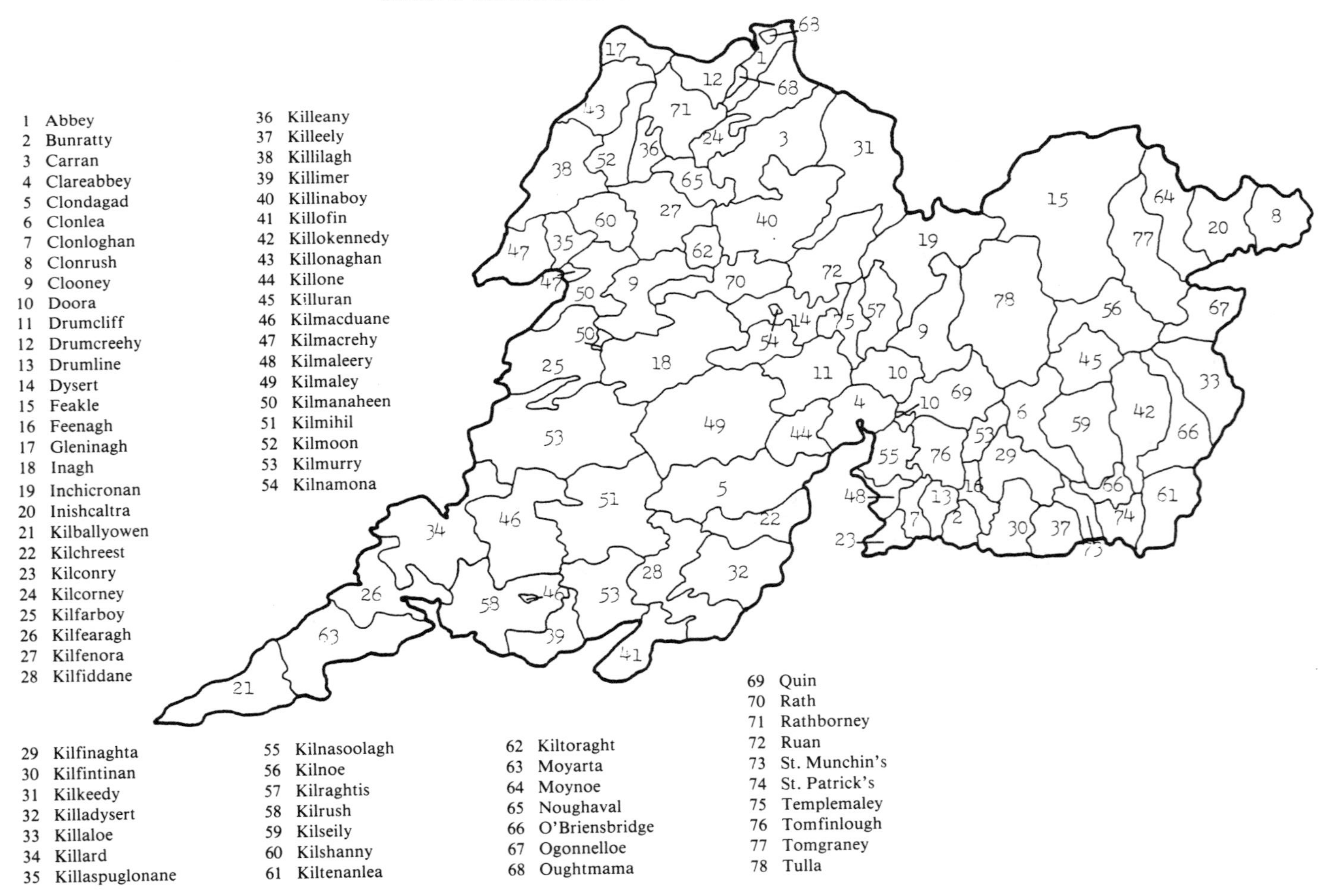

1 Abbey
2 Bunratty
3 Carran
4 Clareabbey
5 Clondagad
6 Clonlea
7 Clonloghan
8 Clonrush
9 Clooney
10 Doora
11 Drumcliff
12 Drumcreehy
13 Drumline
14 Dysert
15 Feakle
16 Feenagh
17 Gleninagh
18 Inagh
19 Inchicronan
20 Inishcaltra
21 Kilballyowen
22 Kilchreest
23 Kilconry
24 Kilcorney
25 Kilfarboy
26 Kilfearagh
27 Kilfenora
28 Kilfiddane
29 Kilfinaghta
30 Kilfintinan
31 Kilkeedy
32 Killadysert
33 Killaloe
34 Killard
35 Killaspuglonane
36 Killeany
37 Killeely
38 Killilagh
39 Killimer
40 Killinaboy
41 Killofin
42 Killokennedy
43 Killonaghan
44 Killone
45 Killuran
46 Kilmacduane
47 Kilmacrehy
48 Kilmaleery
49 Kilmaley
50 Kilmanaheen
51 Kilmihil
52 Kilmoon
53 Kilmurry
54 Kilnamona
55 Kilnasoolagh
56 Kilnoe
57 Kilraghtis
58 Kilrush
59 Kilseily
60 Kilshanny
61 Kiltenanlea
62 Kiltoraght
63 Moyarta
64 Moynoe
65 Noughaval
66 O'Briensbridge
67 Ogonnelloe
68 Oughtmama
69 Quin
70 Rath
71 Rathborney
72 Ruan
73 St. Munchin's
74 St. Patrick's
75 Templemaley
76 Tomfinlough
77 Tomgraney
78 Tulla

THE BARONIES OF COUNTY CLARE

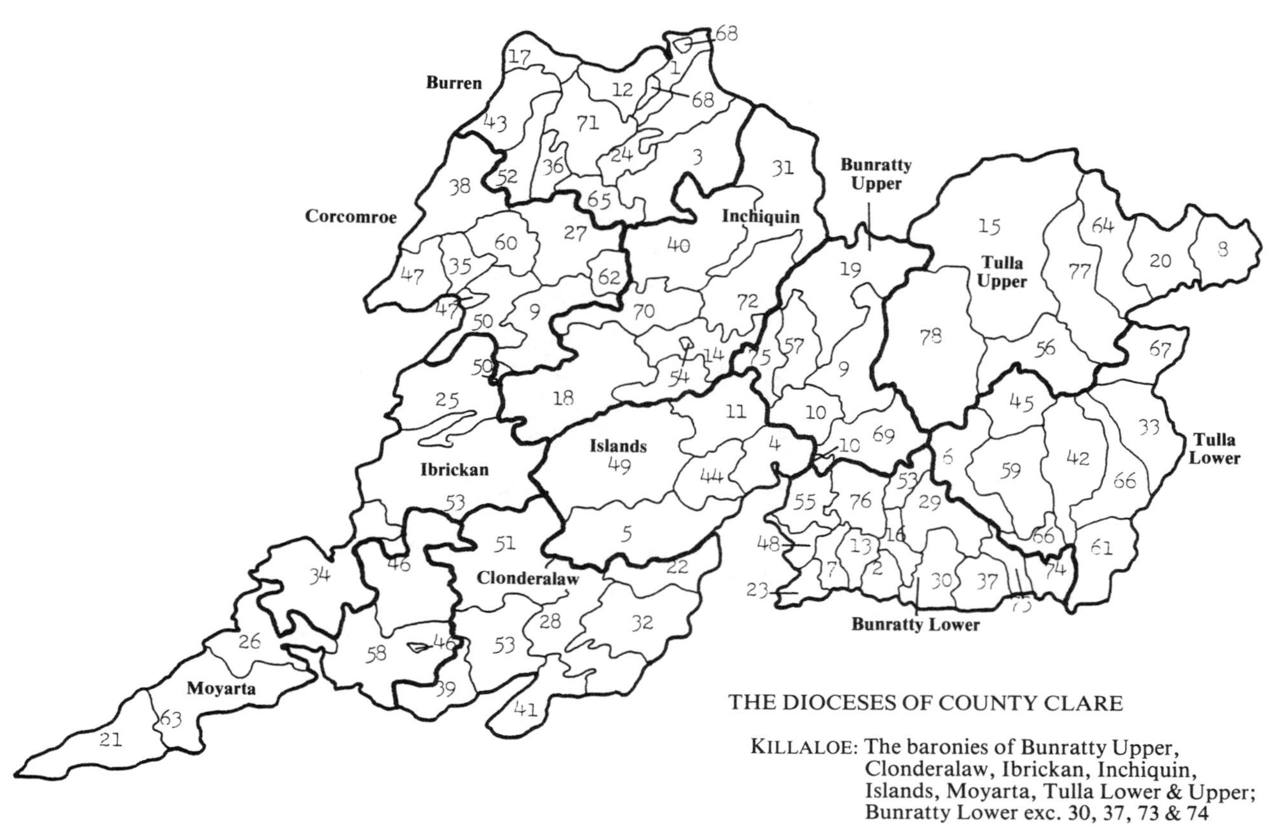

THE DIOCESES OF COUNTY CLARE

KILLALOE: The baronies of Bunratty Upper, Clonderalaw, Ibrickan, Inchiquin, Islands, Moyarta, Tulla Lower & Upper; Bunratty Lower exc. 30, 37, 73 & 74

KILFENORA: The baronies of Burren & Corcomroe

LIMERICK: 30, 37, 73 & 74

THE POOR LAW UNIONS OF COUNTY CLARE

THE PROBATE DISTRICTS OF COUNTY CLARE

LIMERICK: All parishes

THE PARISHES OF COUNTY CORK EAST

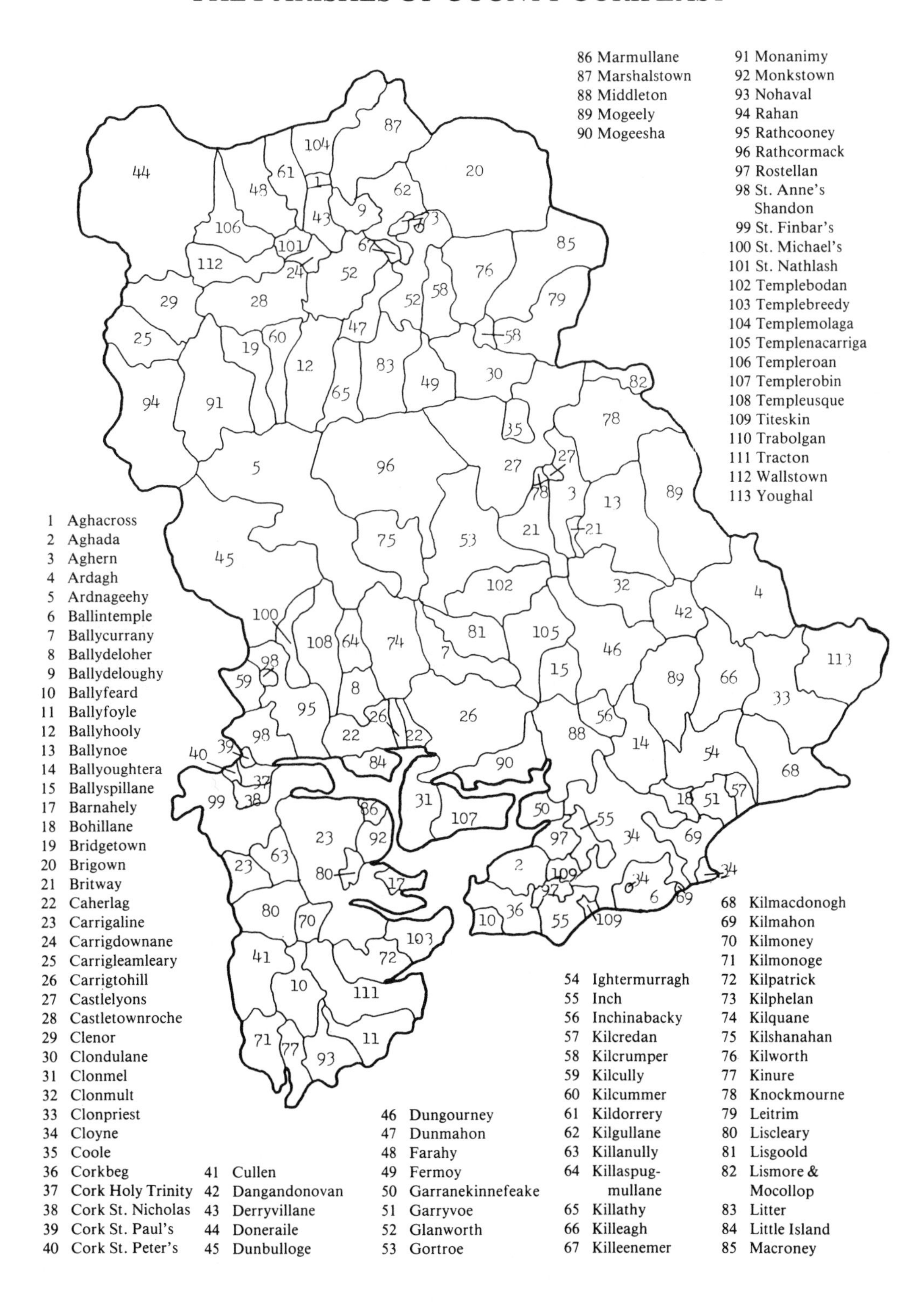

1 Aghacross
2 Aghada
3 Aghern
4 Ardagh
5 Ardnageehy
6 Ballintemple
7 Ballycurrany
8 Ballydeloher
9 Ballydeloughy
10 Ballyfeard
11 Ballyfoyle
12 Ballyhooly
13 Ballynoe
14 Ballyoughtera
15 Ballyspillane
17 Barnahely
18 Bohillane
19 Bridgetown
20 Brigown
21 Britway
22 Caherlag
23 Carrigaline
24 Carrigdownane
25 Carrigleamleary
26 Carrigtohill
27 Castlelyons
28 Castletownroche
29 Clenor
30 Clondulane
31 Clonmel
32 Clonmult
33 Clonpriest
34 Cloyne
35 Coole
36 Corkbeg
37 Cork Holy Trinity
38 Cork St. Nicholas
39 Cork St. Paul's
40 Cork St. Peter's
41 Cullen
42 Dangandonovan
43 Derryvillane
44 Doneraile
45 Dunbulloge
46 Dungourney
47 Dunmahon
48 Farahy
49 Fermoy
50 Garranekinnefeake
51 Garryvoe
52 Glanworth
53 Gortroe
54 Ightermurragh
55 Inch
56 Inchinabacky
57 Kilcredan
58 Kilcrumper
59 Kilcully
60 Kilcummer
61 Kildorrery
62 Kilgullane
63 Killanully
64 Killaspug-mullane
65 Killathy
66 Killeagh
67 Killeenemer
68 Kilmacdonogh
69 Kilmahon
70 Kilmoney
71 Kilmonoge
72 Kilpatrick
73 Kilphelan
74 Kilquane
75 Kilshanahan
76 Kilworth
77 Kinure
78 Knockmourne
79 Leitrim
80 Liscleary
81 Lisgoold
82 Lismore & Mocollop
83 Litter
84 Little Island
85 Macroney
86 Marmullane
87 Marshalstown
88 Middleton
89 Mogeely
90 Mogeesha
91 Monanimy
92 Monkstown
93 Nohaval
94 Rahan
95 Rathcooney
96 Rathcormack
97 Rostellan
98 St. Anne's Shandon
99 St. Finbar's
100 St. Michael's
101 St. Nathlash
102 Templebodan
103 Templebreedy
104 Templemolaga
105 Templenacarriga
106 Templeroan
107 Templerobin
108 Templeusque
109 Titeskin
110 Trabolgan
111 Tracton
112 Wallstown
113 Youghal

THE BARONIES OF COUNTY CORK EAST

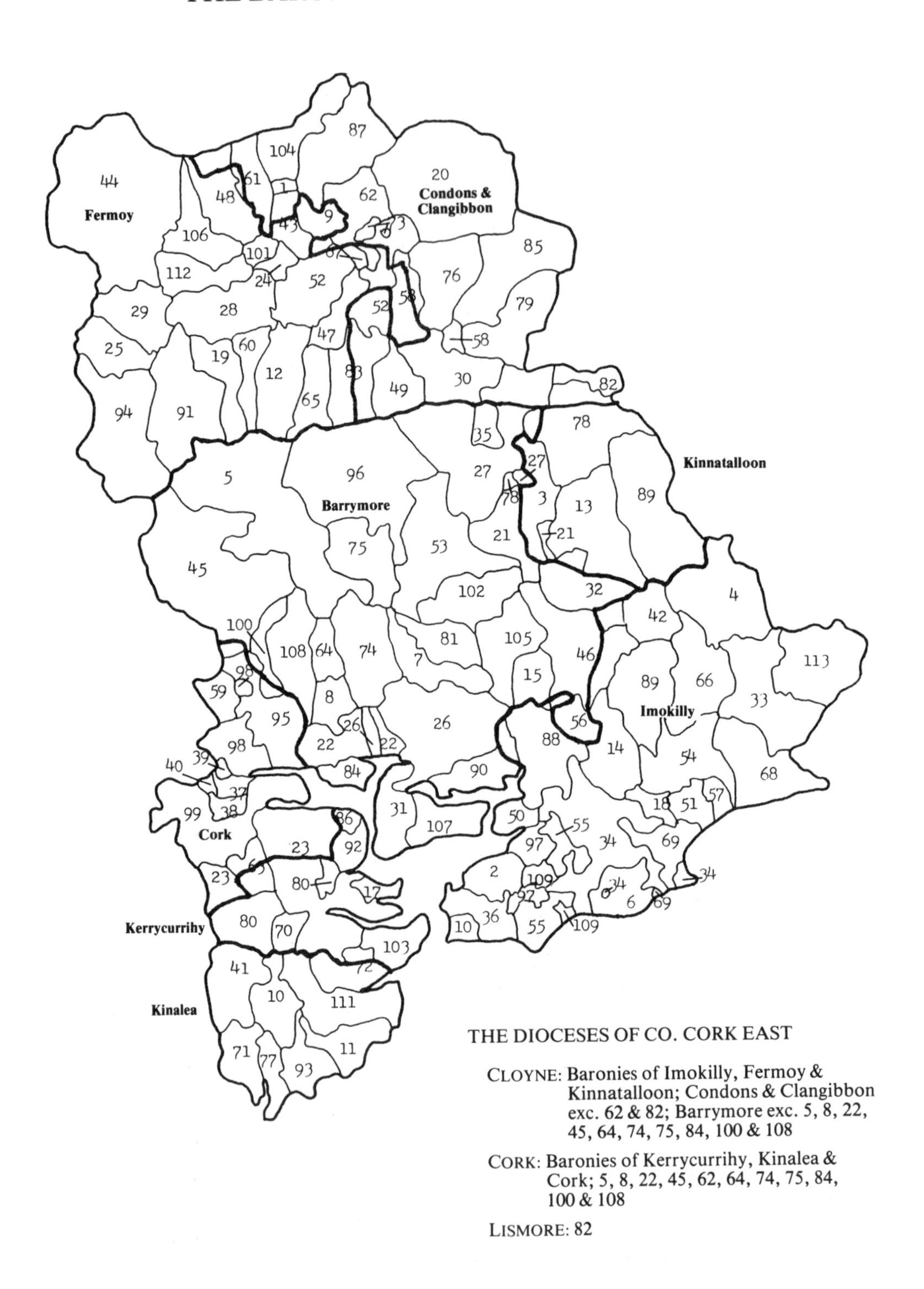

THE DIOCESES OF CO. CORK EAST

CLOYNE: Baronies of Imokilly, Fermoy & Kinnatalloon; Condons & Clangibbon exc. 62 & 82; Barrymore exc. 5, 8, 22, 45, 64, 74, 75, 84, 100 & 108

CORK: Baronies of Kerrycurrihy, Kinalea & Cork; 5, 8, 22, 45, 62, 64, 74, 75, 84, 100 & 108

LISMORE: 82

THE POOR LAW UNIONS OF COUNTY CORK EAST

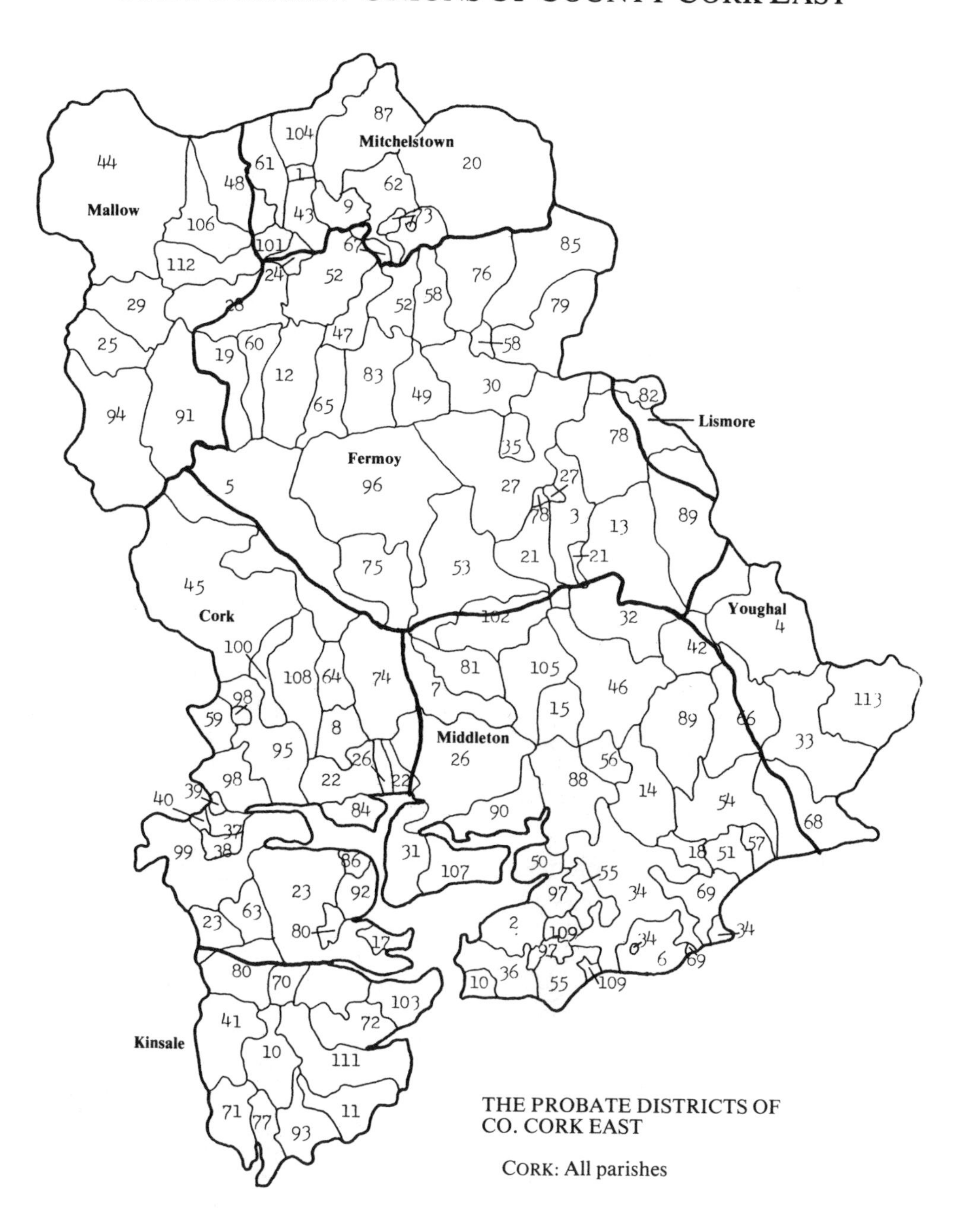

THE PROBATE DISTRICTS OF
CO. CORK EAST

CORK: All parishes

THE PARISHES OF COUNTY CORK MIDDLE

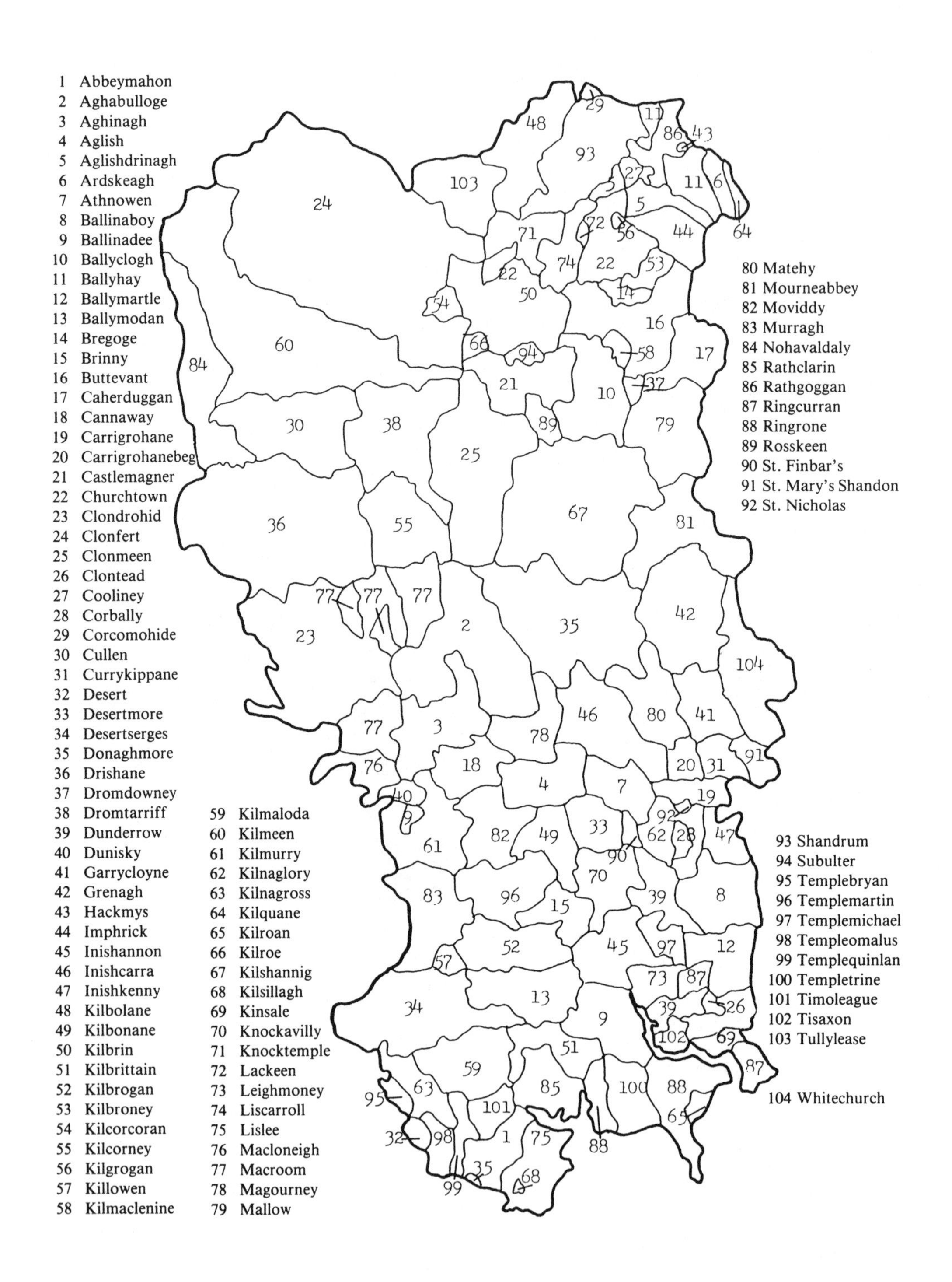

THE BARONIES OF COUNTY CORK MIDDLE

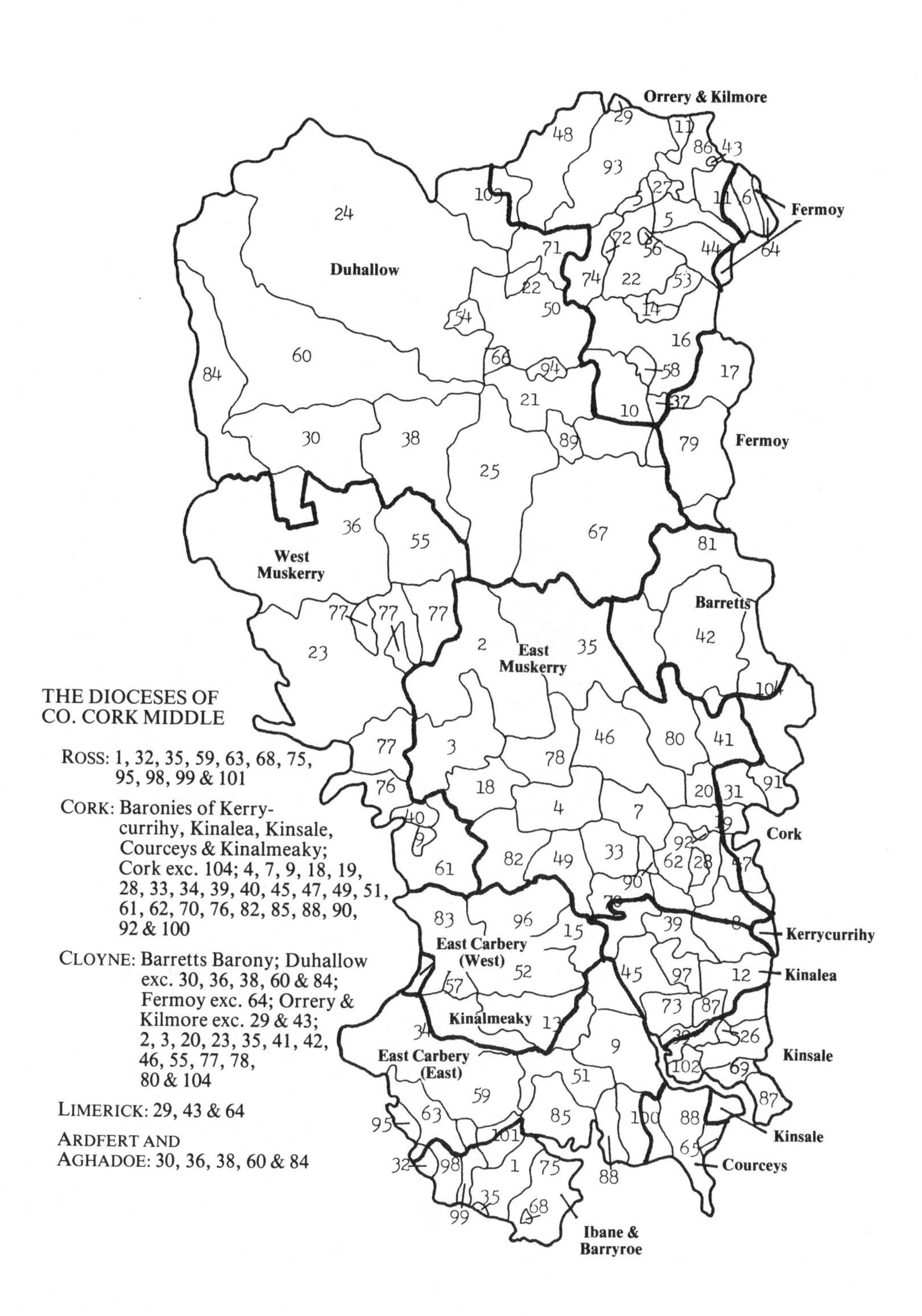

THE POOR LAW UNIONS OF COUNTY CORK MIDDLE

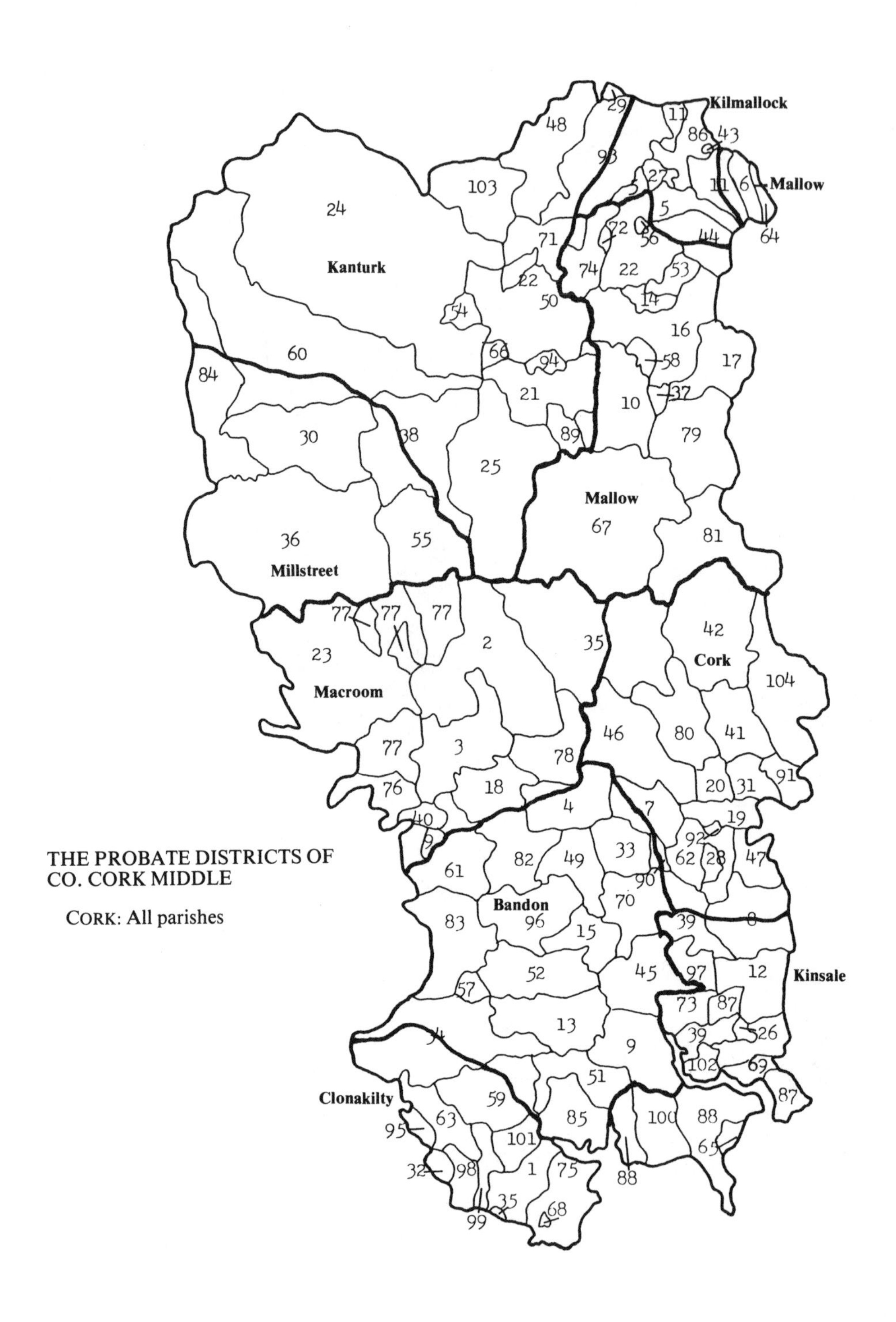

THE PROBATE DISTRICTS OF
CO. CORK MIDDLE

CORK: All parishes

THE PARISHES OF COUNTY CORK WEST

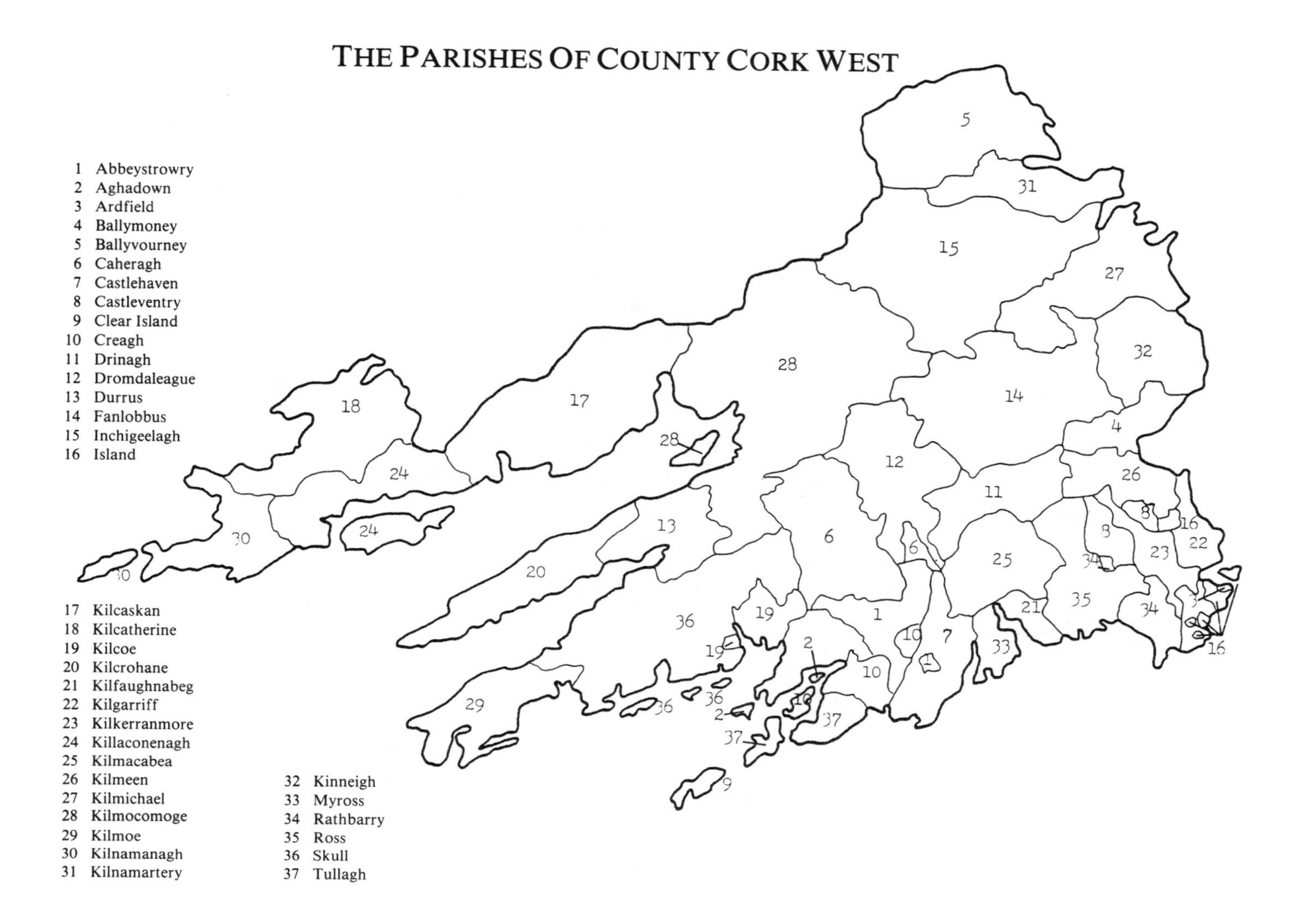

The Baronies of County Cork West

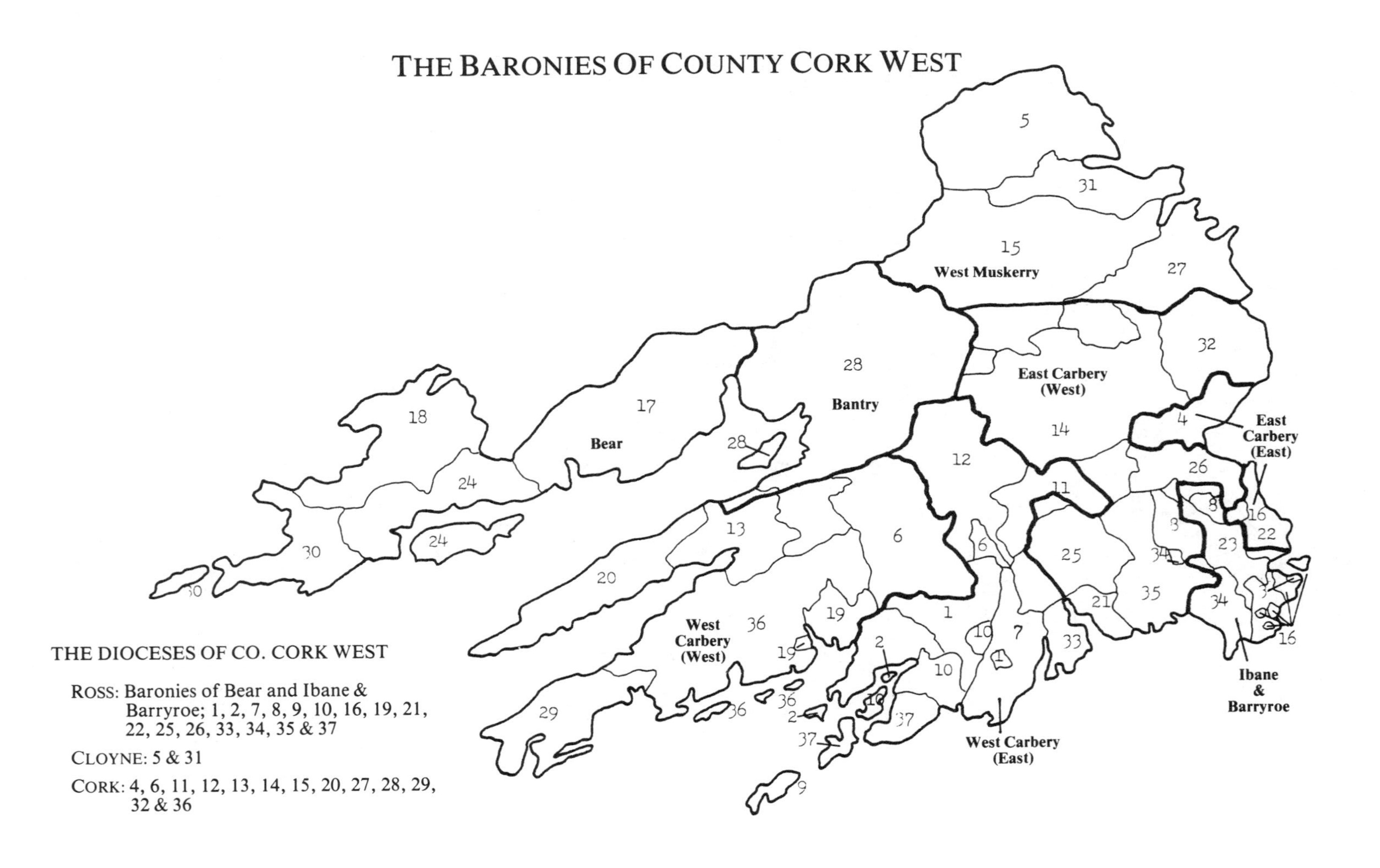

THE DIOCESES OF CO. CORK WEST

ROSS: Baronies of Bear and Ibane & Barryroe; 1, 2, 7, 8, 9, 10, 16, 19, 21, 22, 25, 26, 33, 34, 35 & 37

CLOYNE: 5 & 31

CORK: 4, 6, 11, 12, 13, 14, 15, 20, 27, 28, 29, 32 & 36

THE POOR LAW UNIONS OF COUNTY CORK WEST

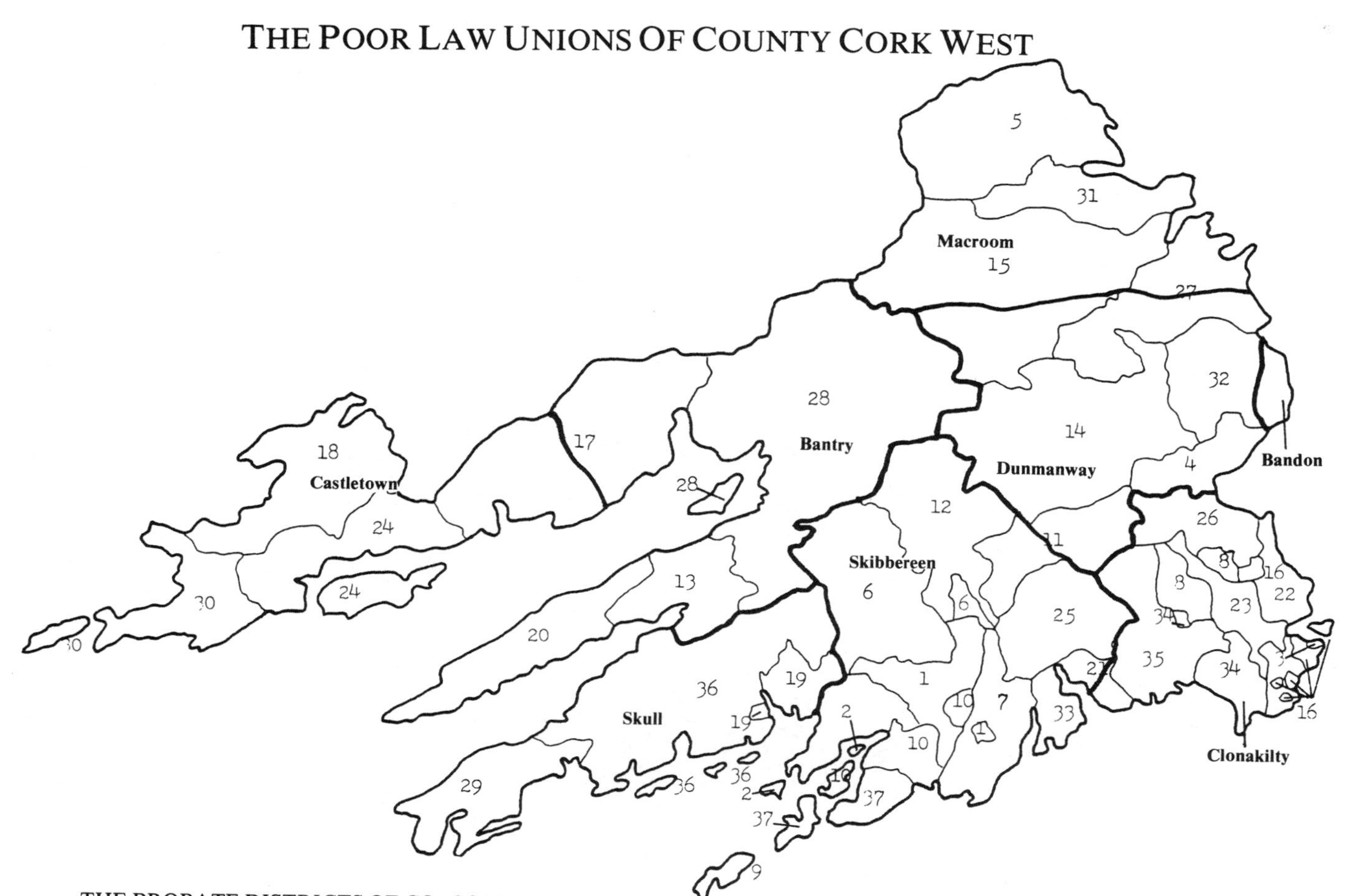

THE PROBATE DISTRICTS OF CO. CORK WEST

CORK: All parishes

THE PARISHES OF COUNTY DONEGAL

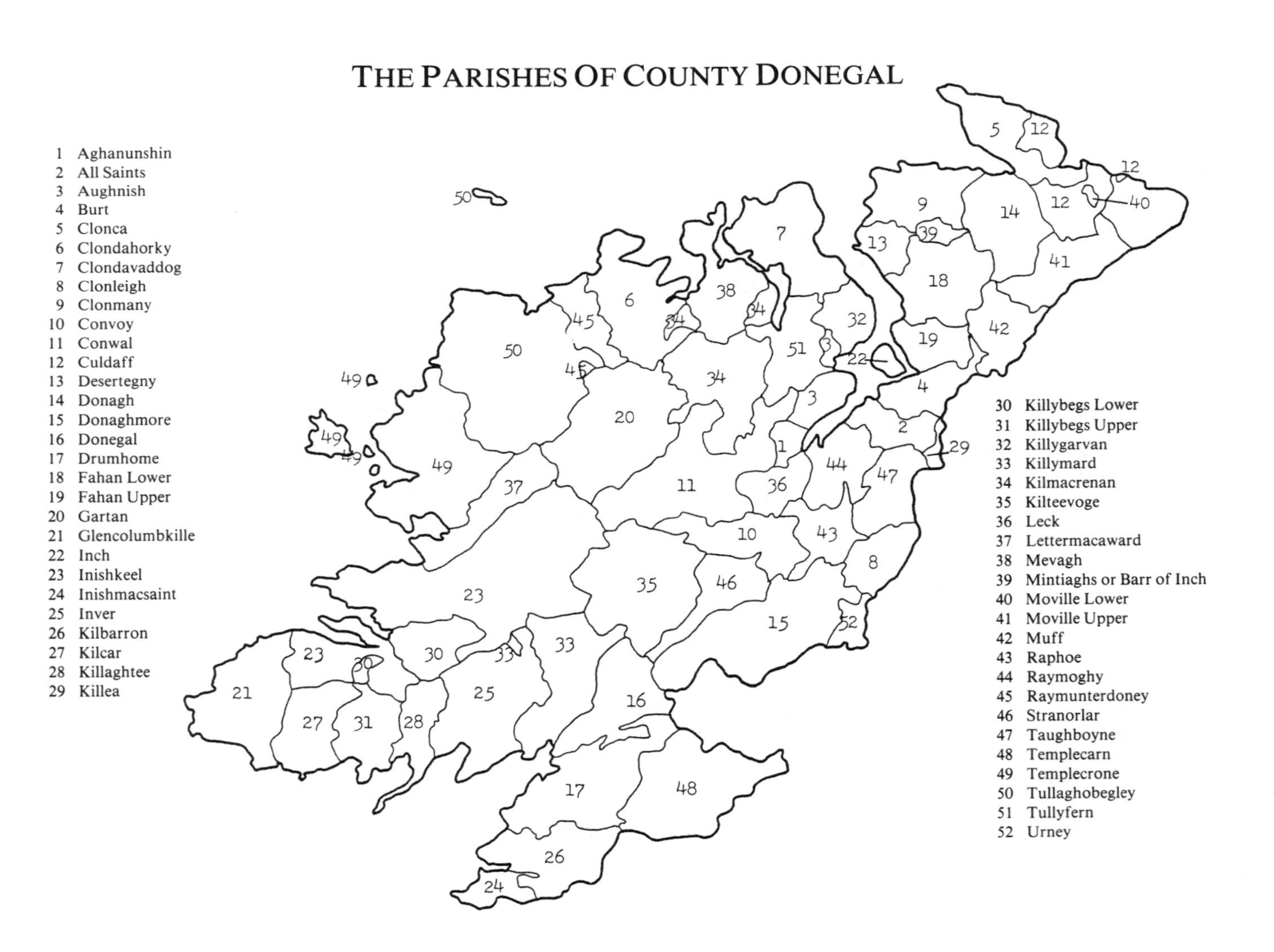

1 Aghanunshin
2 All Saints
3 Aughnish
4 Burt
5 Clonca
6 Clondahorky
7 Clondavaddog
8 Clonleigh
9 Clonmany
10 Convoy
11 Conwal
12 Culdaff
13 Desertegny
14 Donagh
15 Donaghmore
16 Donegal
17 Drumhome
18 Fahan Lower
19 Fahan Upper
20 Gartan
21 Glencolumbkille
22 Inch
23 Inishkeel
24 Inishmacsaint
25 Inver
26 Kilbarron
27 Kilcar
28 Killaghtee
29 Killea
30 Killybegs Lower
31 Killybegs Upper
32 Killygarvan
33 Killymard
34 Kilmacrenan
35 Kilteevoge
36 Leck
37 Lettermacaward
38 Mevagh
39 Mintiaghs or Barr of Inch
40 Moville Lower
41 Moville Upper
42 Muff
43 Raphoe
44 Raymoghy
45 Raymunterdoney
46 Stranorlar
47 Taughboyne
48 Templecarn
49 Templecrone
50 Tullaghobegley
51 Tullyfern
52 Urney

THE BARONIES OF COUNTY DONEGAL

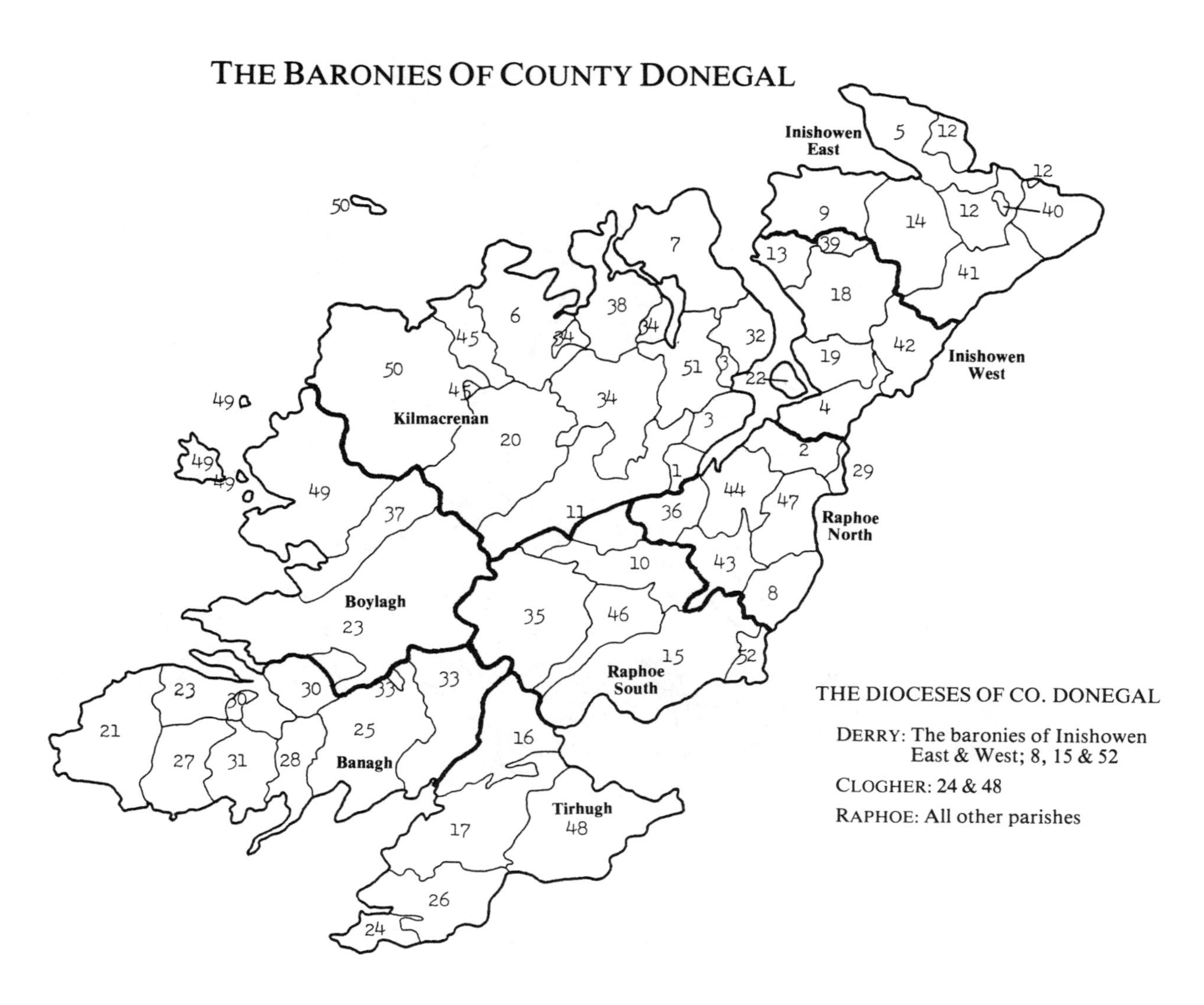

THE DIOCESES OF CO. DONEGAL

DERRY: The baronies of Inishowen East & West; 8, 15 & 52

CLOGHER: 24 & 48

RAPHOE: All other parishes

THE POOR LAW UNIONS OF COUNTY DONEGAL

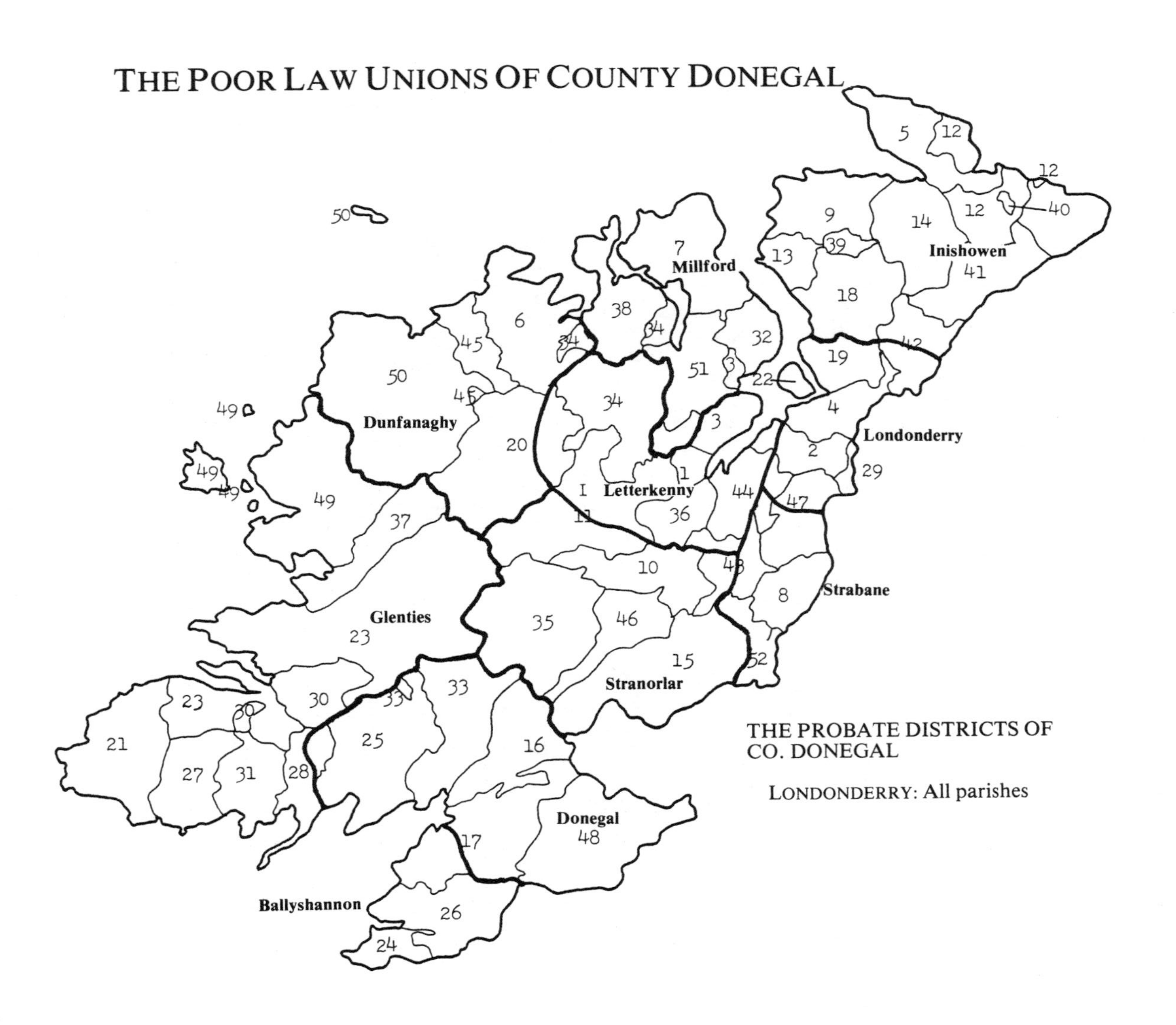

The Parishes Of County Down

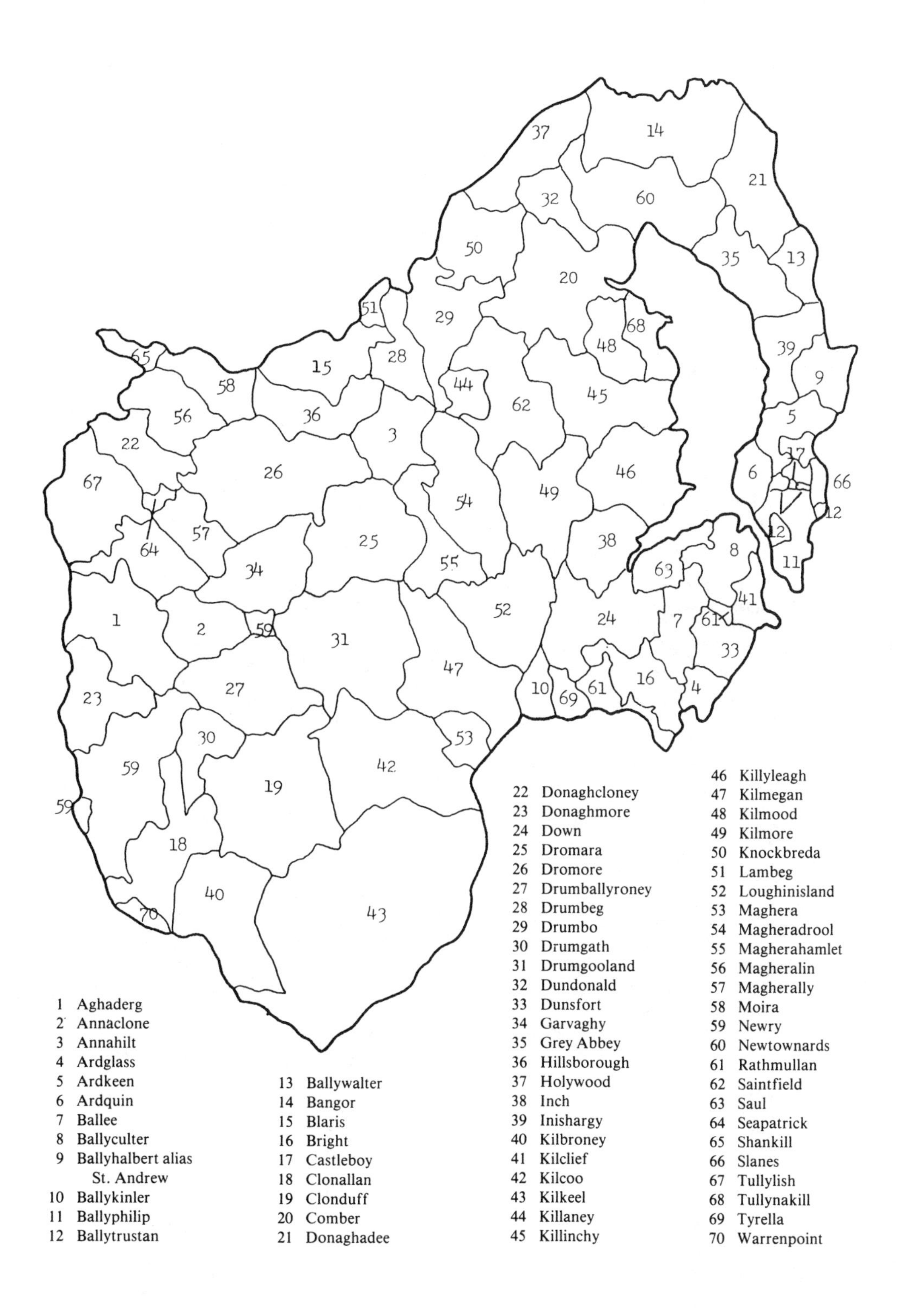

THE BARONIES OF COUNTY DOWN

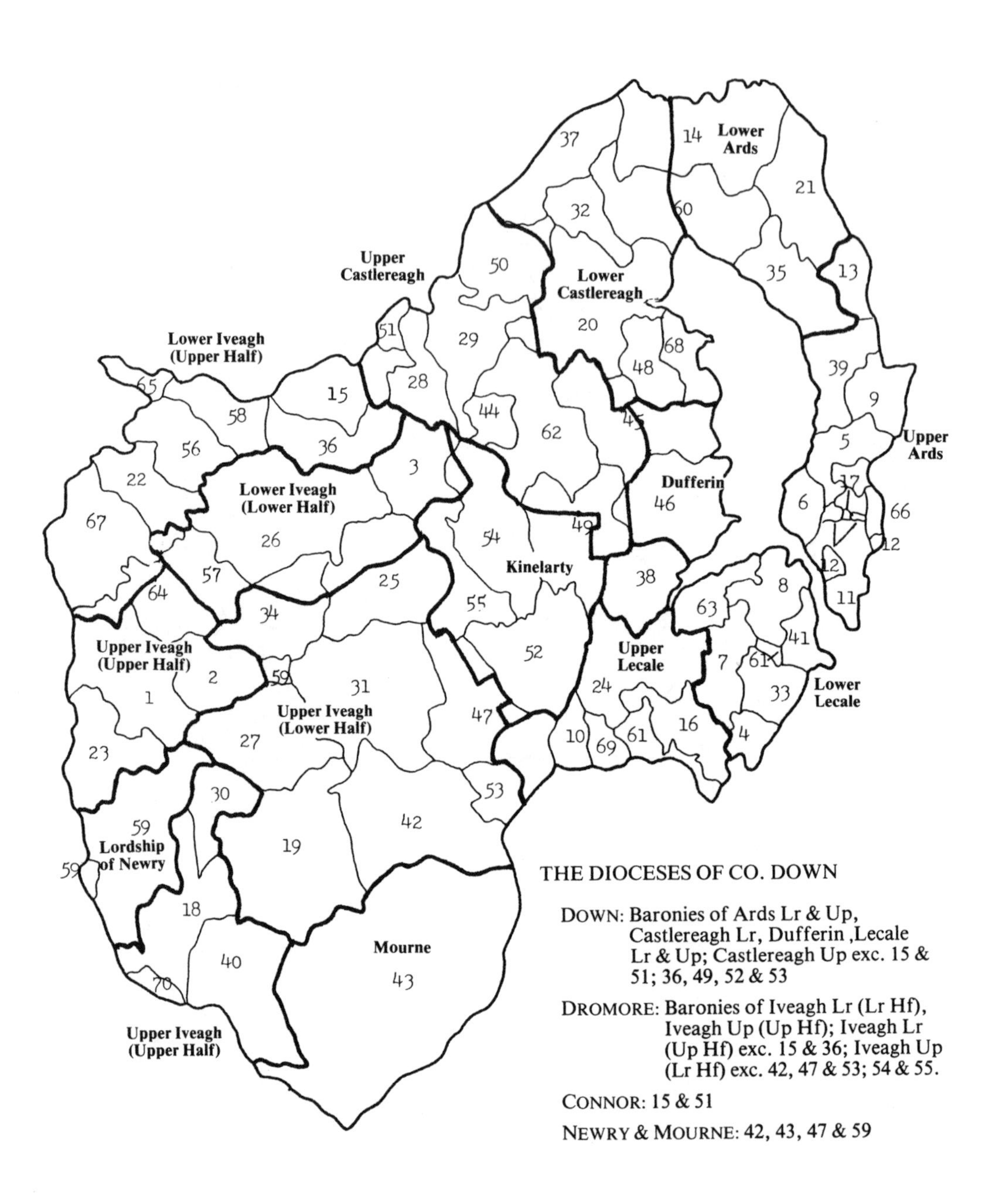

THE DIOCESES OF CO. DOWN

DOWN: Baronies of Ards Lr & Up, Castlereagh Lr, Dufferin ,Lecale Lr & Up; Castlereagh Up exc. 15 & 51; 36, 49, 52 & 53

DROMORE: Baronies of Iveagh Lr (Lr Hf), Iveagh Up (Up Hf); Iveagh Lr (Up Hf) exc. 15 & 36; Iveagh Up (Lr Hf) exc. 42, 47 & 53; 54 & 55.

CONNOR: 15 & 51

NEWRY & MOURNE: 42, 43, 47 & 59

THE POOR LAW UNIONS OF COUNTY DOWN

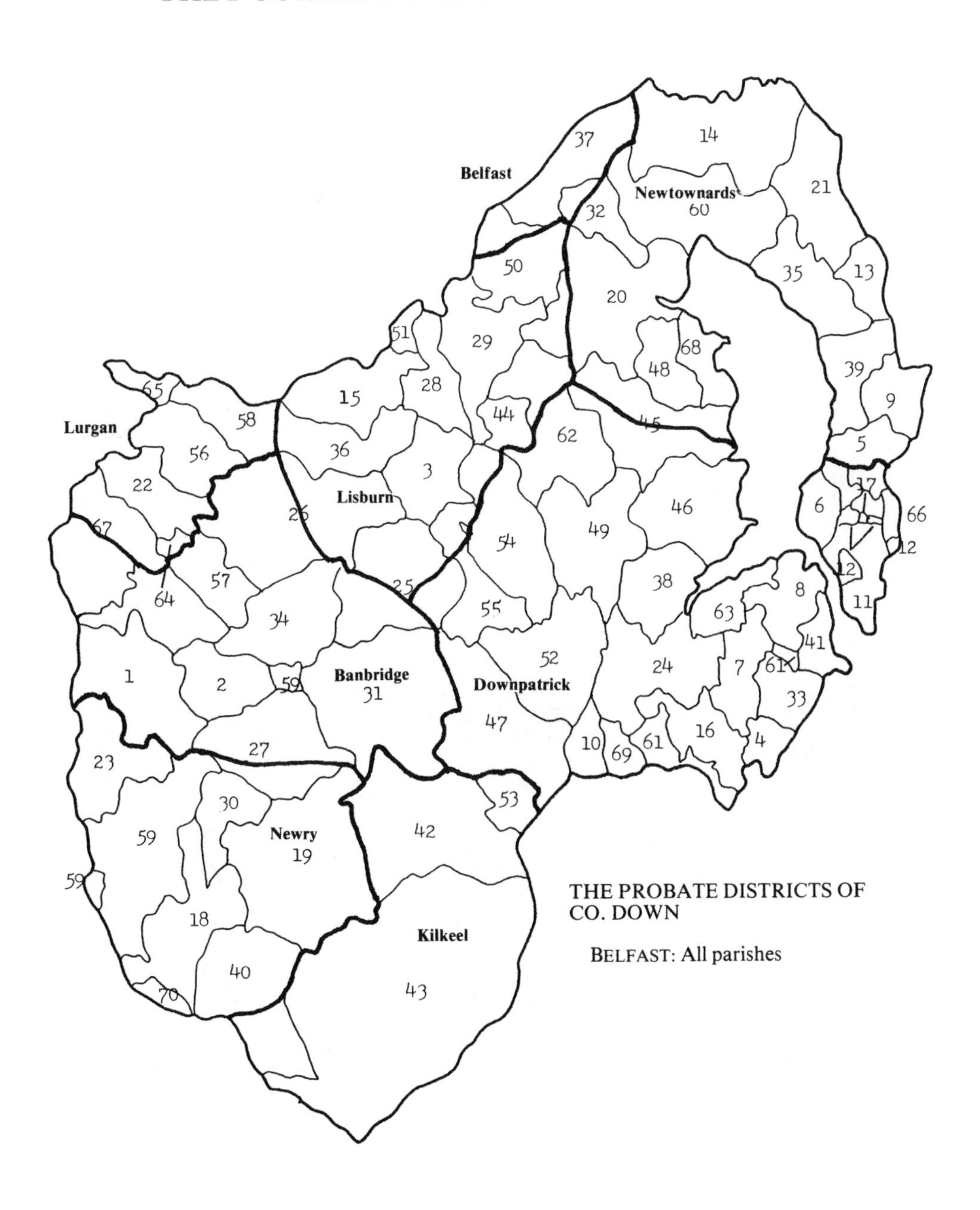

THE PROBATE DISTRICTS OF CO. DOWN

BELFAST: All parishes

THE PARISHES OF COUNTY DUBLIN

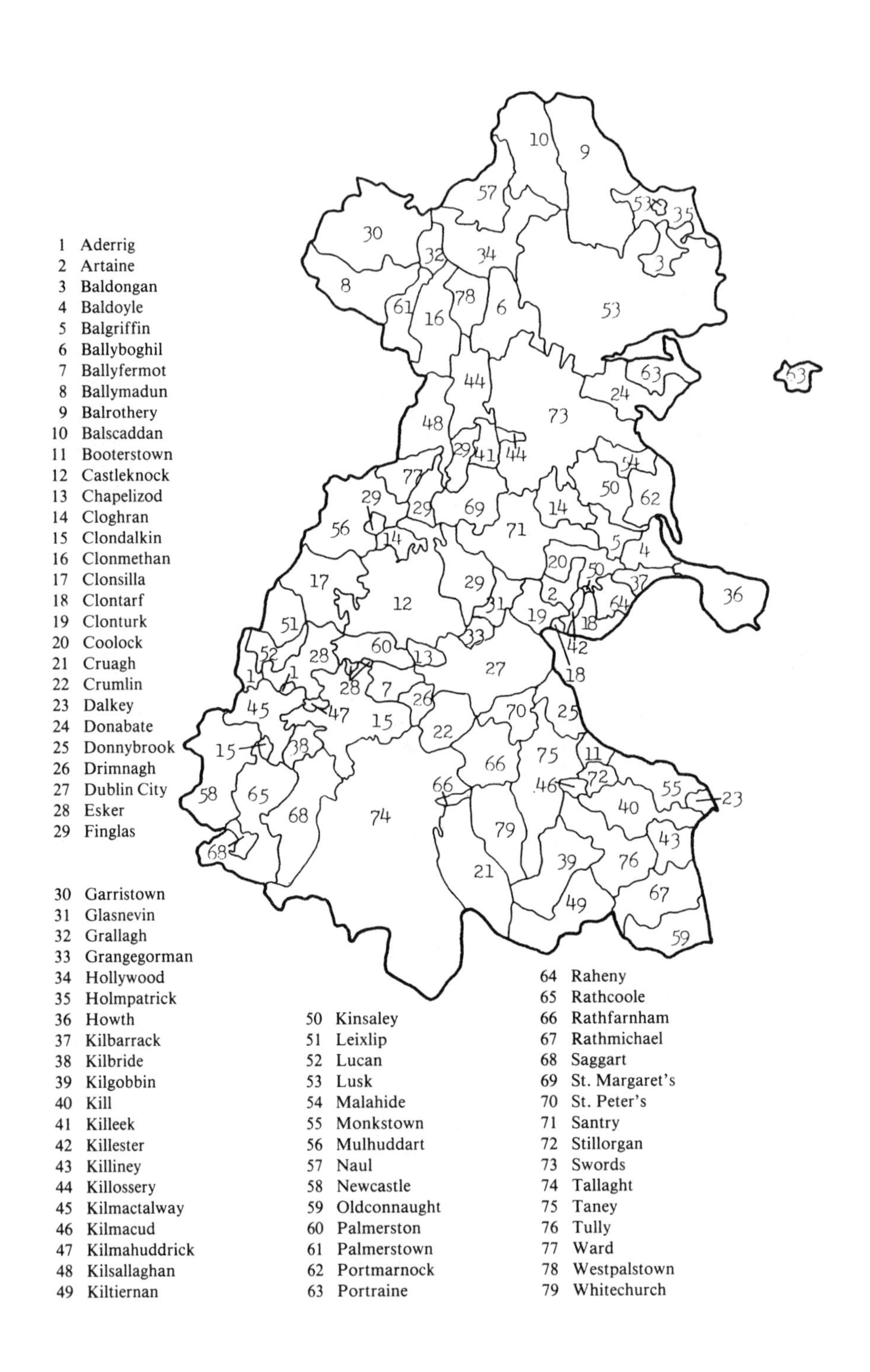

1 Aderrig
2 Artaine
3 Baldongan
4 Baldoyle
5 Balgriffin
6 Ballyboghil
7 Ballyfermot
8 Ballymadun
9 Balrothery
10 Balscaddan
11 Booterstown
12 Castleknock
13 Chapelizod
14 Cloghran
15 Clondalkin
16 Clonmethan
17 Clonsilla
18 Clontarf
19 Clonturk
20 Coolock
21 Cruagh
22 Crumlin
23 Dalkey
24 Donabate
25 Donnybrook
26 Drimnagh
27 Dublin City
28 Esker
29 Finglas

30 Garristown
31 Glasnevin
32 Grallagh
33 Grangegorman
34 Hollywood
35 Holmpatrick
36 Howth
37 Kilbarrack
38 Kilbride
39 Kilgobbin
40 Kill
41 Killeek
42 Killester
43 Killiney
44 Killossery
45 Kilmactalway
46 Kilmacud
47 Kilmahuddrick
48 Kilsallaghan
49 Kiltiernan

50 Kinsaley
51 Leixlip
52 Lucan
53 Lusk
54 Malahide
55 Monkstown
56 Mulhuddart
57 Naul
58 Newcastle
59 Oldconnaught
60 Palmerston
61 Palmerstown
62 Portmarnock
63 Portraine

64 Raheny
65 Rathcoole
66 Rathfarnham
67 Rathmichael
68 Saggart
69 St. Margaret's
70 St. Peter's
71 Santry
72 Stillorgan
73 Swords
74 Tallaght
75 Taney
76 Tully
77 Ward
78 Westpalstown
79 Whitechurch

THE BARONIES OF COUNTY DUBLIN

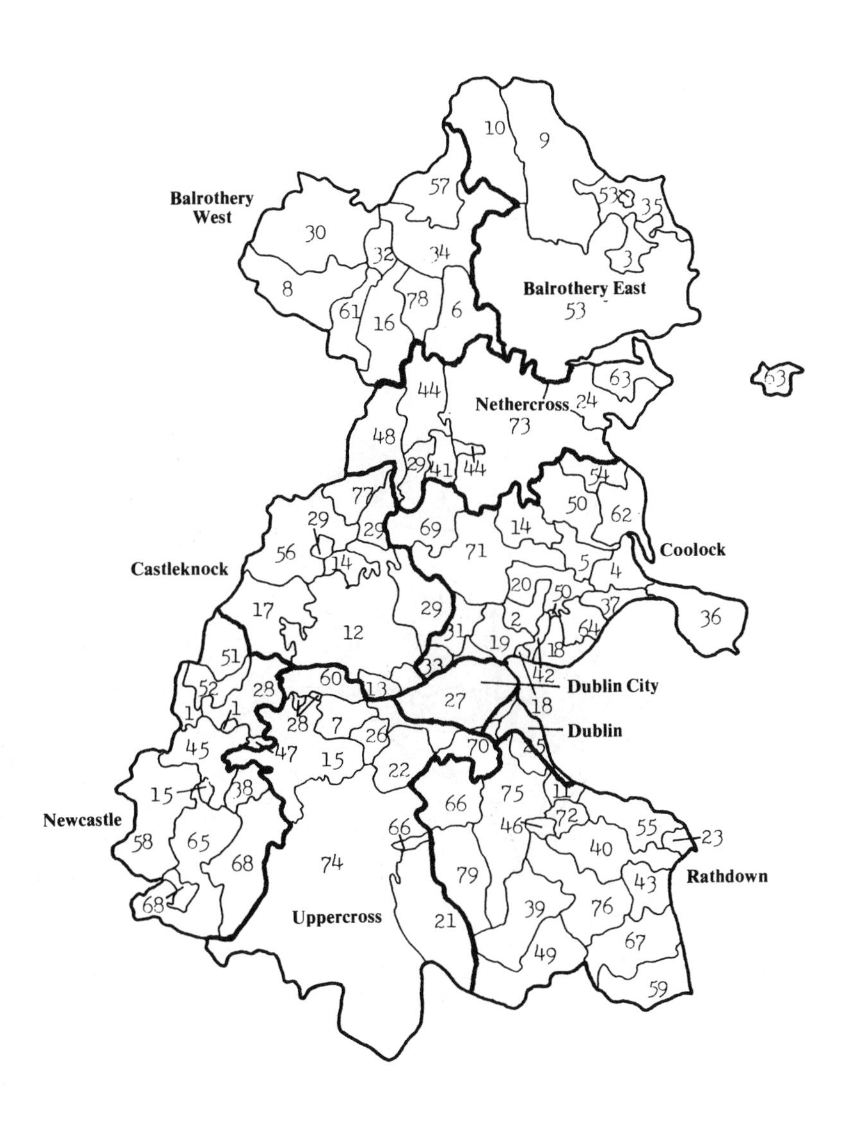

THE DIOCESES OF COUNTY DUBLIN

DUBLIN: All parishes

THE POOR LAW UNIONS OF COUNTY DUBLIN

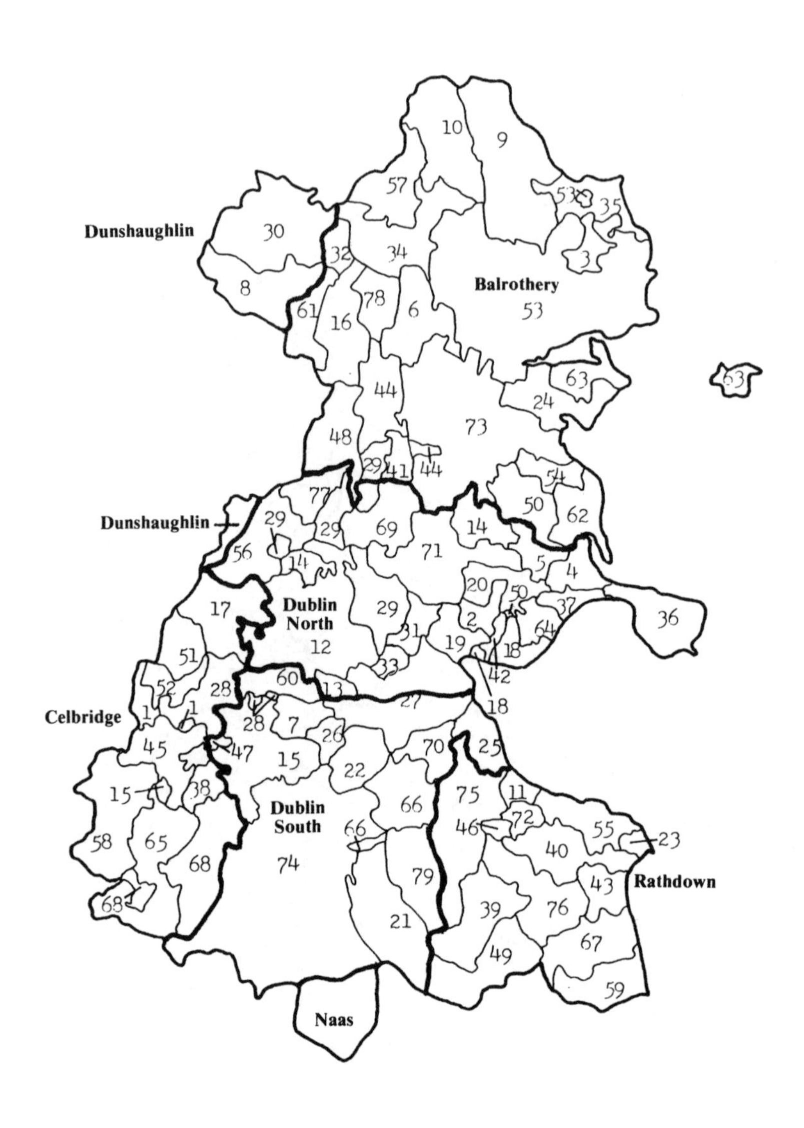

THE PROBATE DISTRICTS OF COUNTY DUBLIN

DUBLIN: All parishes

THE PARISHES OF DUBLIN CITY

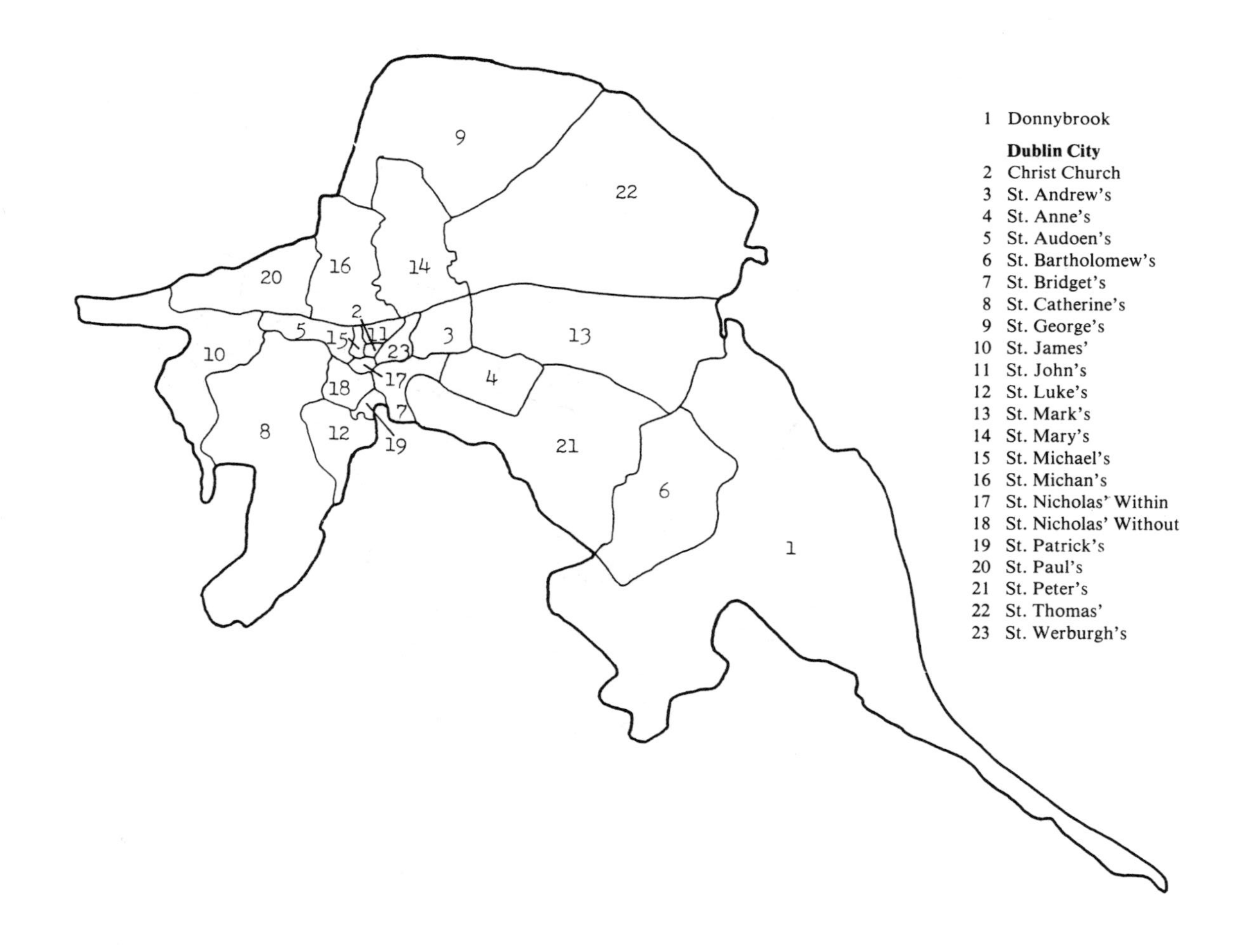

THE BARONIES OF DUBLIN CITY

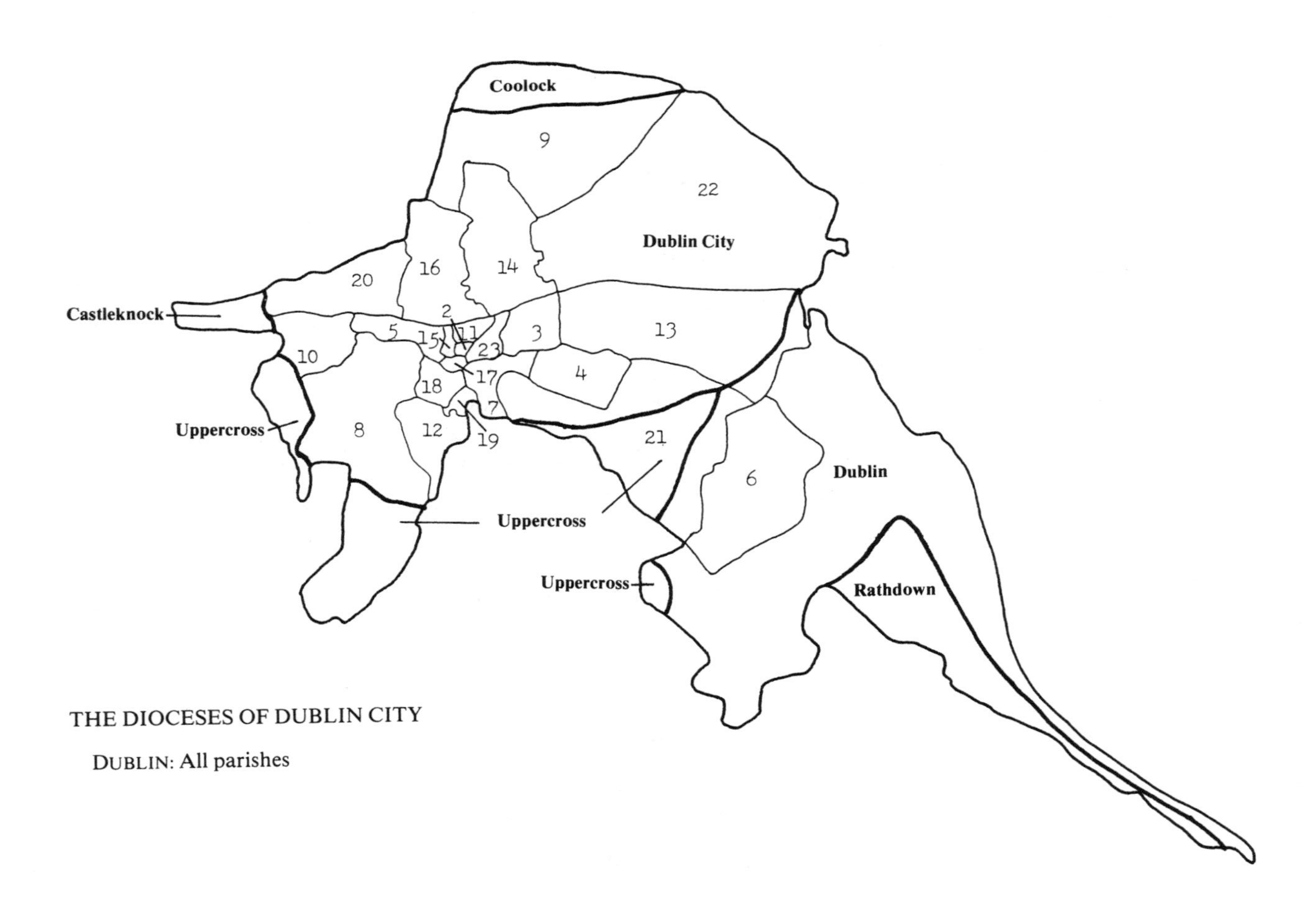

THE DIOCESES OF DUBLIN CITY

DUBLIN: All parishes

THE POOR LAW UNIONS OF DUBLIN CITY

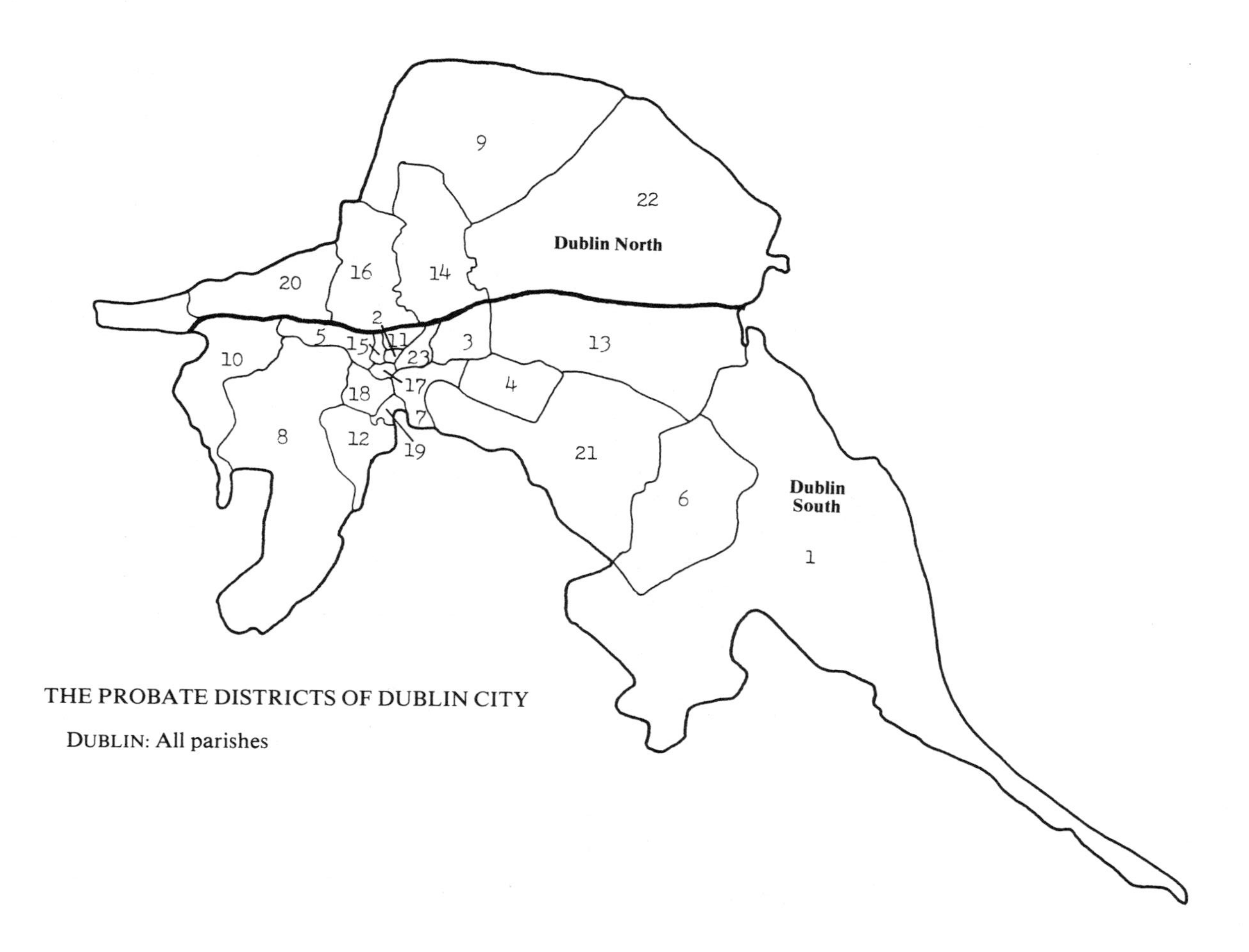

THE PROBATE DISTRICTS OF DUBLIN CITY

DUBLIN: All parishes

THE PARISHES OF COUNTY FERMANAGH

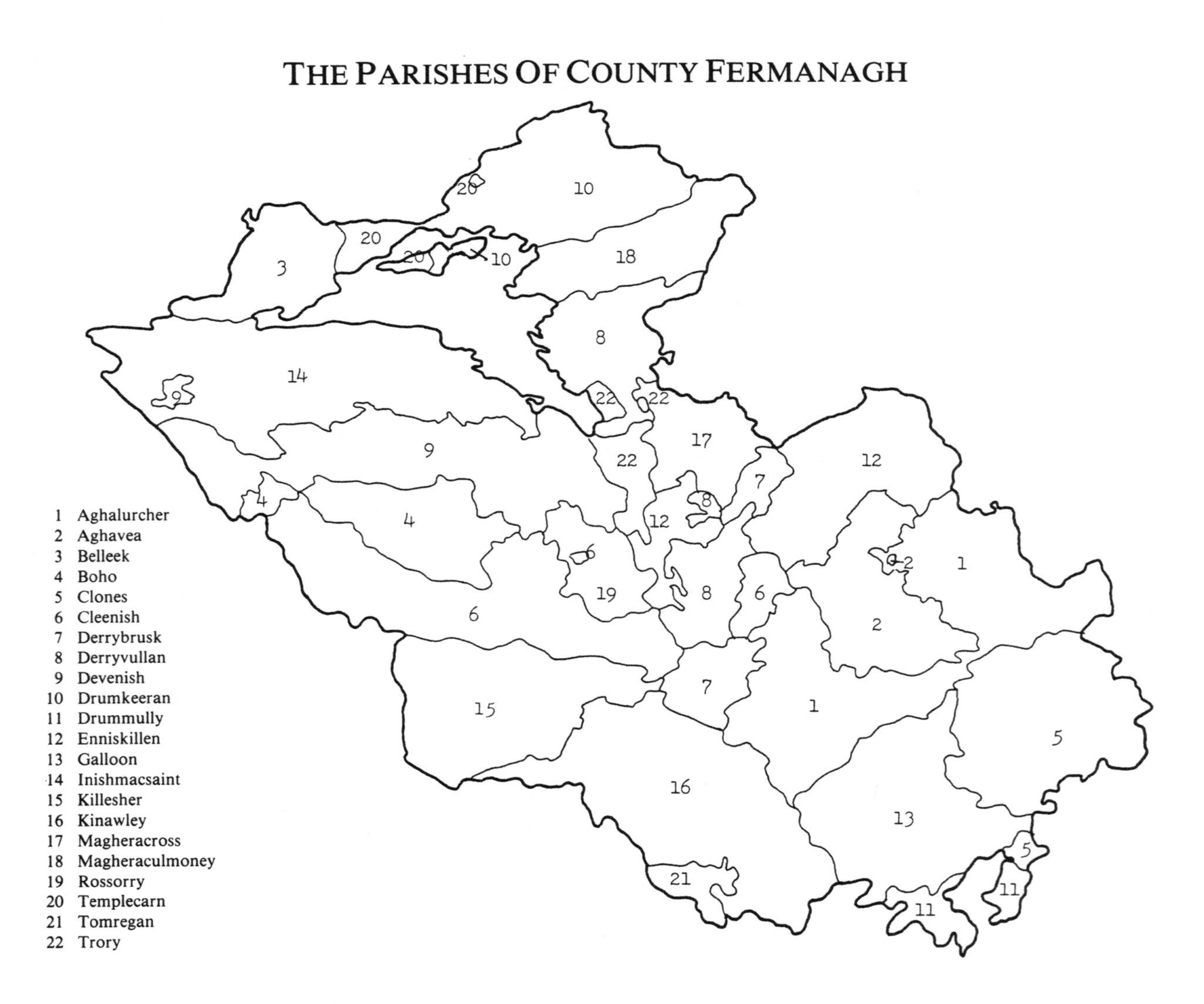

THE BARONIES OF COUNTY FERMANAGH

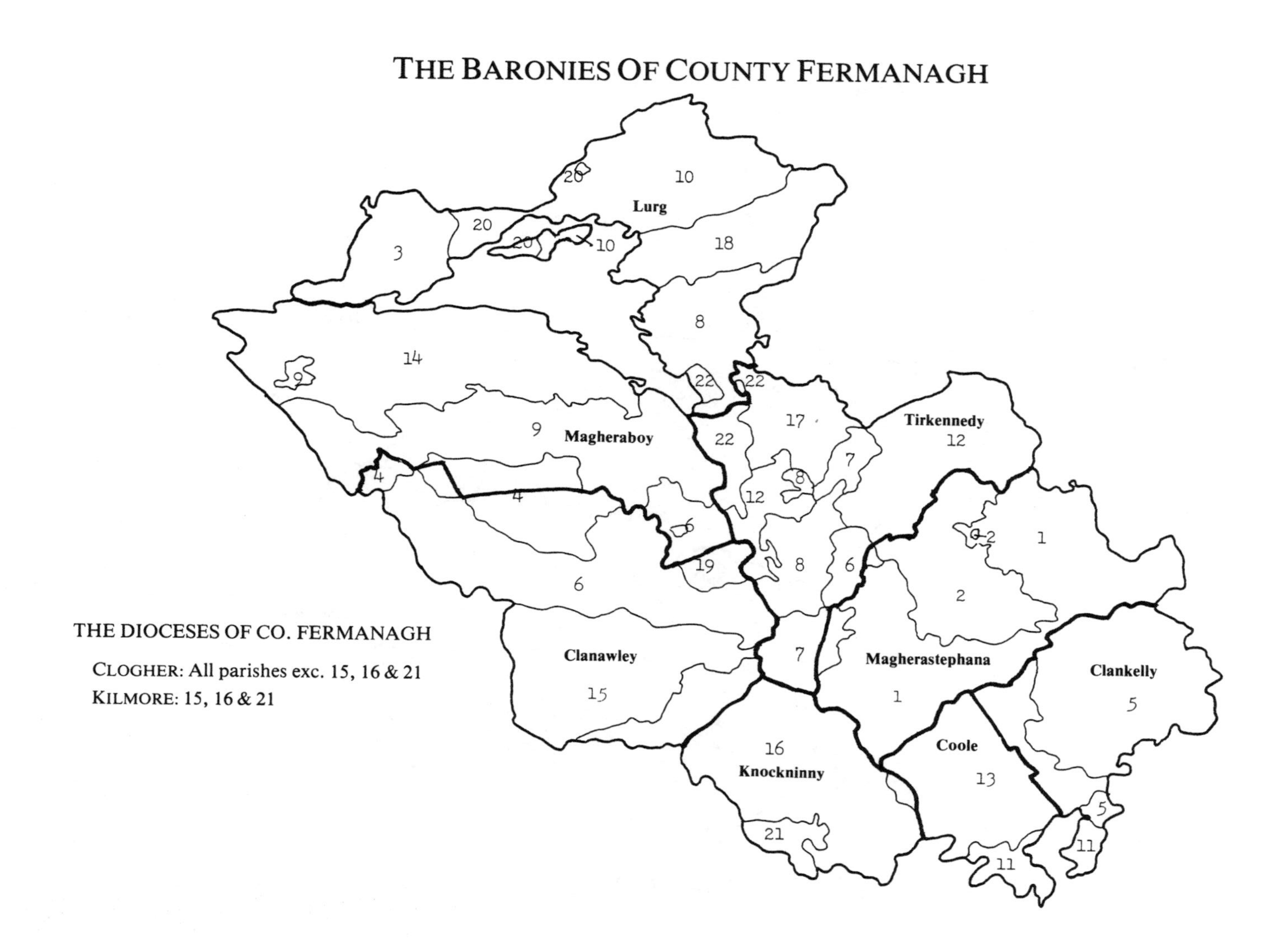

THE DIOCESES OF CO. FERMANAGH

CLOGHER: All parishes exc. 15, 16 & 21
KILMORE: 15, 16 & 21

THE POOR LAW UNIONS OF COUNTY FERMANAGH

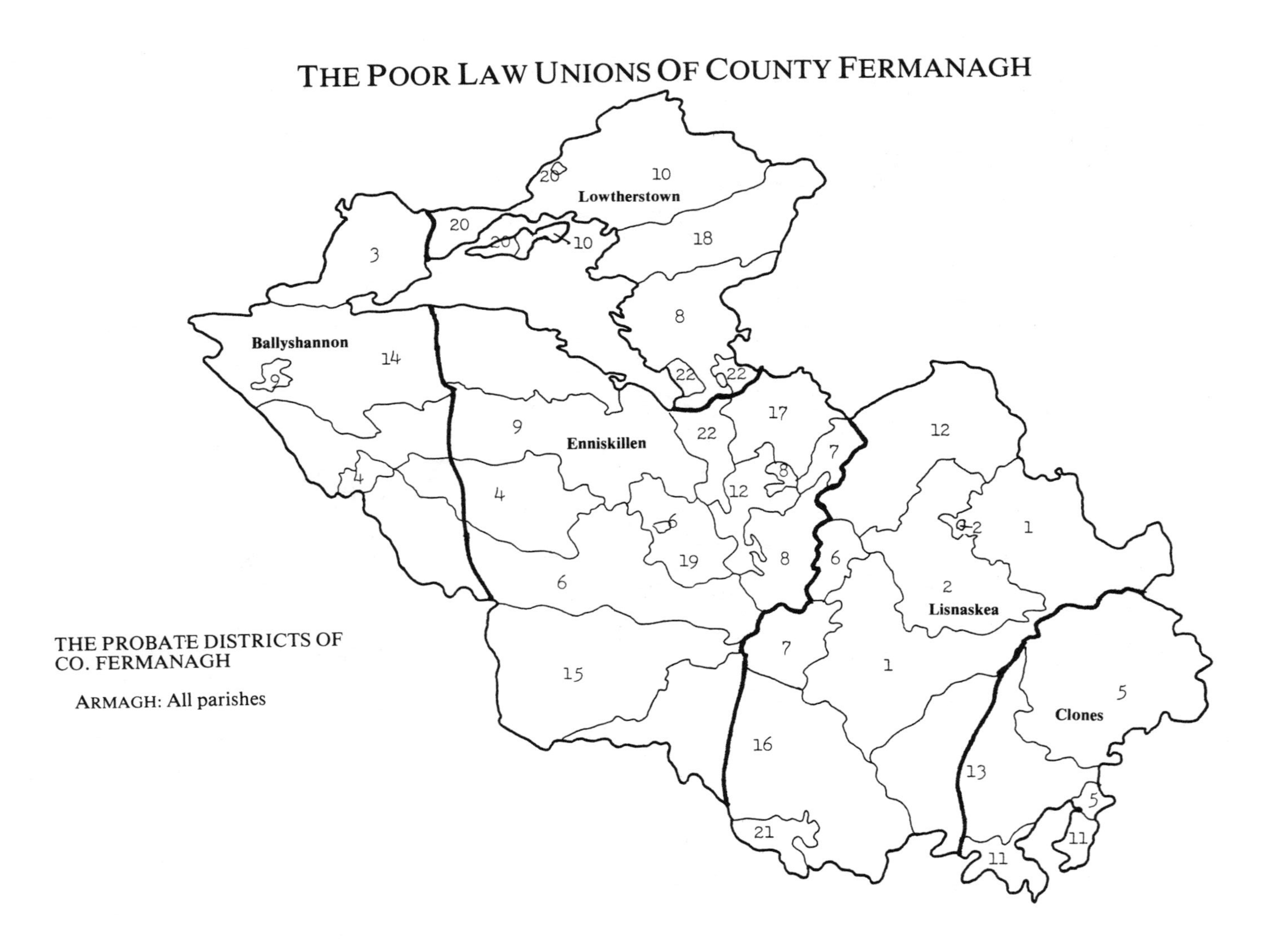

THE PROBATE DISTRICTS OF
CO. FERMANAGH

ARMAGH: All parishes

THE PARISHES OF COUNTY GALWAY

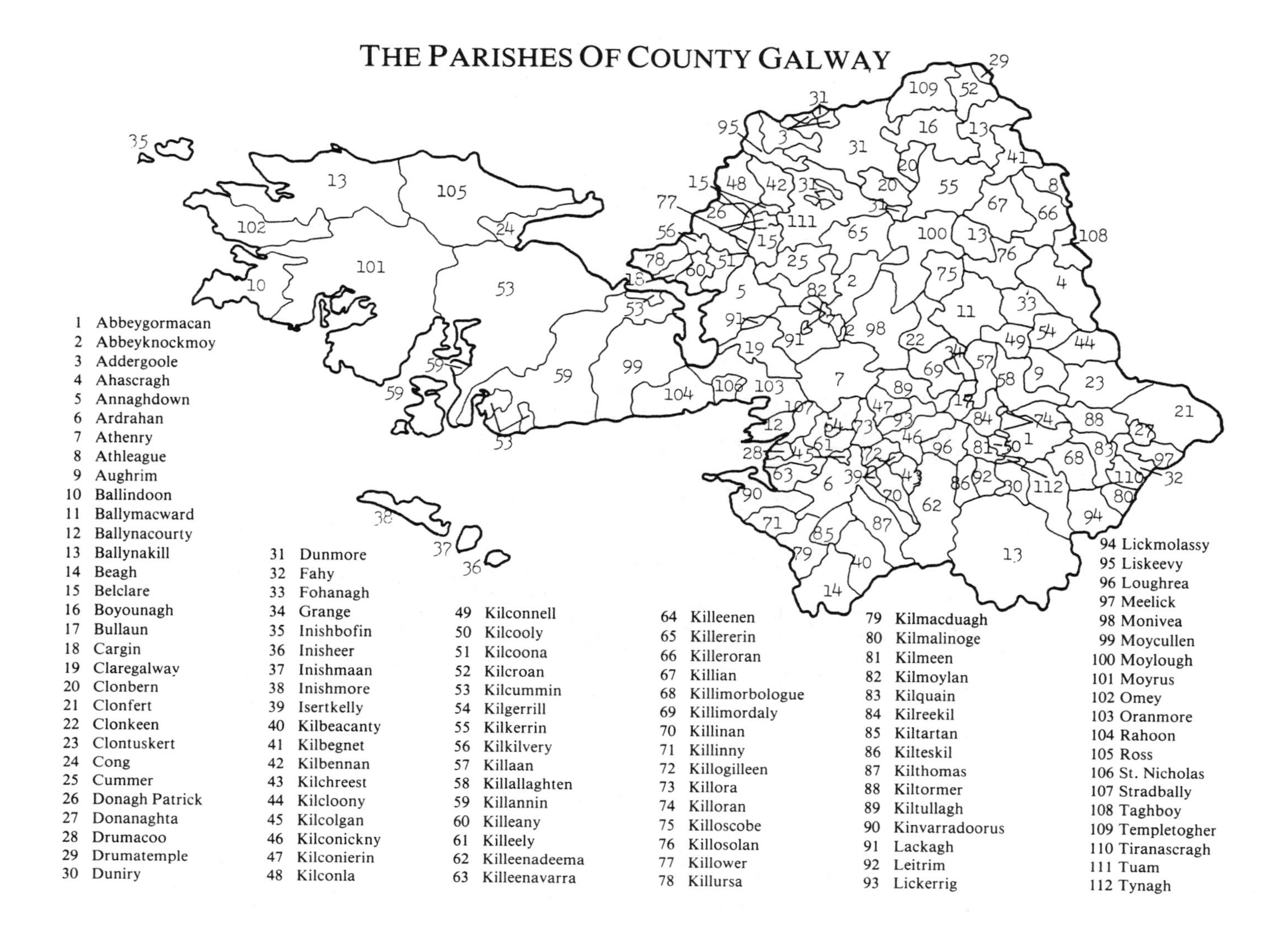

1 Abbeygormacan
2 Abbeyknockmoy
3 Addergoole
4 Ahascragh
5 Annaghdown
6 Ardrahan
7 Athenry
8 Athleague
9 Aughrim
10 Ballindoon
11 Ballymacward
12 Ballynacourty
13 Ballynakill
14 Beagh
15 Belclare
16 Boyounagh
17 Bullaun
18 Cargin
19 Claregalway
20 Clonbern
21 Clonfert
22 Clonkeen
23 Clontuskert
24 Cong
25 Cummer
26 Donagh Patrick
27 Donanaghta
28 Drumacoo
29 Drumatemple
30 Duniry
31 Dunmore
32 Fahy
33 Fohanagh
34 Grange
35 Inishbofin
36 Inisheer
37 Inishmaan
38 Inishmore
39 Isertkelly
40 Kilbeacanty
41 Kilbegnet
42 Kilbennan
43 Kilchreest
44 Kilcloony
45 Kilcolgan
46 Kilconickny
47 Kilconierin
48 Kilconla
49 Kilconnell
50 Kilcooly
51 Kilcoona
52 Kilcroan
53 Kilcummin
54 Kilgerrill
55 Kilkerrin
56 Kilkilvery
57 Killaan
58 Killallaghten
59 Killannin
60 Killeany
61 Killeely
62 Killeenadeema
63 Killeenavarra
64 Killeenen
65 Killererin
66 Killeroran
67 Killian
68 Killimorbologue
69 Killimordaly
70 Killinan
71 Killinny
72 Killogilleen
73 Killora
74 Killoran
75 Killoscobe
76 Killosolan
77 Killower
78 Killursa
79 Kilmacduagh
80 Kilmalinoge
81 Kilmeen
82 Kilmoylan
83 Kilquain
84 Kilreekil
85 Kiltartan
86 Kilteskil
87 Kilthomas
88 Kiltormer
89 Kiltullagh
90 Kinvarradoorus
91 Lackagh
92 Leitrim
93 Lickerrig
94 Lickmolassy
95 Liskeevy
96 Loughrea
97 Meelick
98 Monivea
99 Moycullen
100 Moylough
101 Moyrus
102 Omey
103 Oranmore
104 Rahoon
105 Ross
106 St. Nicholas
107 Stradbally
108 Taghboy
109 Templetogher
110 Tiranascragh
111 Tuam
112 Tynagh

THE BARONIES OF COUNTY GALWAY

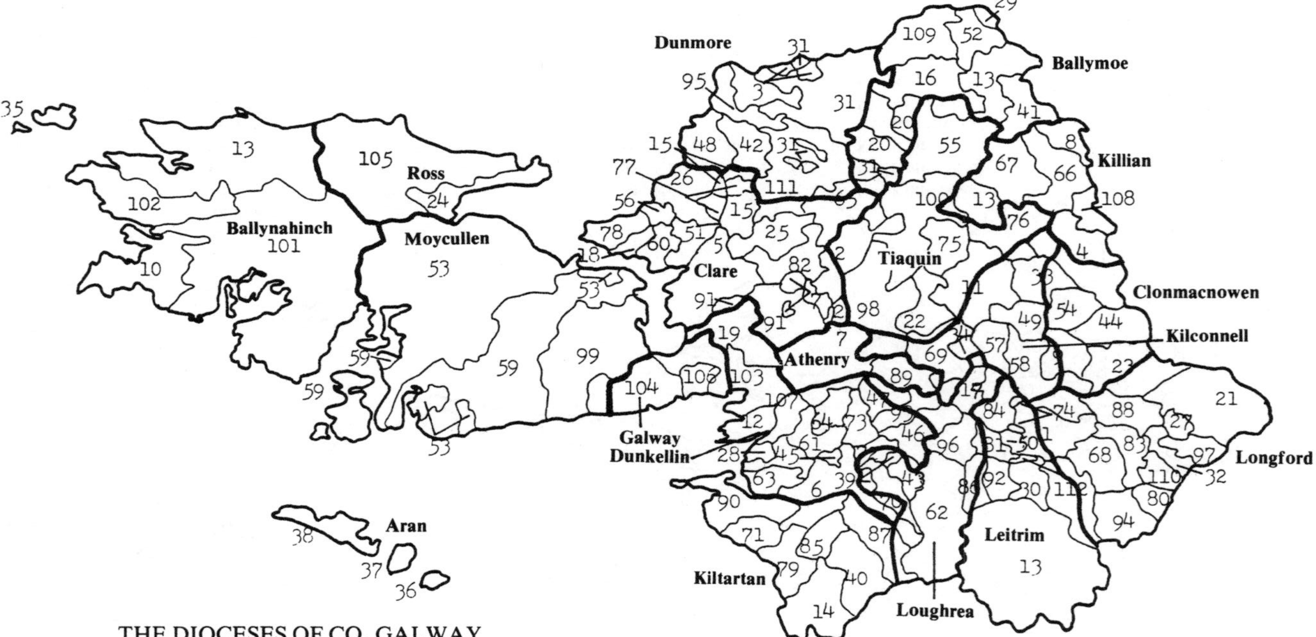

THE DIOCESES OF CO. GALWAY

TUAM: Aran, Ballynahinch, Ross, Moycullen, Dunmore & Galway Baronies; Ballymoe exc. 13, 29, 41 & 52; Tiaquin exc. 11, 22, 69 & 76; Clare exc. 60; 7, 12, 13, 19, 71, 81, 98 & 103

ELPHIN: Killian Barony exc. 13; 13, 29, 41 & 52 in Ballymoe; 4 & 76

KILMACDUAGH: Kiltartan exc. 71; Dunkellin exc. 12, 19, 46, 47, 93 & 103; Loughrea exc. 34, 57, 62, 86 & 96; 50 & 60

CLONFERT: Longford Barony; Athenry exc. 7; Clonmacnowen exc. 4; Kilconnell exc. 4, 76 & 98; Leitrim exc. 50 & 81; 11, 22, 34, 46, 47, 57, 62, 69, 86, 93 & 96

THE POOR LAW UNIONS OF COUNTY GALWAY

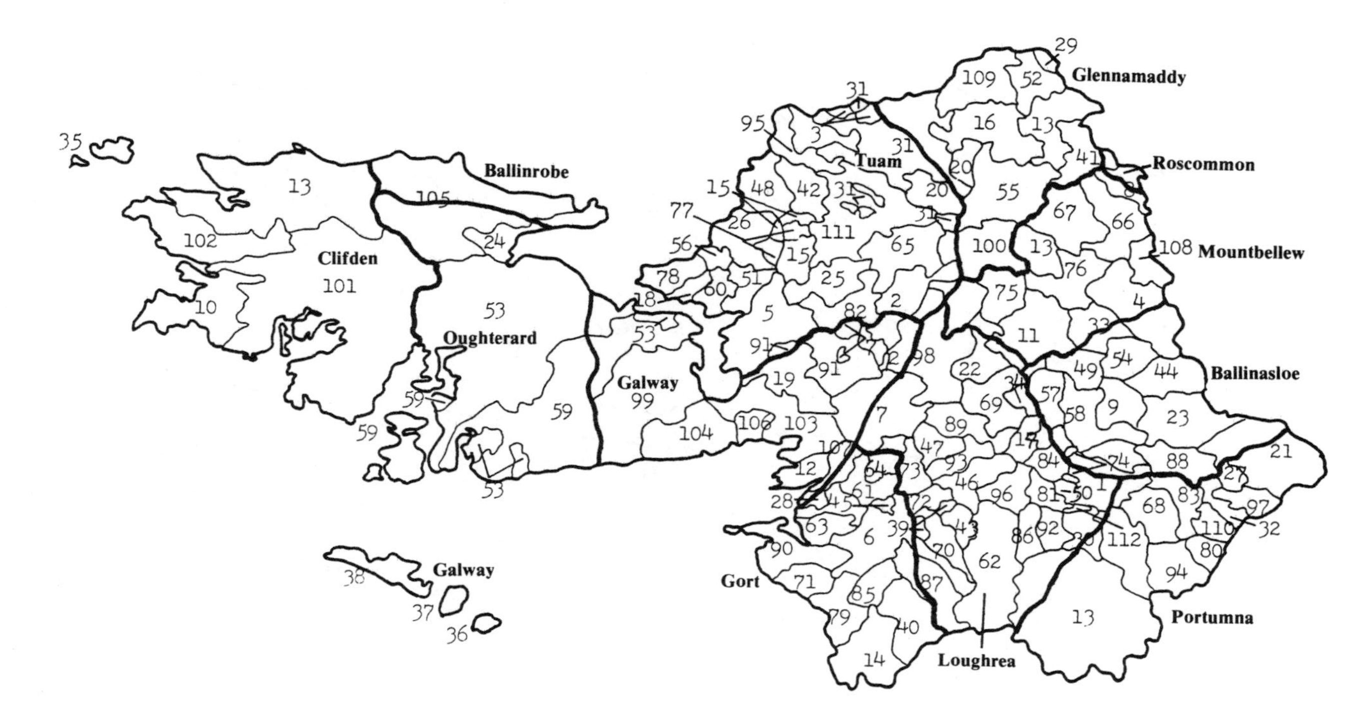

THE PROBATE DISTRICTS OF CO. GALWAY

TUAM: All parishes

THE PARISHES OF COUNTY KERRY

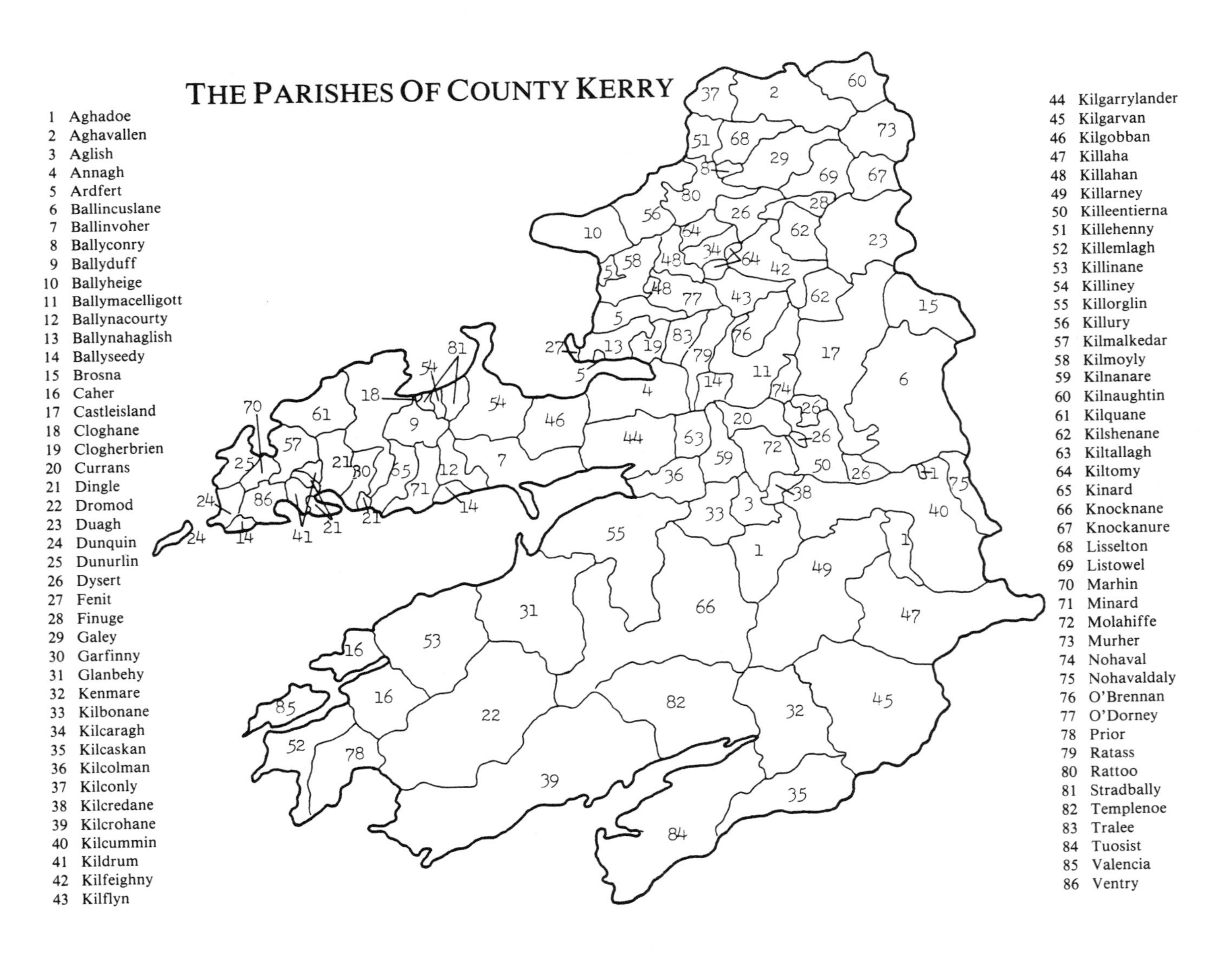

1 Aghadoe
2 Aghavallen
3 Aglish
4 Annagh
5 Ardfert
6 Ballincuslane
7 Ballinvoher
8 Ballyconry
9 Ballyduff
10 Ballyheige
11 Ballymacelligott
12 Ballynacourty
13 Ballynahaglish
14 Ballyseedy
15 Brosna
16 Caher
17 Castleisland
18 Cloghane
19 Clogherbrien
20 Currans
21 Dingle
22 Dromod
23 Duagh
24 Dunquin
25 Dunurlin
26 Dysert
27 Fenit
28 Finuge
29 Galey
30 Garfinny
31 Glanbehy
32 Kenmare
33 Kilbonane
34 Kilcaragh
35 Kilcaskan
36 Kilcolman
37 Kilconly
38 Kilcredane
39 Kilcrohane
40 Kilcummin
41 Kildrum
42 Kilfeighny
43 Kilflyn
44 Kilgarrylander
45 Kilgarvan
46 Kilgobban
47 Killaha
48 Killahan
49 Killarney
50 Killeentierna
51 Killehenny
52 Killemlagh
53 Killinane
54 Killiney
55 Killorglin
56 Killury
57 Kilmalkedar
58 Kilmoyly
59 Kilnanare
60 Kilnaughtin
61 Kilquane
62 Kilshenane
63 Kiltallagh
64 Kiltomy
65 Kinard
66 Knocknane
67 Knockanure
68 Lisselton
69 Listowel
70 Marhin
71 Minard
72 Molahiffe
73 Murher
74 Nohaval
75 Nohavaldaly
76 O'Brennan
77 O'Dorney
78 Prior
79 Ratass
80 Rattoo
81 Stradbally
82 Templenoe
83 Tralee
84 Tuosist
85 Valencia
86 Ventry

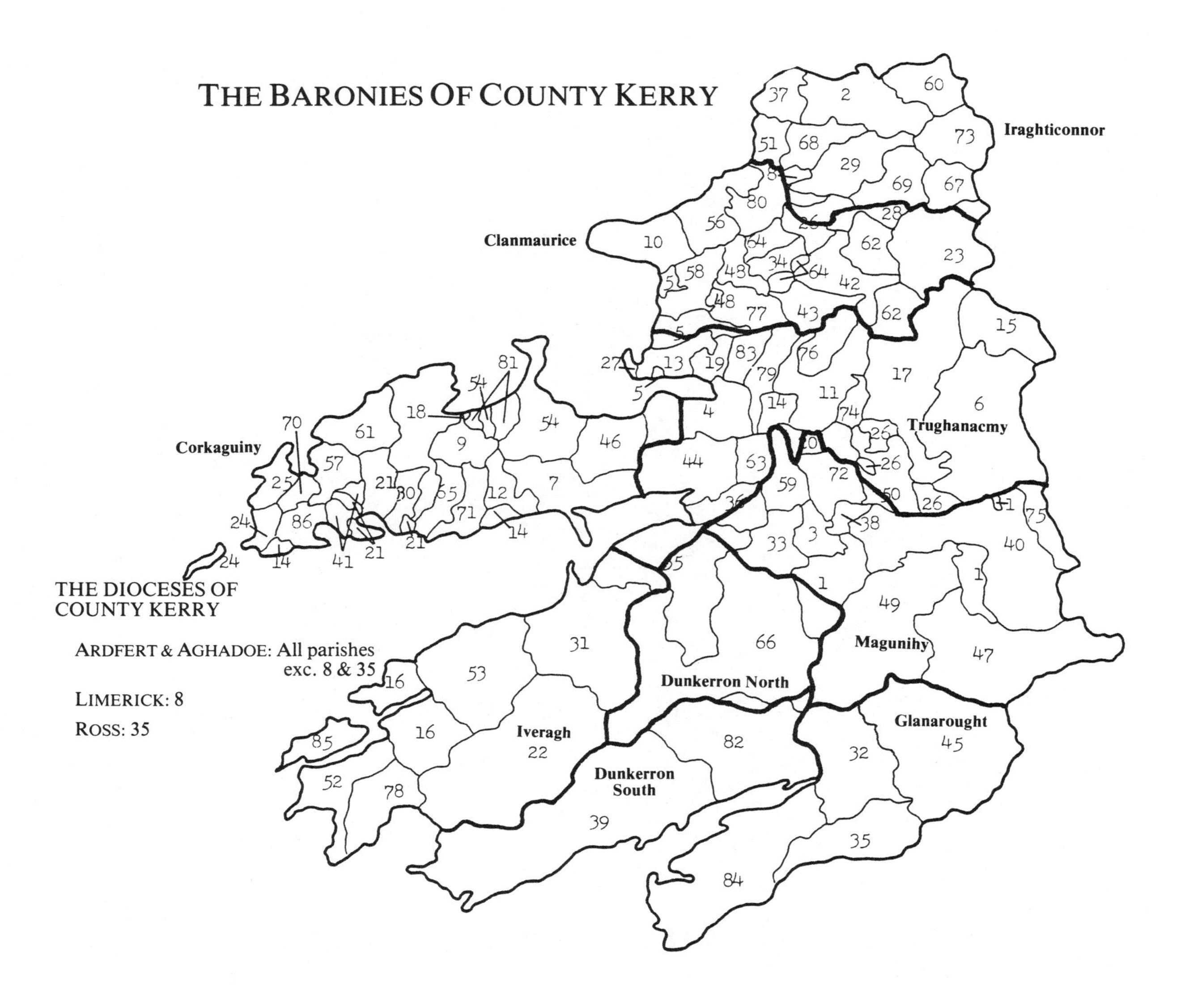
THE BARONIES OF COUNTY KERRY
Iraghticonnor
Clanmaurice
Trughanacmy
Corkaguiny
Magunihy
Dunkerron North
Glanarought
Iveragh
Dunkerron South
THE DIOCESES OF COUNTY KERRY
ARDFERT & AGHADOE: All parishes exc. 8 & 35
LIMERICK: 8
ROSS: 35

THE POOR LAW UNIONS OF COUNTY KERRY

THE PROBATE DISTRICTS OF COUNTY KERRY

LIMERICK: Baronies of Clanmaurice & Iraghticonnor

CORK: All parishes exc. the Baronies of Clanmaurice & Iraghticonnor

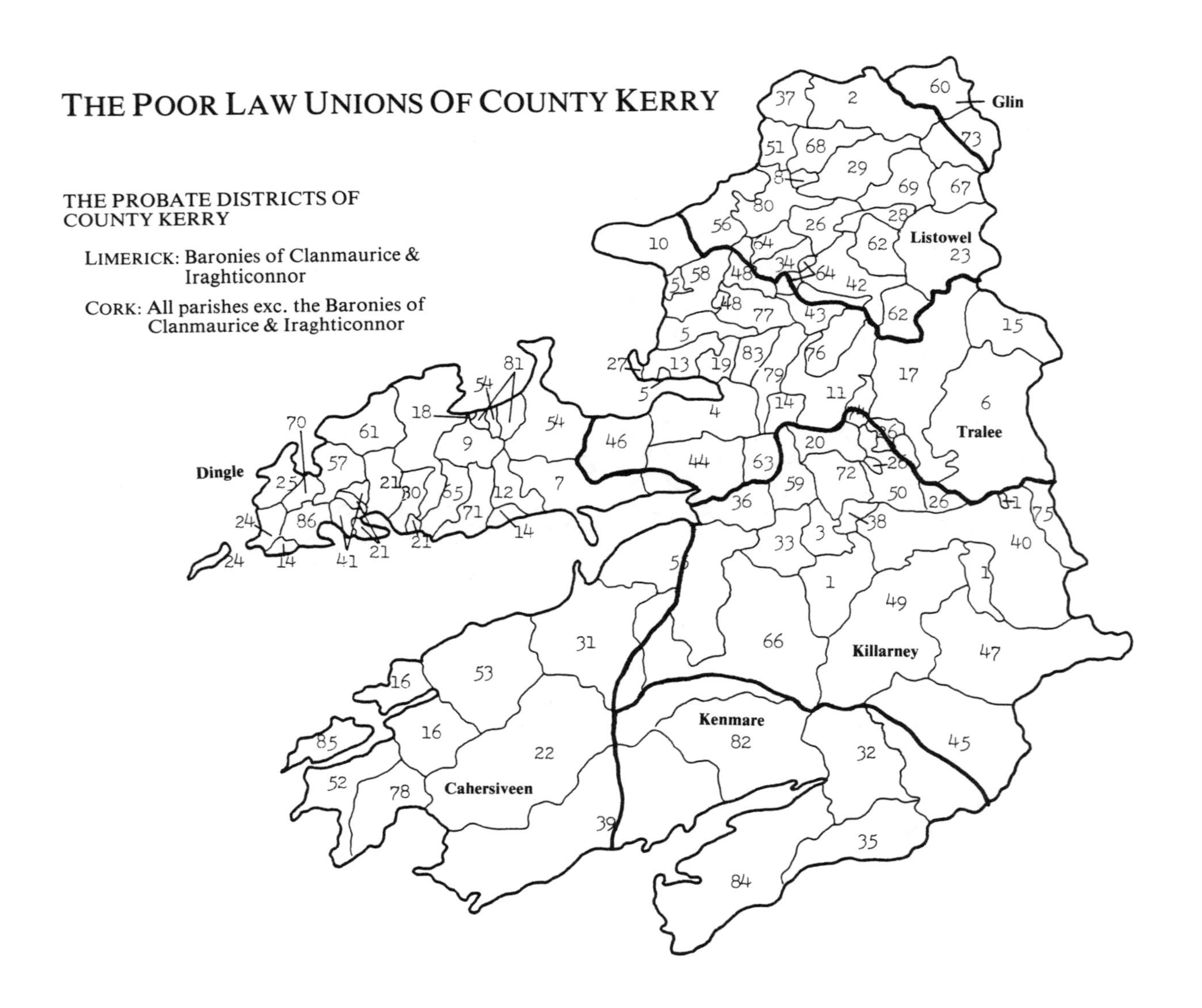

THE PARISHES OF COUNTY KILDARE

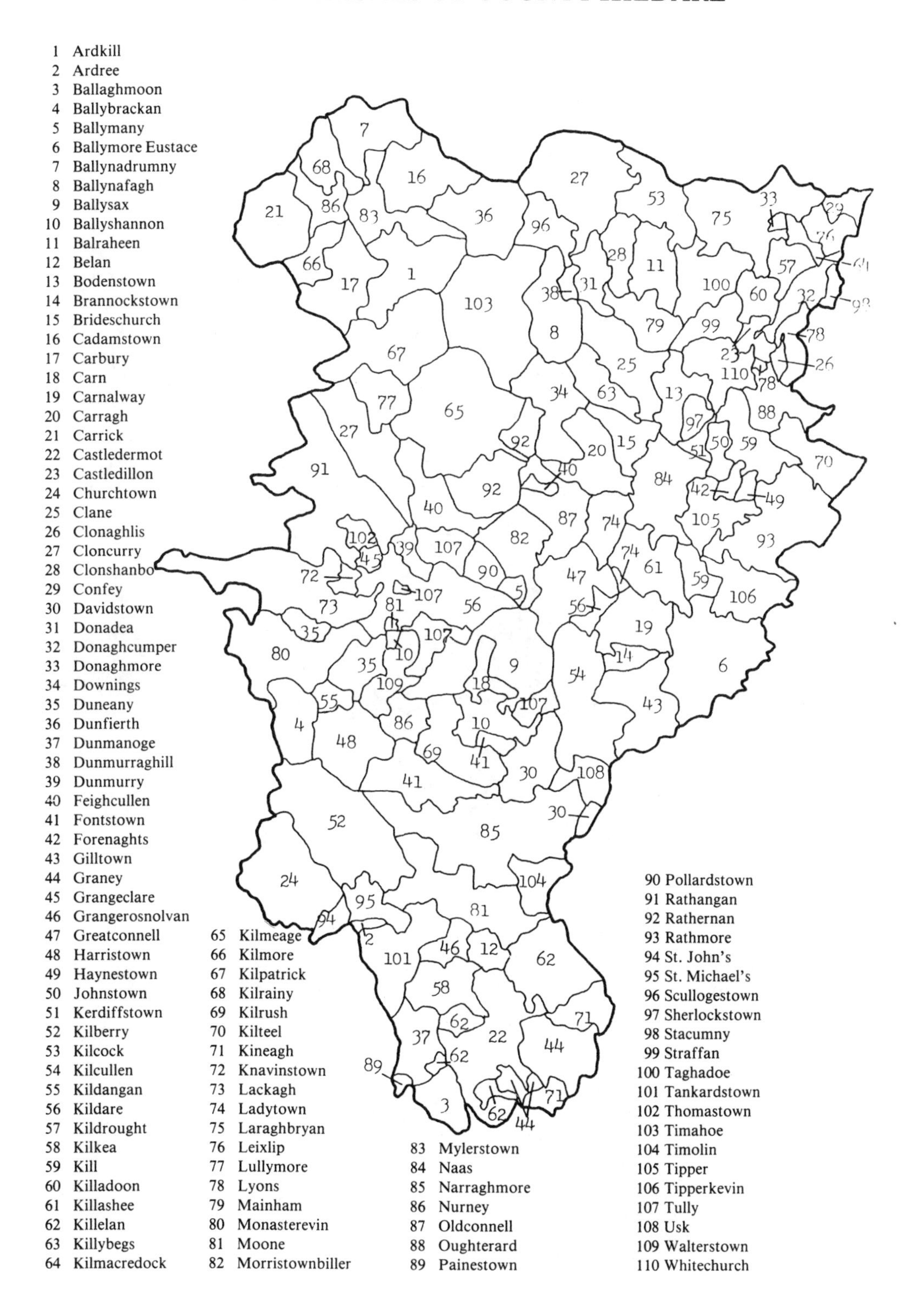

THE BARONIES OF COUNTY KILDARE

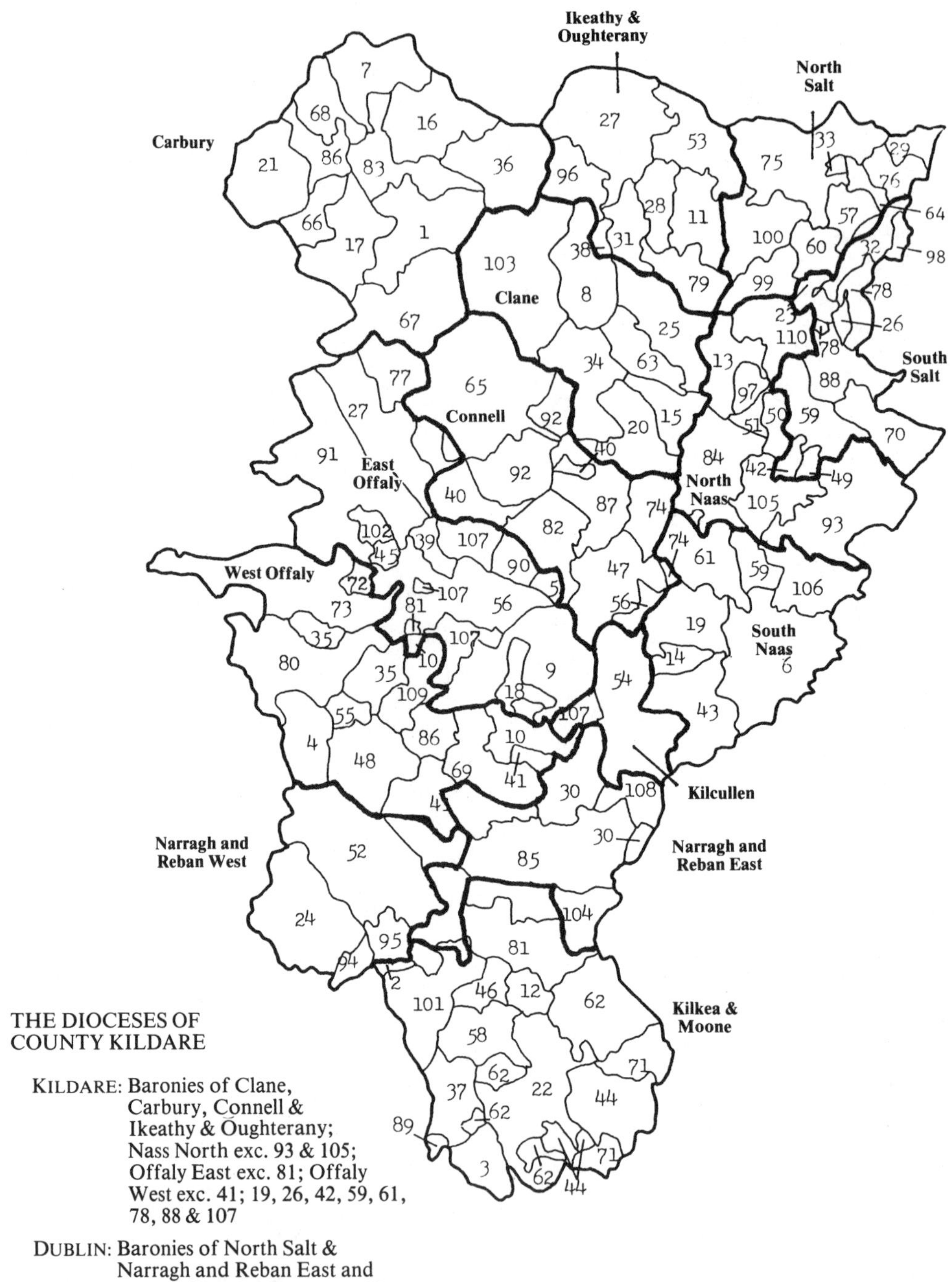

THE DIOCESES OF
COUNTY KILDARE

KILDARE: Baronies of Clane, Carbury, Connell & Ikeathy & Oughterany; Nass North exc. 93 & 105; Offaly East exc. 81; Offaly West exc. 41; 19, 26, 42, 59, 61, 78, 88 & 107

DUBLIN: Baronies of North Salt & Narragh and Reban East and West; Kilkea & Moone exc. 89; South Naas exc. 19, 59 & 61; 23, 32, 41, 49, 54, 70, 81, 93, 98 & 105

LEIGHLIN: 89

THE POOR LAW UNIONS OF COUNTY KILDARE

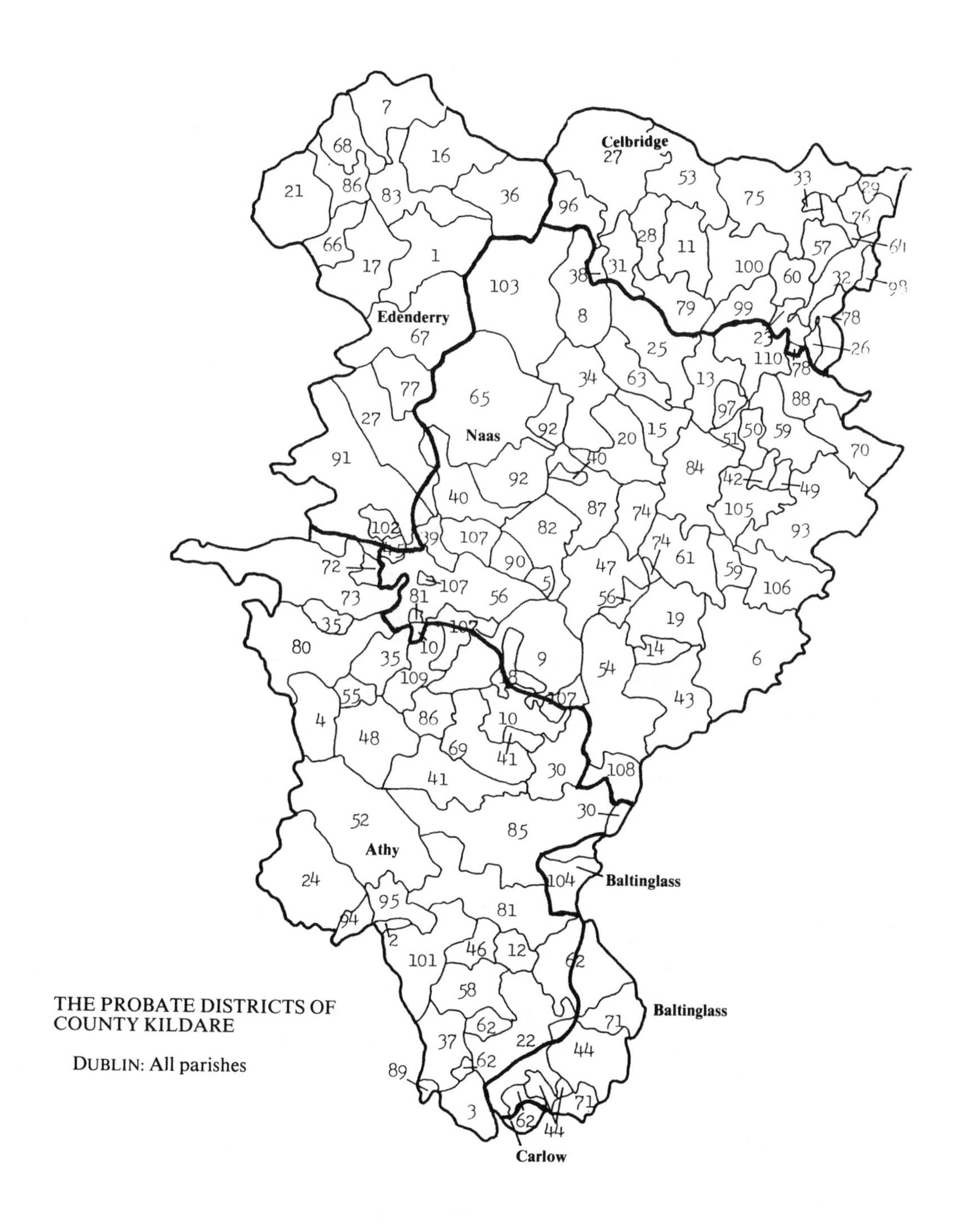

THE PROBATE DISTRICTS OF COUNTY KILDARE

DUBLIN: All parishes

THE PARISHES OF COUNTY KILKENNY

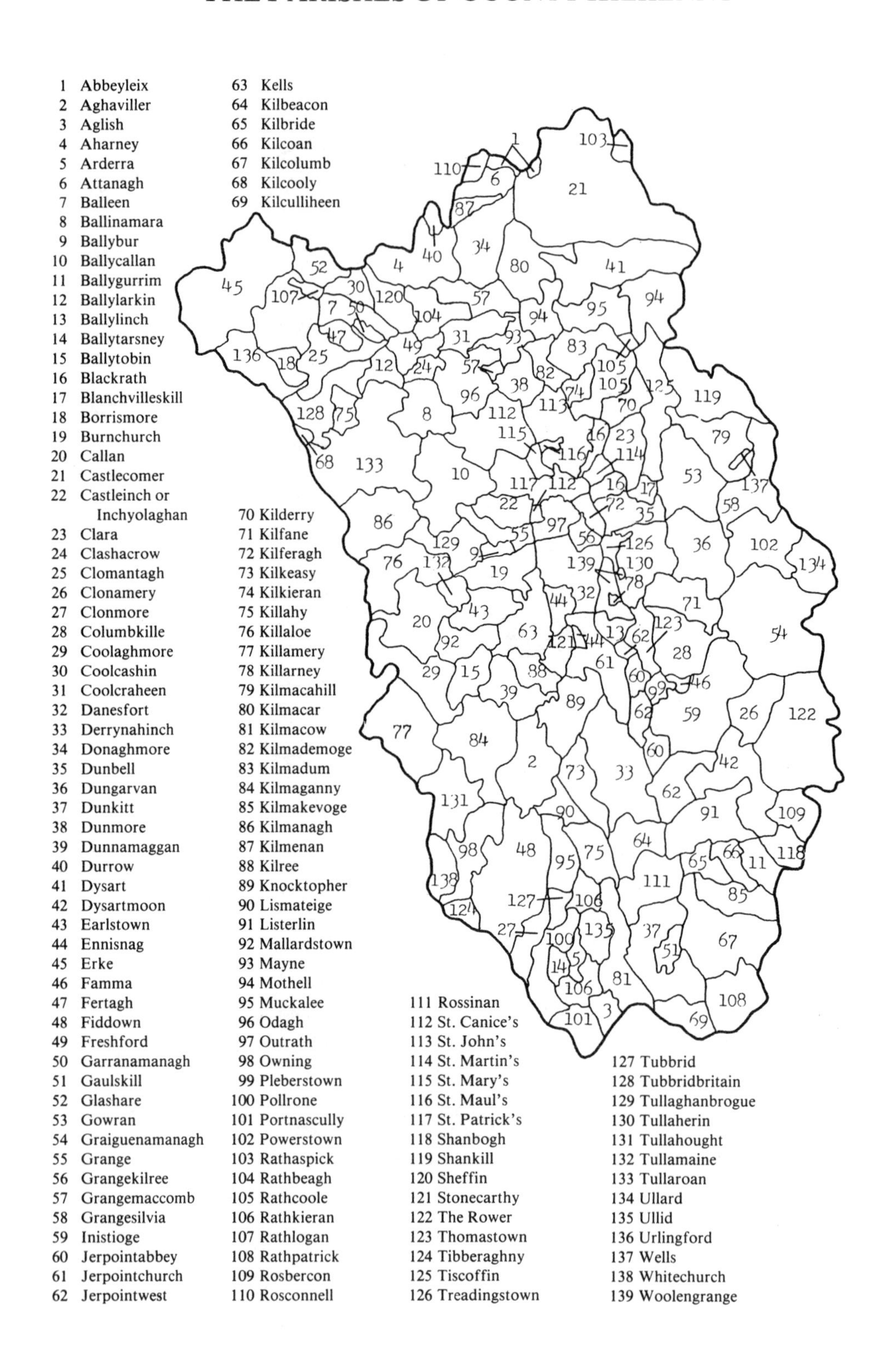

1 Abbeyleix
2 Aghaviller
3 Aglish
4 Aharney
5 Arderra
6 Attanagh
7 Balleen
8 Ballinamara
9 Ballybur
10 Ballycallan
11 Ballygurrim
12 Ballylarkin
13 Ballylinch
14 Ballytarsney
15 Ballytobin
16 Blackrath
17 Blanchvilleskill
18 Borrismore
19 Burnchurch
20 Callan
21 Castlecomer
22 Castleinch or Inchyolaghan
23 Clara
24 Clashacrow
25 Clomantagh
26 Clonamery
27 Clonmore
28 Columbkille
29 Coolaghmore
30 Coolcashin
31 Coolcraheen
32 Danesfort
33 Derrynahinch
34 Donaghmore
35 Dunbell
36 Dungarvan
37 Dunkitt
38 Dunmore
39 Dunnamaggan
40 Durrow
41 Dysart
42 Dysartmoon
43 Earlstown
44 Ennisnag
45 Erke
46 Famma
47 Fertagh
48 Fiddown
49 Freshford
50 Garranamanagh
51 Gaulskill
52 Glashare
53 Gowran
54 Graiguenamanagh
55 Grange
56 Grangekilree
57 Grangemaccomb
58 Grangesilvia
59 Inistioge
60 Jerpointabbey
61 Jerpointchurch
62 Jerpointwest
63 Kells
64 Kilbeacon
65 Kilbride
66 Kilcoan
67 Kilcolumb
68 Kilcooly
69 Kilculliheen
70 Kilderry
71 Kilfane
72 Kilferagh
73 Kilkeasy
74 Kilkieran
75 Killahy
76 Killaloe
77 Killamery
78 Killarney
79 Kilmacahill
80 Kilmacar
81 Kilmacow
82 Kilmademoge
83 Kilmadum
84 Kilmaganny
85 Kilmakevoge
86 Kilmanagh
87 Kilmenan
88 Kilree
89 Knocktopher
90 Lismateige
91 Listerlin
92 Mallardstown
93 Mayne
94 Mothell
95 Muckalee
96 Odagh
97 Outrath
98 Owning
99 Pleberstown
100 Pollrone
101 Portnascully
102 Powerstown
103 Rathaspick
104 Rathbeagh
105 Rathcoole
106 Rathkieran
107 Rathlogan
108 Rathpatrick
109 Rosbercon
110 Rosconnell
111 Rossinan
112 St. Canice's
113 St. John's
114 St. Martin's
115 St. Mary's
116 St. Maul's
117 St. Patrick's
118 Shanbogh
119 Shankill
120 Sheffin
121 Stonecarthy
122 The Rower
123 Thomastown
124 Tibberaghny
125 Tiscoffin
126 Treadingstown
127 Tubbrid
128 Tubbridbritain
129 Tullaghanbrogue
130 Tullaherin
131 Tullahought
132 Tullamaine
133 Tullaroan
134 Ullard
135 Ullid
136 Urlingford
137 Wells
138 Whitechurch
139 Woolengrange

THE BARONIES OF COUNTY KILKENNY

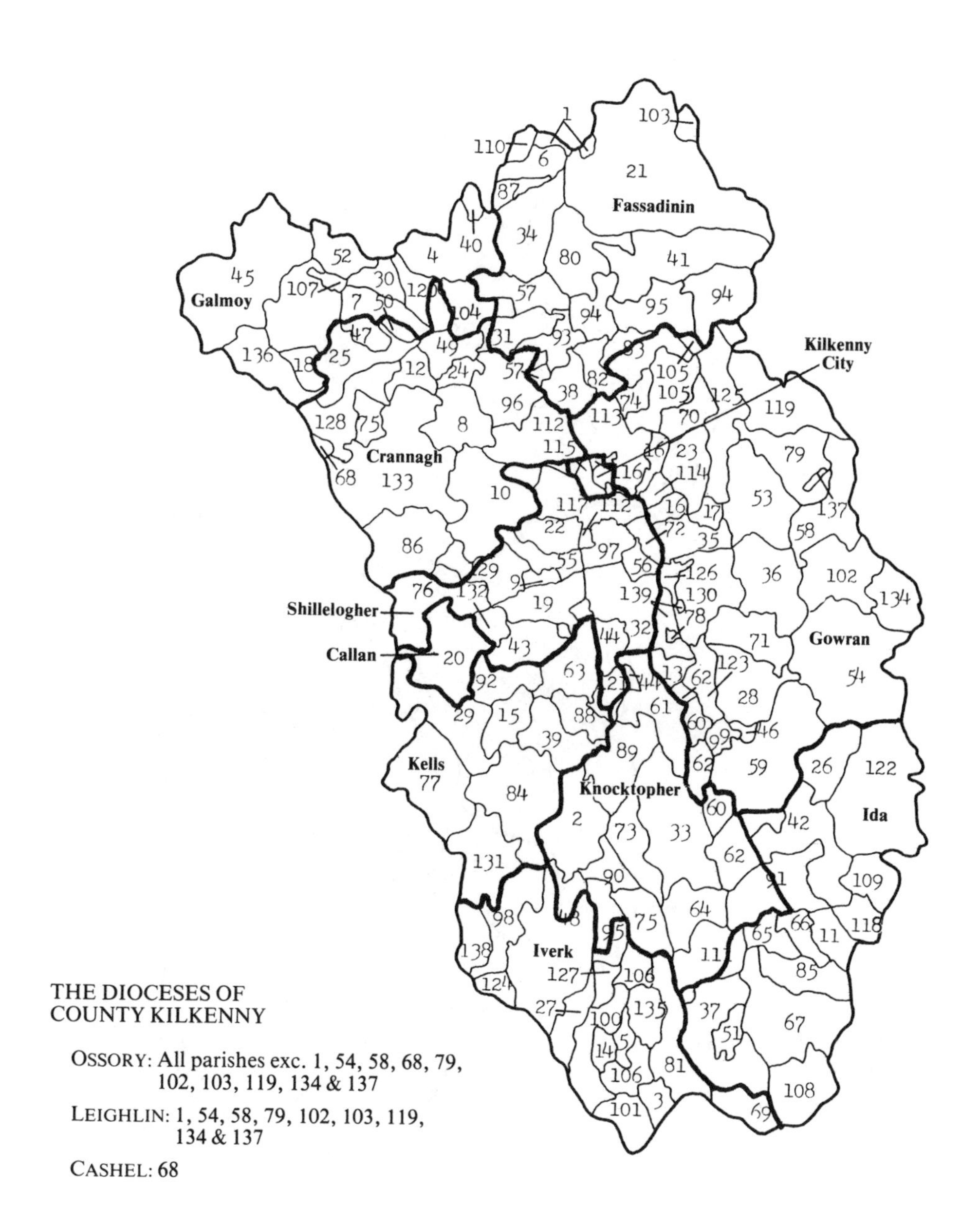

THE DIOCESES OF
COUNTY KILKENNY

OSSORY: All parishes exc. 1, 54, 58, 68, 79, 102, 103, 119, 134 & 137

LEIGHLIN: 1, 54, 58, 79, 102, 103, 119, 134 & 137

CASHEL: 68

THE POOR LAW UNIONS OF COUNTY KILKENNY

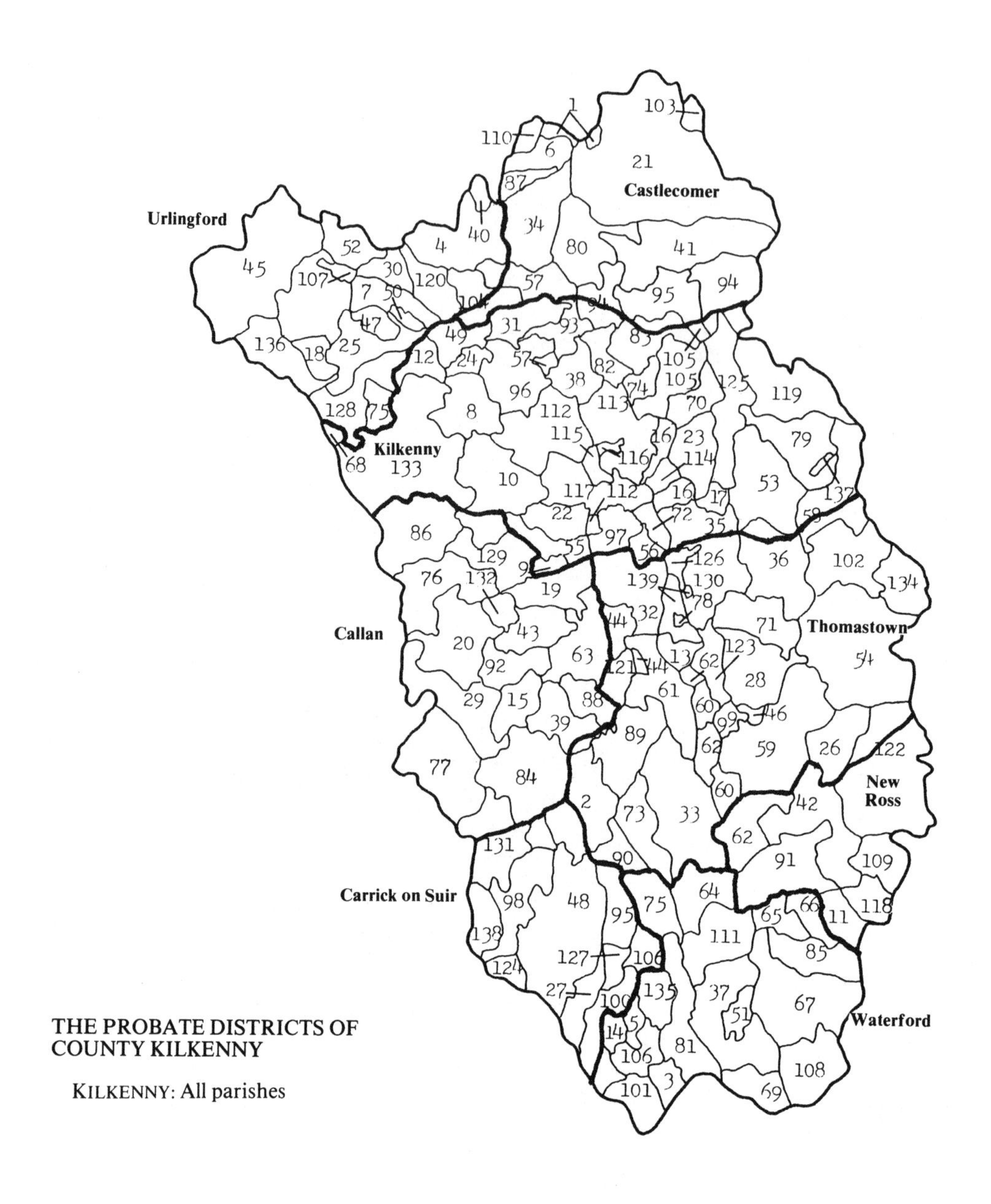

THE PROBATE DISTRICTS OF COUNTY KILKENNY

KILKENNY: All parishes

THE PARISHES OF COUNTY LEITRIM

THE BARONIES OF COUNTY LEITRIM

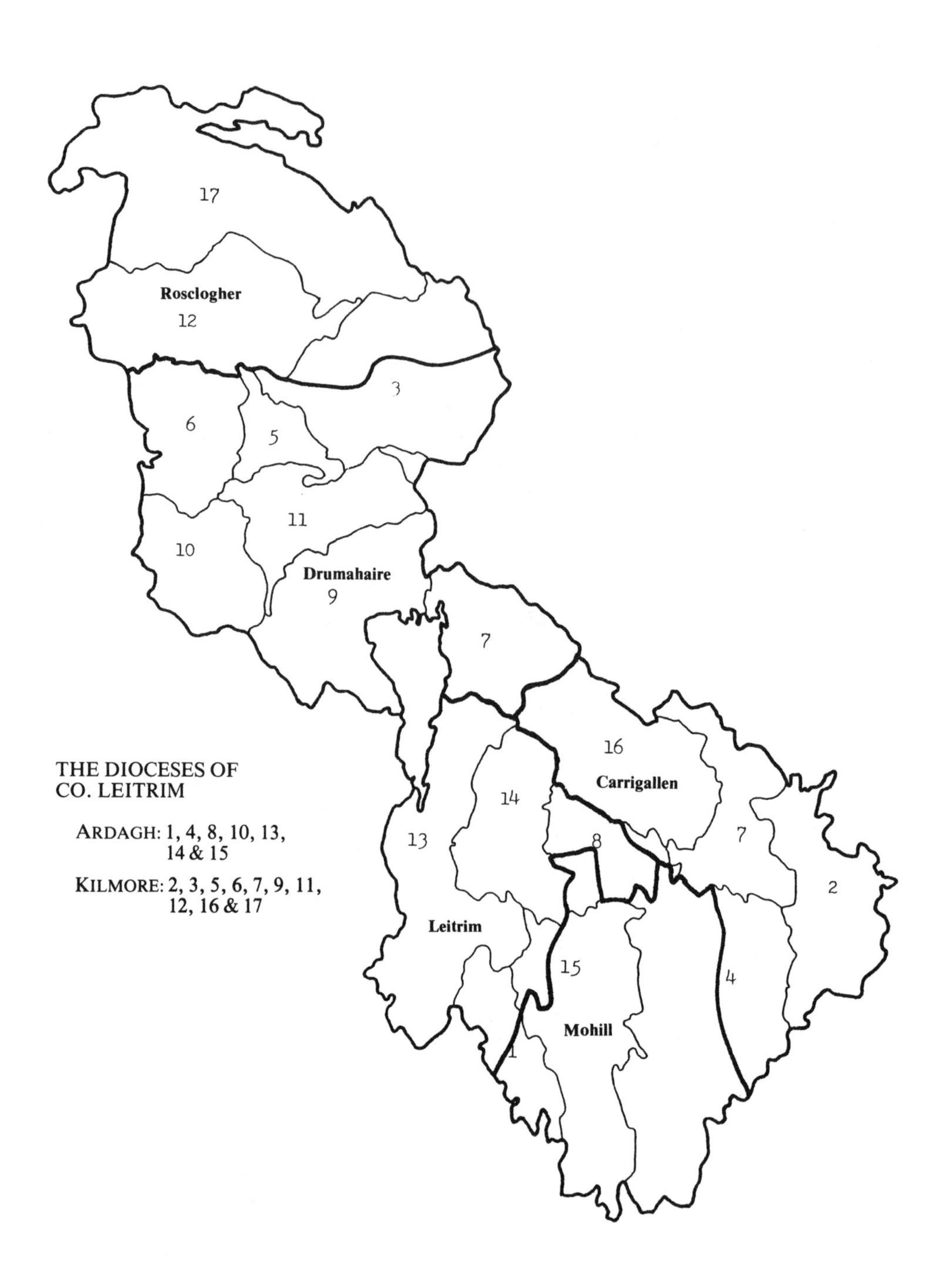

THE POOR LAW UNIONS OF COUNTY LEITRIM

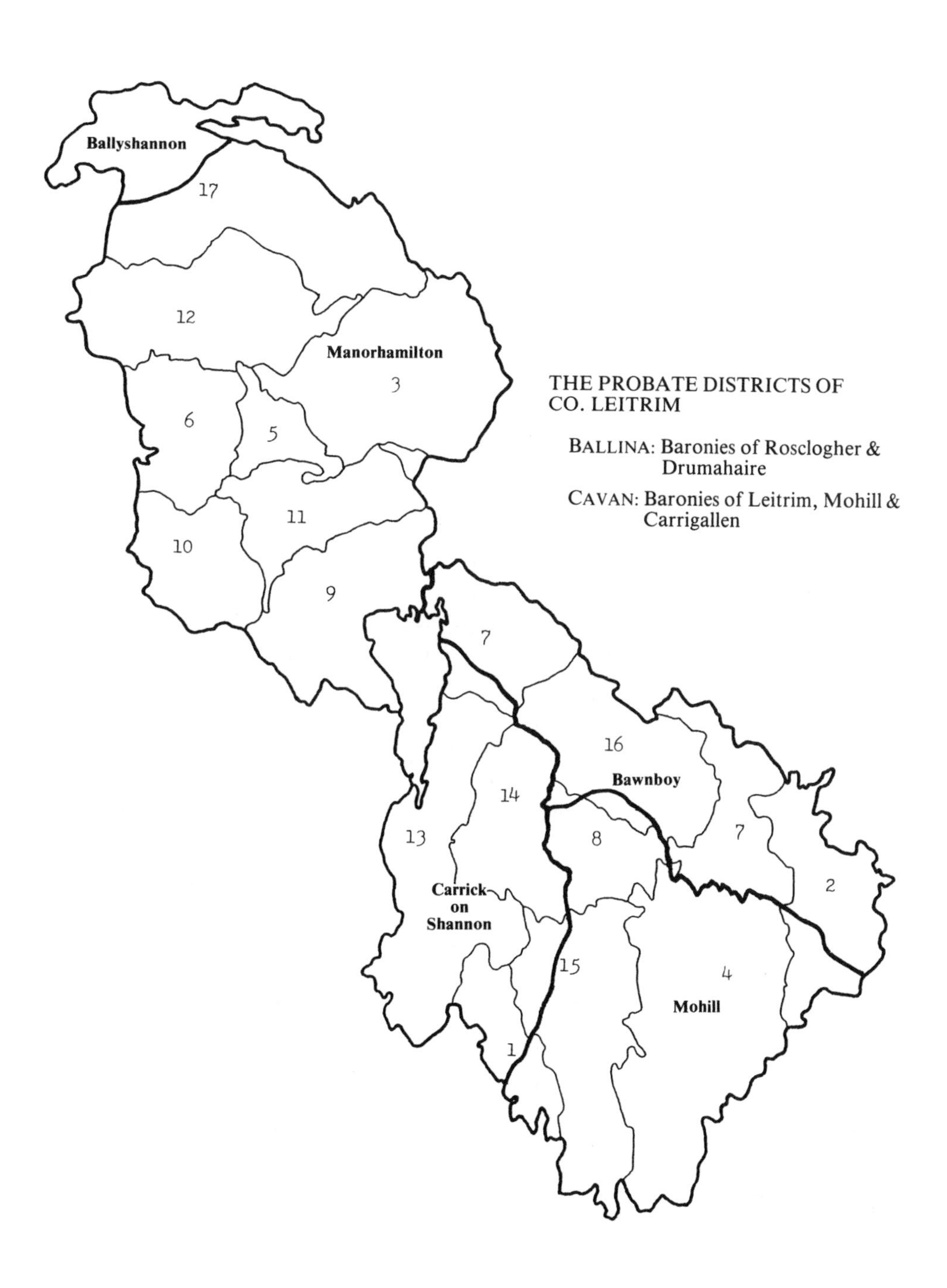

THE PROBATE DISTRICTS OF CO. LEITRIM

BALLINA: Baronies of Rosclogher & Drumahaire

CAVAN: Baronies of Leitrim, Mohill & Carrigallen

THE PARISHES OF COUNTY LEIX (QUEEN'S COUNTY)

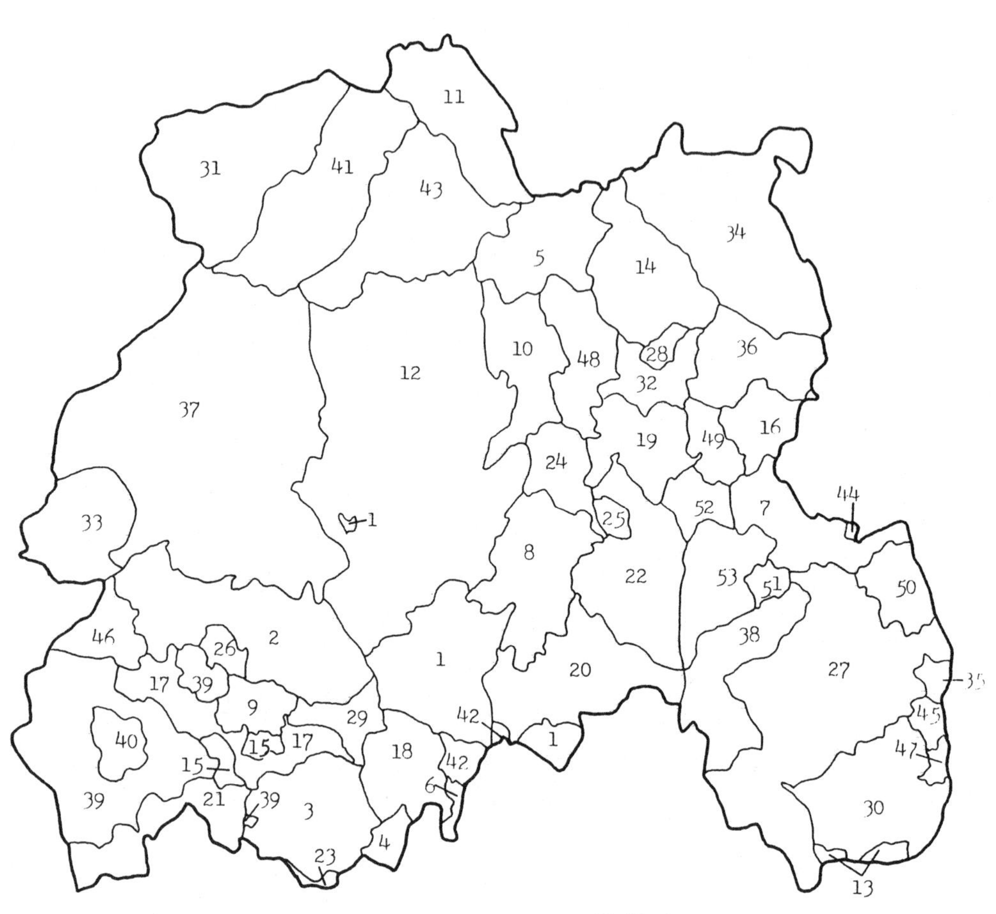

1 Abbeyleix
2 Aghaboe
3 Aghmacart
4 Aharney
5 Ardea
6 Attanagh
7 Ballyadams
8 Ballyroan
9 Bordwell
10 Borris
11 Castlebrack
12 Clonenagh and Clonagheen
13 Cloydagh
14 Coolbanagher
15 Coolkerry
16 Curraclone
17 Donaghmore
18 Durrow
19 Dysartenos
20 Dysartgallen
21 Erke
22 Fossy or Timahoe
23 Glashare
24 Kilcolmanbane
25 Kilcolmanbrack
26 Kildellig
27 Killabban
28 Killenny
29 Killermogh
30 Killeshin
31 Kilmanman
32 Kilteale
33 Kyle
34 Lea
35 Monksgrange
36 Moyanna
37 Offerlane
38 Rathaspick
39 Rathdowney
40 Rathsaran
41 Rearymore
42 Rosconnell
43 Rosenallis
44 St. John's
45 Shrule
46 Skirk
47 Sleaty
48 Straboe
49 Stradbally
50 Tankardstown
51 Tecolm
52 Timogue
53 Tullomoy

THE BARONIES OF COUNTY LEIX (QUEEN'S COUNTY)

THE DIOCESES OF COUNTY LEIX

KILDARE: Baronies of Portnahinch & Tinnahinch

LEIGHLIN: Baronies of Slievemargy, Stradbally and Maryborough East & West; Cullenagh exc. 42; Ballyadams exc. 44 & 50; 1

OSSORY: Clandonagh Barony exc. 33; Clarmallagh exc. 1; 37 & 42

DUBLIN: 44 & 50

KILLALOE: 33

THE POOR LAW UNIONS OF COUNTY LEIX (QUEEN'S COUNTY)

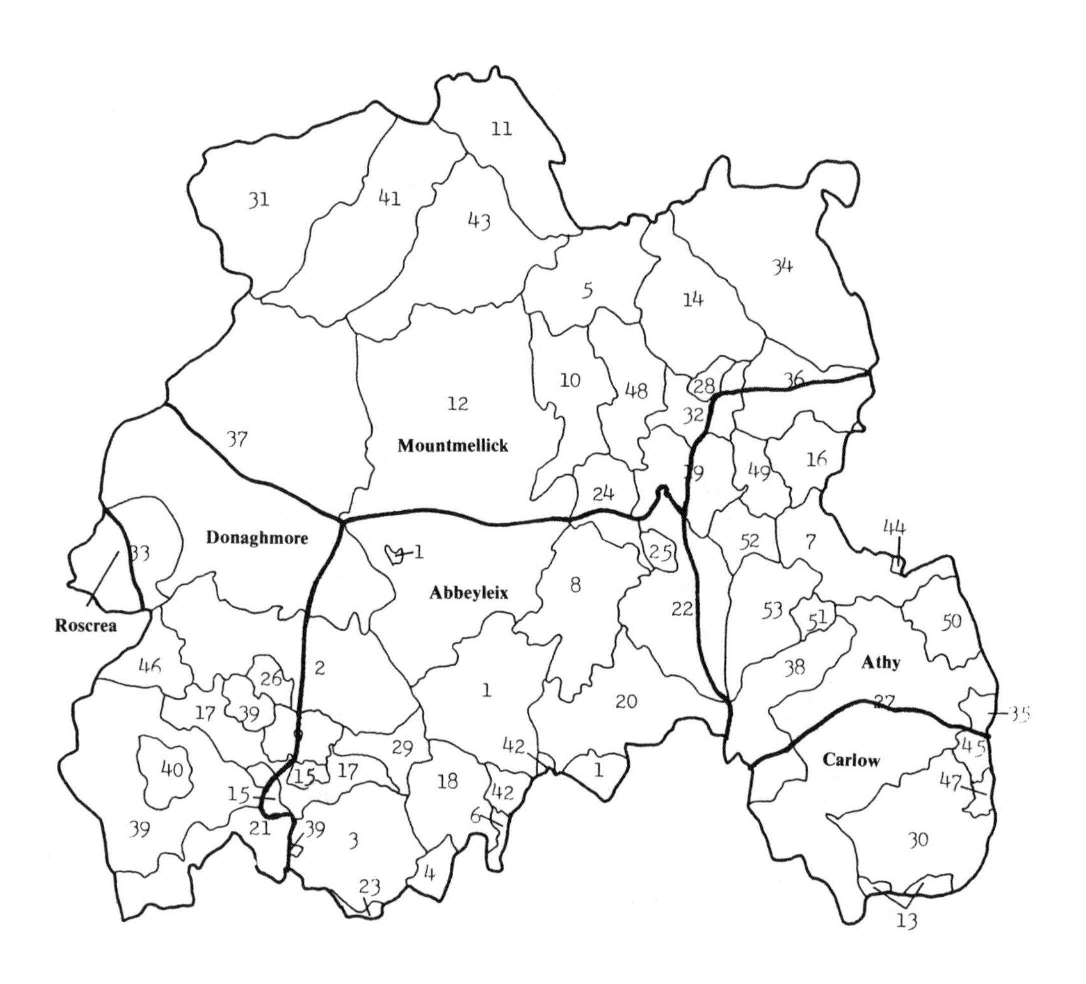

THE PROBATE DISTRICTS OF COUNTY LEIX

KILKENNY: All parishes

The Parishes Of County Limerick

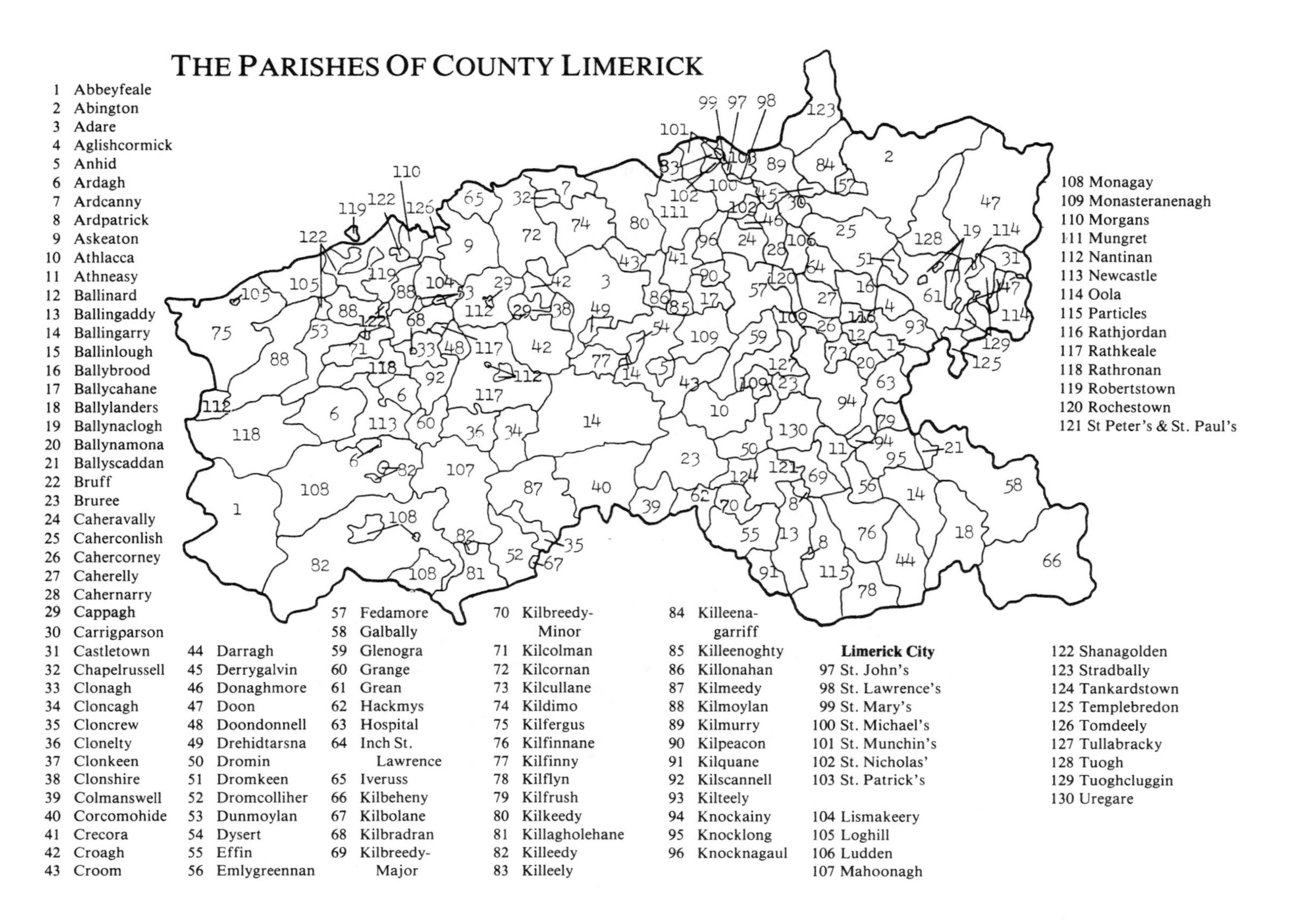

1 Abbeyfeale
2 Abington
3 Adare
4 Aglishcormick
5 Anhid
6 Ardagh
7 Ardcanny
8 Ardpatrick
9 Askeaton
10 Athlacca
11 Athneasy
12 Ballinard
13 Ballingaddy
14 Ballingarry
15 Ballinlough
16 Ballybrood
17 Ballycahane
18 Ballylanders
19 Ballynaclogh
20 Ballynamona
21 Ballyscaddan
22 Bruff
23 Bruree
24 Caheravally
25 Caherconlish
26 Cahercorney
27 Caherelly
28 Cahernarry
29 Cappagh
30 Carrigparson
31 Castletown
32 Chapelrussell
33 Clonagh
34 Cloncagh
35 Cloncrew
36 Clonelty
37 Clonkeen
38 Clonshire
39 Colmanswell
40 Corcomohide
41 Crecora
42 Croagh
43 Croom
44 Darragh
45 Derrygalvin
46 Donaghmore
47 Doon
48 Doondonnell
49 Drehidtarsna
50 Dromin
51 Dromkeen
52 Dromcolliher
53 Dunmoylan
54 Dysert
55 Effin
56 Emlygreennan
57 Fedamore
58 Galbally
59 Glenogra
60 Grange
61 Grean
62 Hackmys
63 Hospital
64 Inch St. Lawrence
65 Iveruss
66 Kilbeheny
67 Kilbolane
68 Kilbradran
69 Kilbreedy-Major
70 Kilbreedy-Minor
71 Kilcolman
72 Kilcornan
73 Kilcullane
74 Kildimo
75 Kilfergus
76 Kilfinnane
77 Kilfinny
78 Kilflyn
79 Kilfrush
80 Kilkeedy
81 Killagholehane
82 Killeedy
83 Killeely
84 Killeena-garriff
85 Killeenoghty
86 Killonahan
87 Kilmeedy
88 Kilmoylan
89 Kilmurry
90 Kilpeacon
91 Kilquane
92 Kilscannell
93 Kilteely
94 Knockainy
95 Knocklong
96 Knocknagaul

Limerick City
97 St. John's
98 St. Lawrence's
99 St. Mary's
100 St. Michael's
101 St. Munchin's
102 St. Nicholas'
103 St. Patrick's

104 Lismakeery
105 Loghill
106 Ludden
107 Mahoonagh
108 Monagay
109 Monasteranenagh
110 Morgans
111 Mungret
112 Nantinan
113 Newcastle
114 Oola
115 Particles
116 Rathjordan
117 Rathkeale
118 Rathronan
119 Robertstown
120 Rochestown
121 St Peter's & St. Paul's
122 Shanagolden
123 Stradbally
124 Tankardstown
125 Templebredon
126 Tomdeely
127 Tullabracky
128 Tuogh
129 Tuoghcluggin
130 Uregare

THE BARONIES OF COUNTY LIMERICK

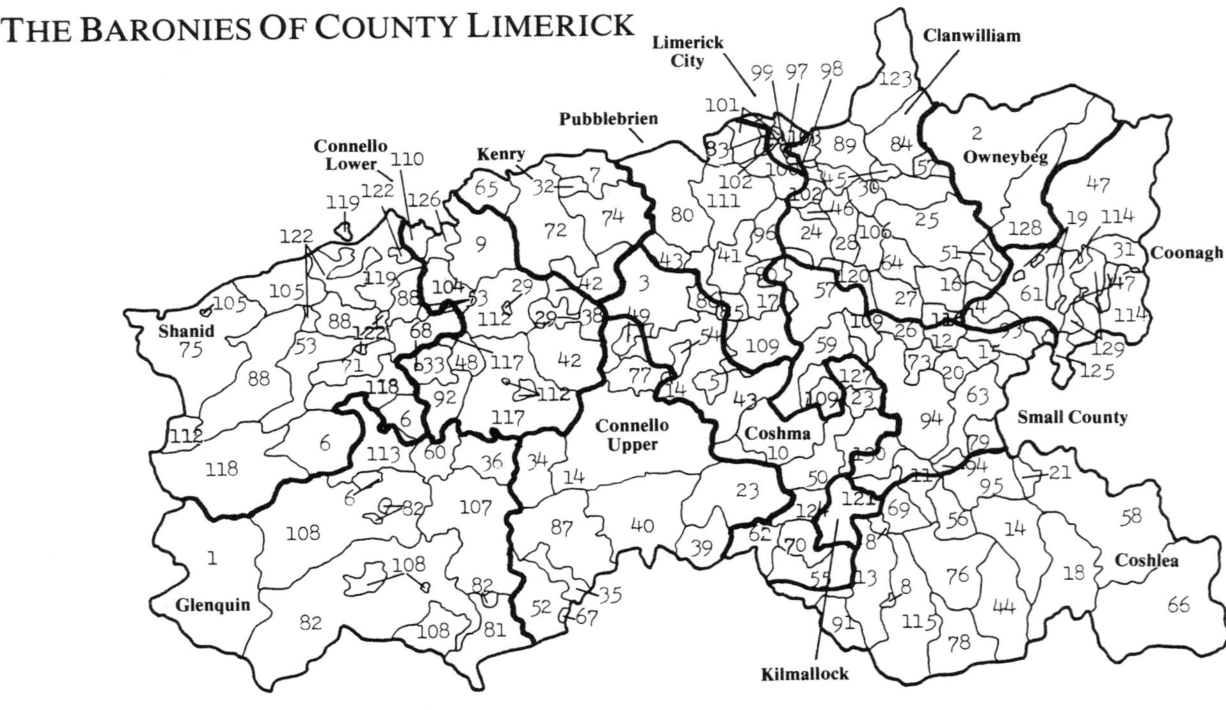

THE DIOCESES OF COUNTY LIMERICK

LIMERICK: Baronies of Connello Lower, Coshma, Glenquin, Kenry, Kilmallock, Limerick City, Pubblebrien & Shanid; Connello Upper exc. 67; Coshlea exc. 14, 18, 21, 58, 66 & 95; 11, 17, 57, 59, 69, 90, 109, 127 & 130 in Small County; 24, 28, 45, 46, 57, 97, 98, 102 & 103 in Clanwilliam

EMLY: Owneybeg Barony; Coonagh exc. 31; Clanwilliam exc. 24, 28, 45, 46, 57, 84, 97, 98, 102, 103 & 123; 14, 18, 21, 58, 66 & 95 in Coshlea; 12, 15, 20, 63, 79, 93 & 94 in Small County

CASHEL: 26, 31 & 73

KILLALOE: 84 & 123

CLOYNE: 67

THE POOR LAW UNIONS OF COUNTY LIMERICK

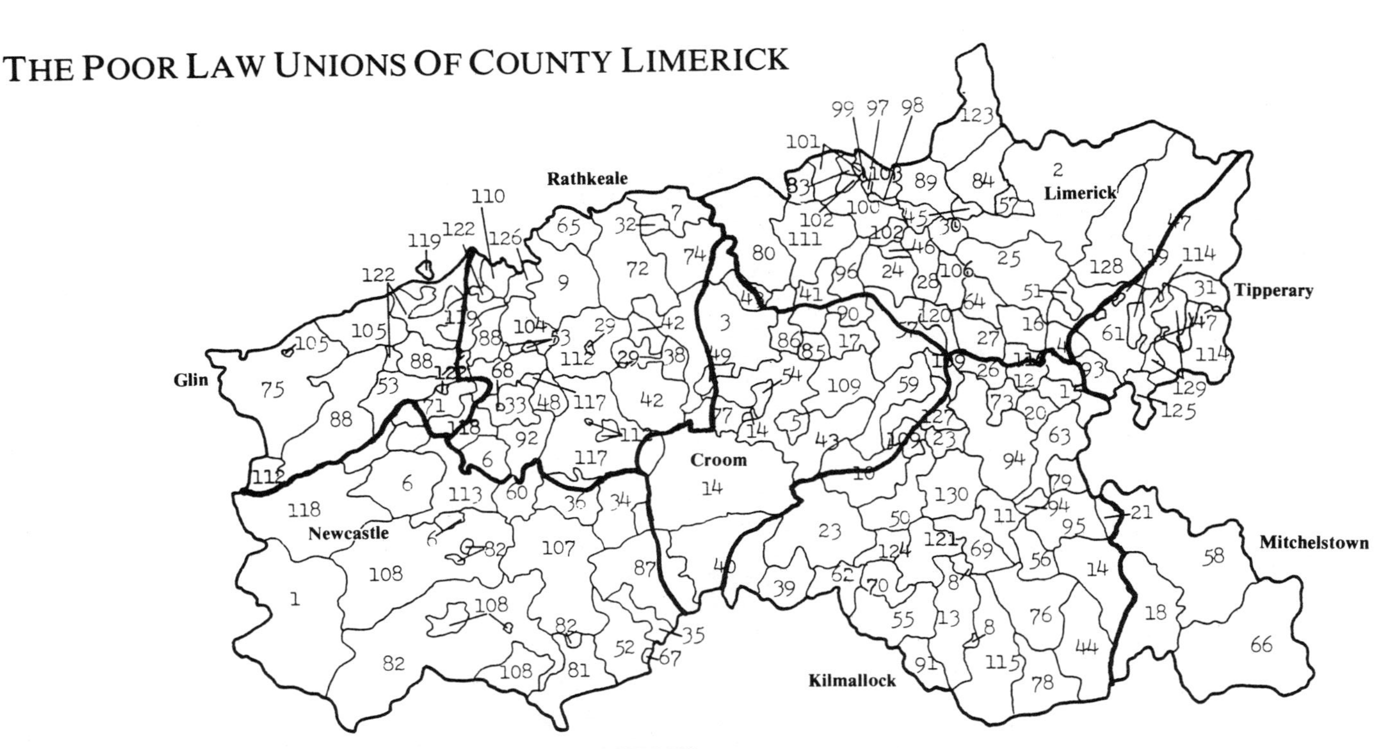

THE PROBATE DISTRICTS OF COUNTY LIMERICK

LIMERICK: All parishes

THE PARISHES OF COUNTY LONDONDERRY

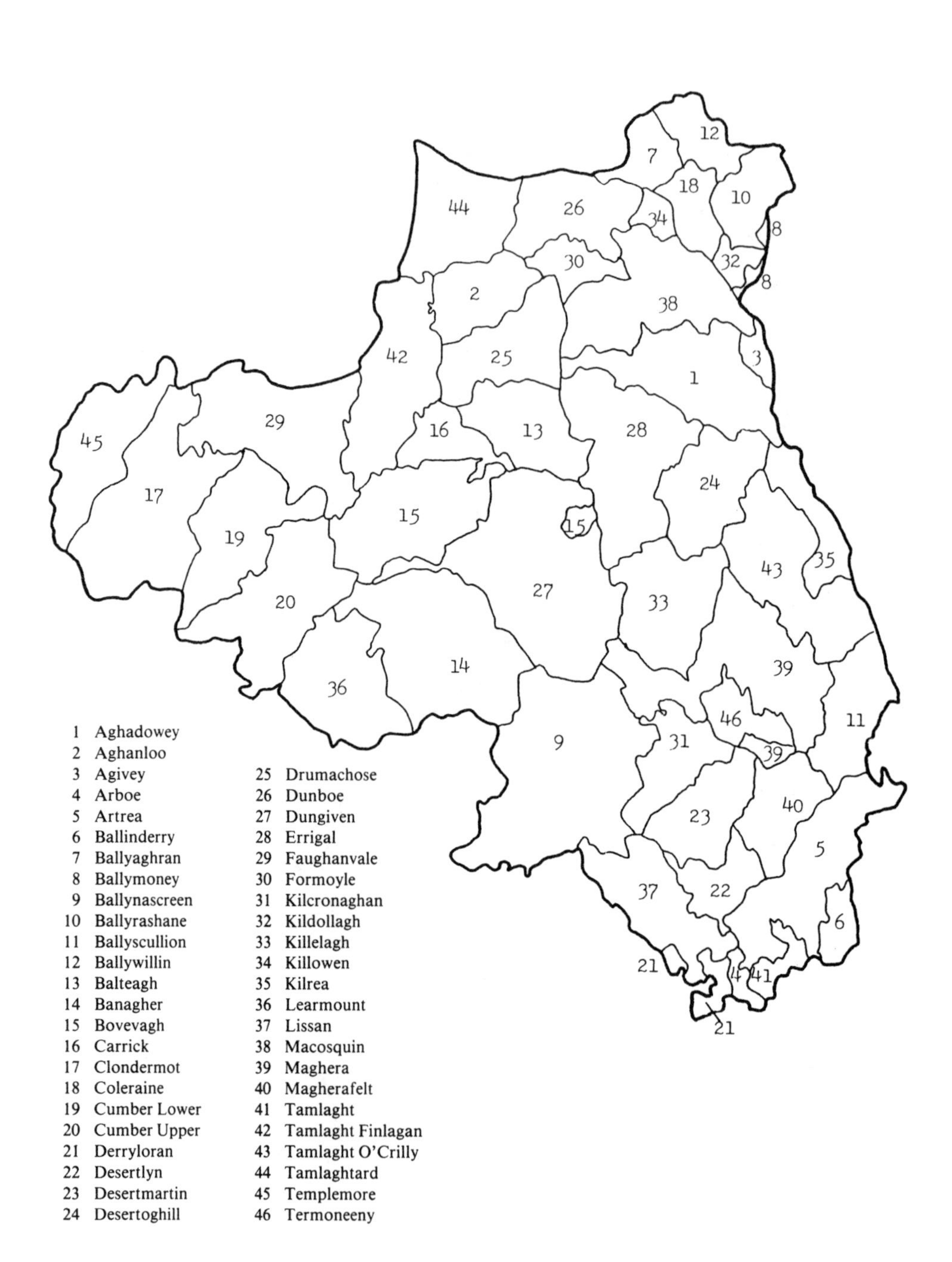

THE BARONIES OF COUNTY LONDONDERRY

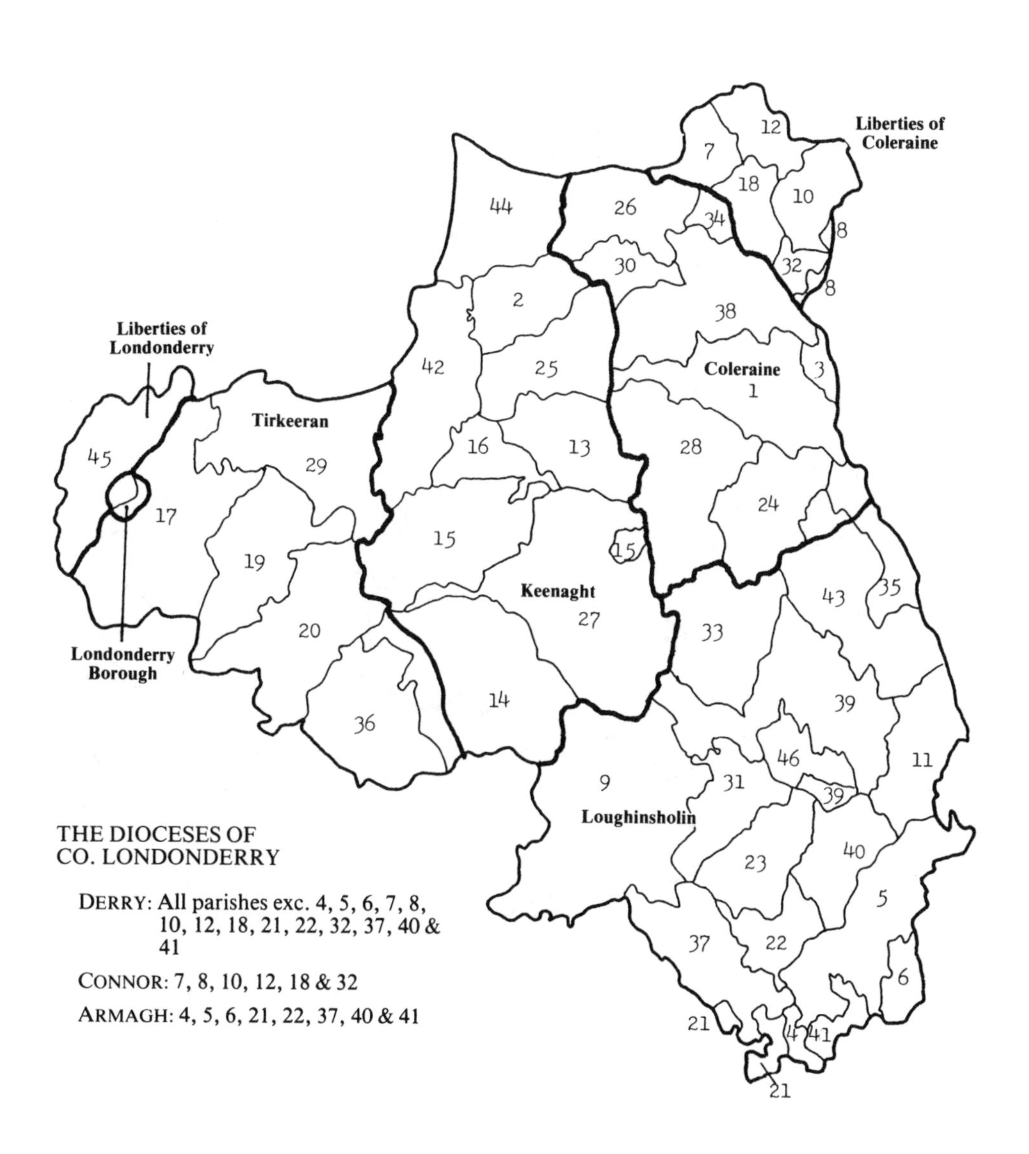

THE POOR LAW UNIONS OF COUNTY LONDONDERRY

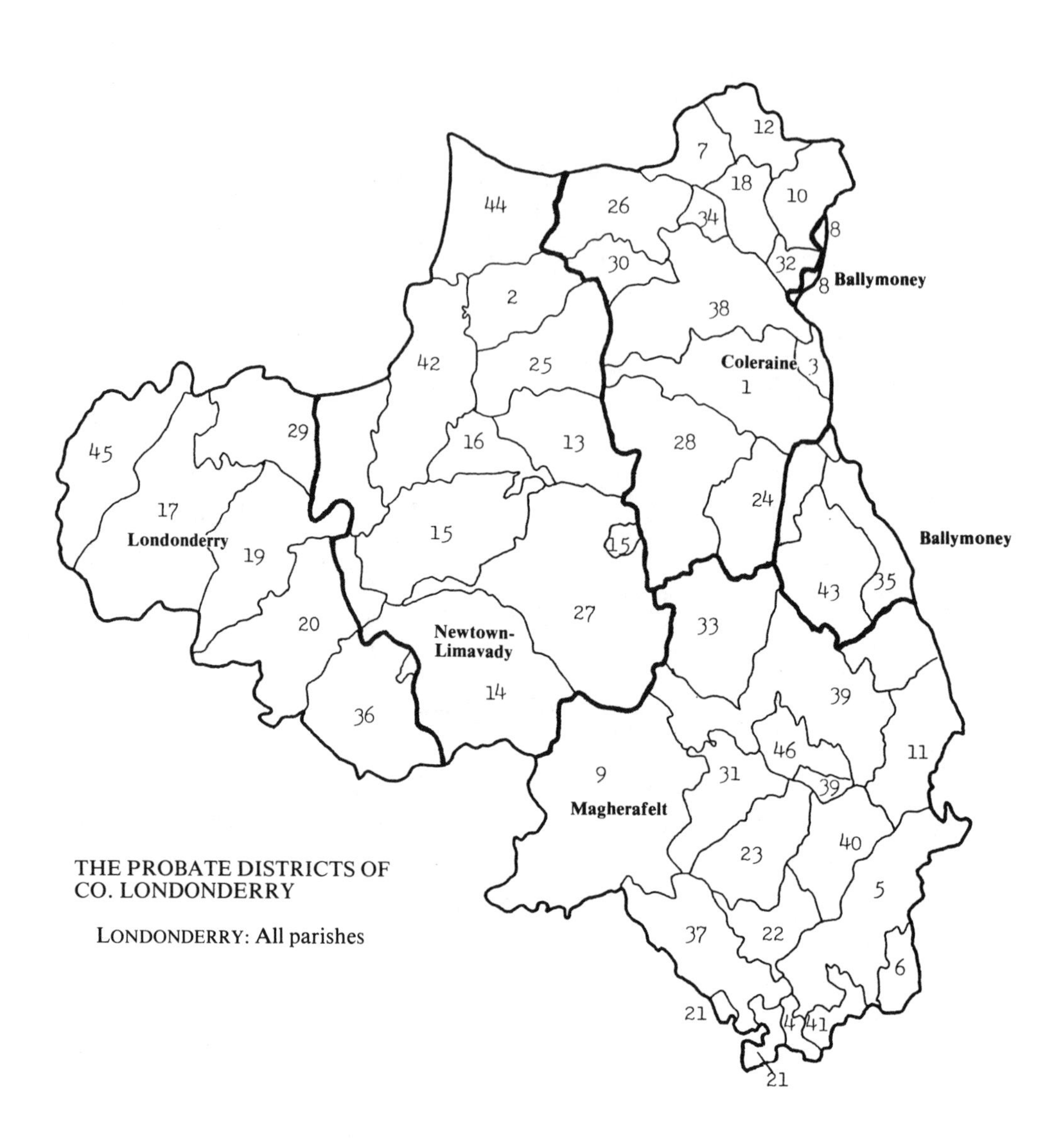

THE PROBATE DISTRICTS OF
CO. LONDONDERRY

LONDONDERRY: All parishes

THE PARISHES OF COUNTY LONGFORD

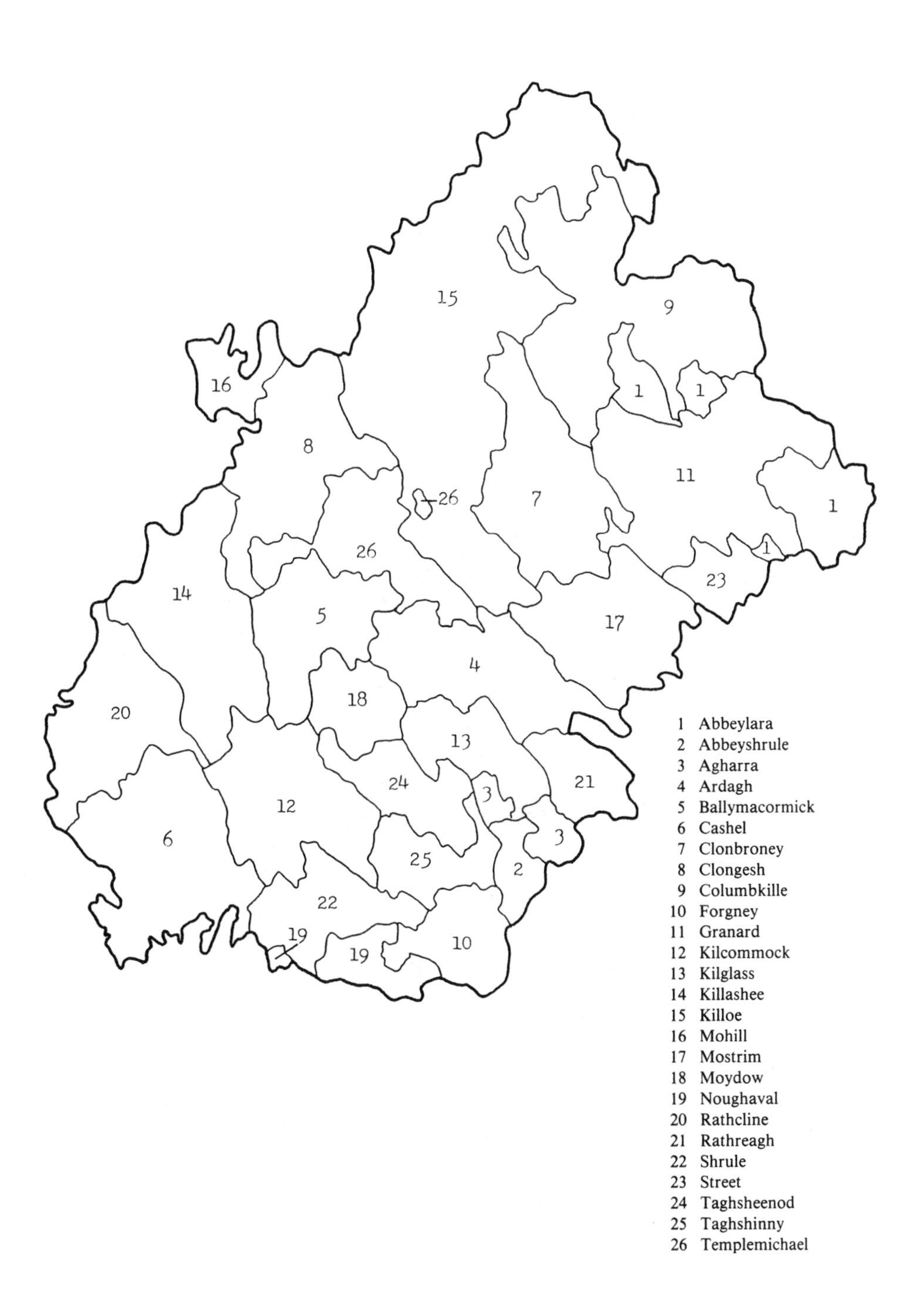

THE BARONIES OF COUNTY LONGFORD

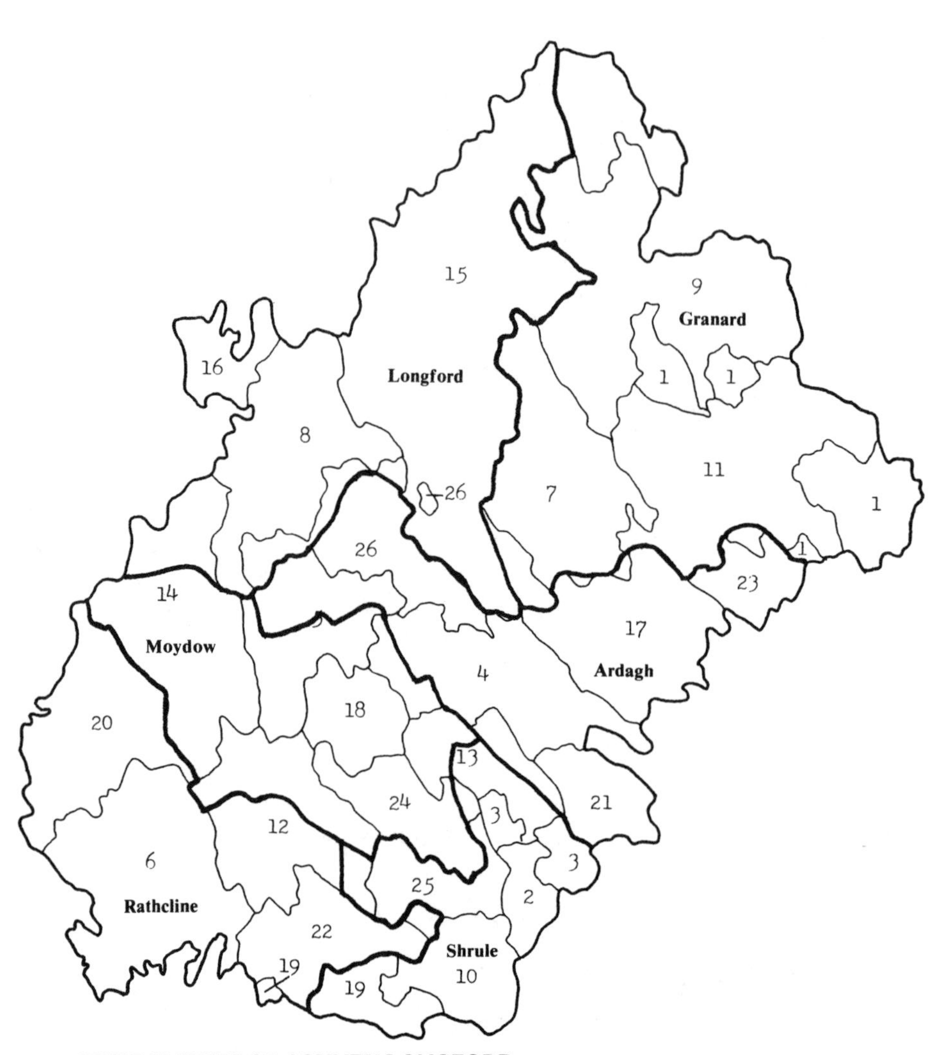

THE DIOCESES OF COUNTY LONGFORD

ARDAGH: All parishes exc. 10 & 19

MEATH: 10 & 19

THE POOR LAW UNIONS OF COUNTY LONGFORD

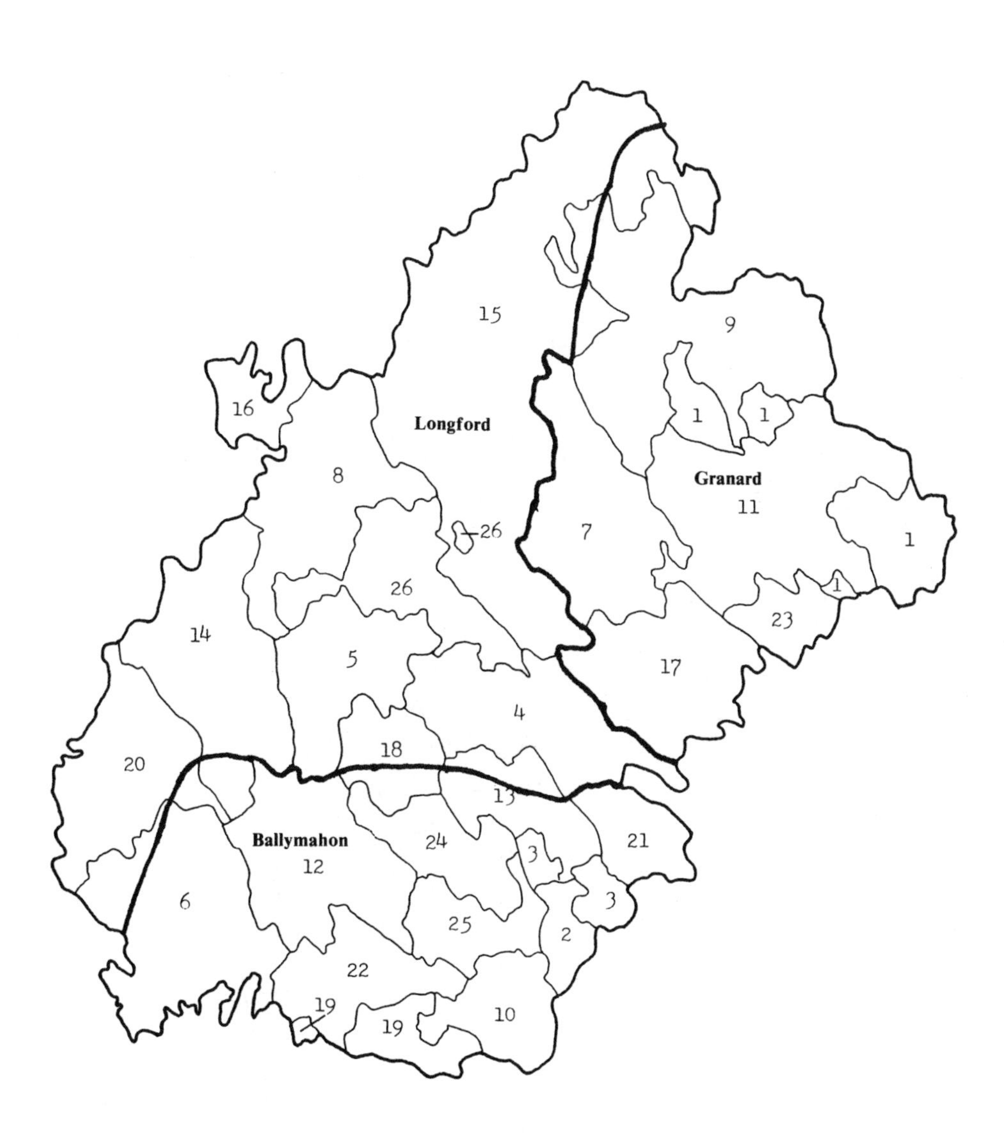

THE PROBATE DISTRICTS OF COUNTY LONGFORD

CAVAN: All parishes

THE PARISHES OF COUNTY LOUTH

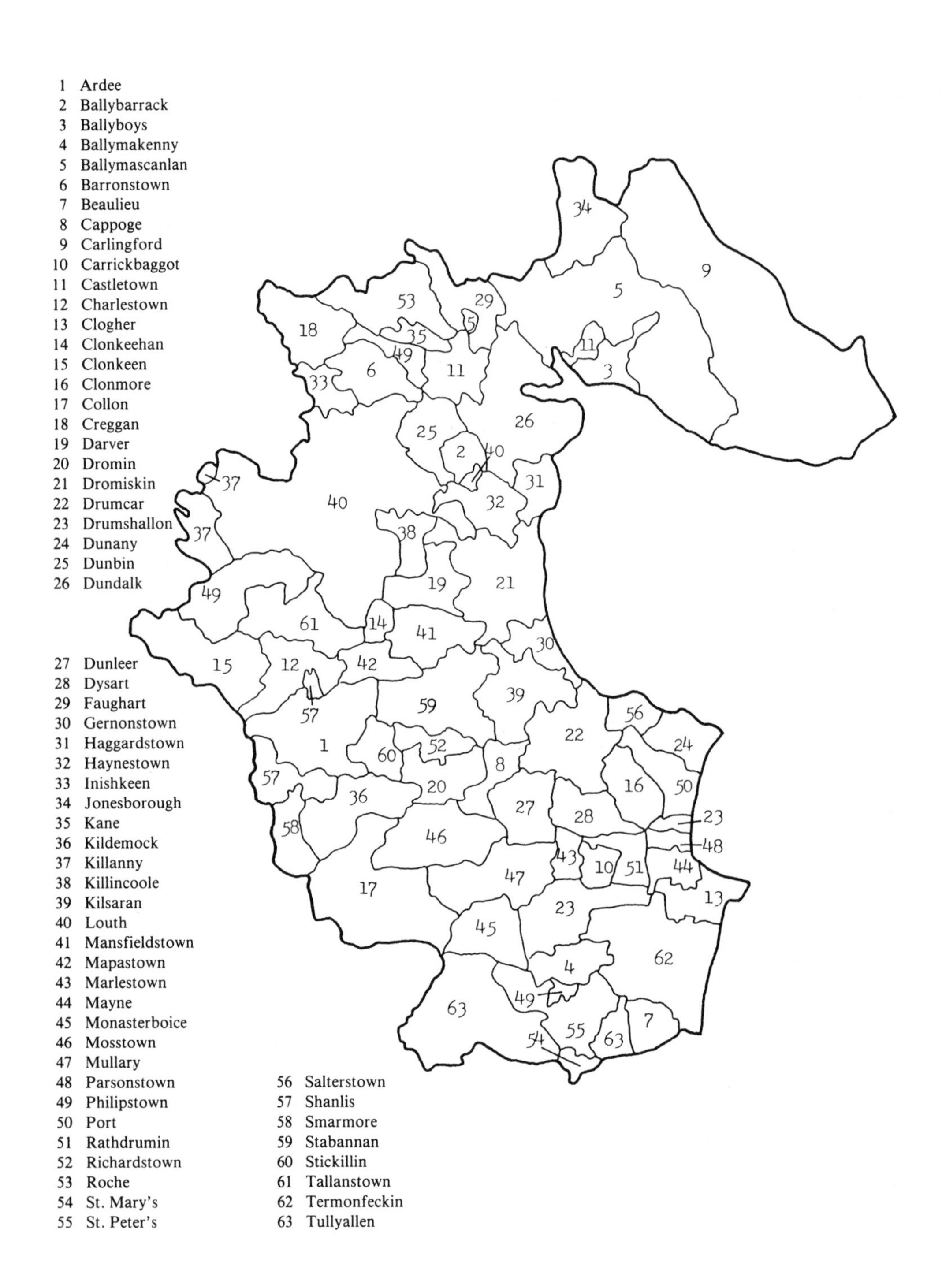

THE BARONIES OF COUNTY LOUTH

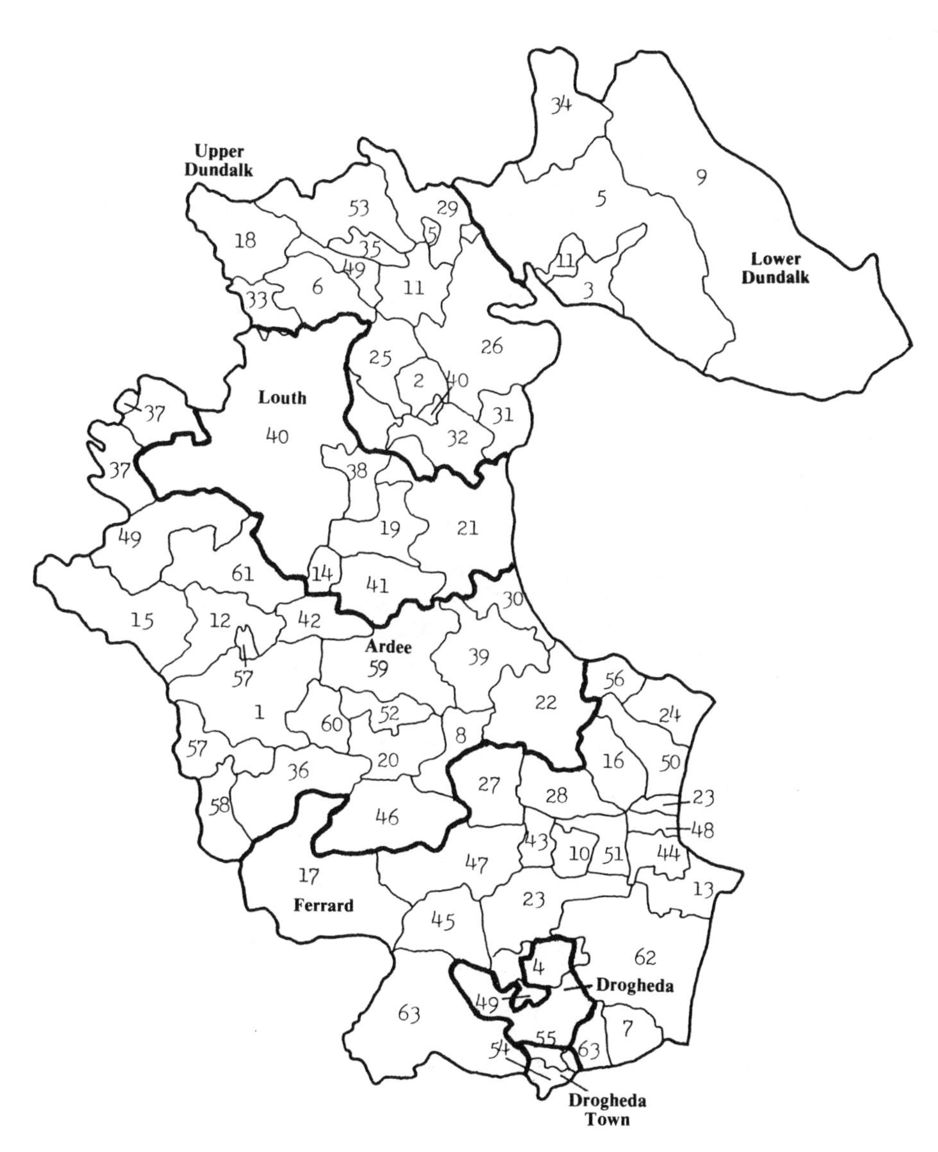

THE DIOCESES OF COUNTY LOUTH

ARMAGH: All parishes exc. 33 & 37

CLOGHER: 33 & 37

THE POOR LAW UNIONS OF COUNTY LOUTH

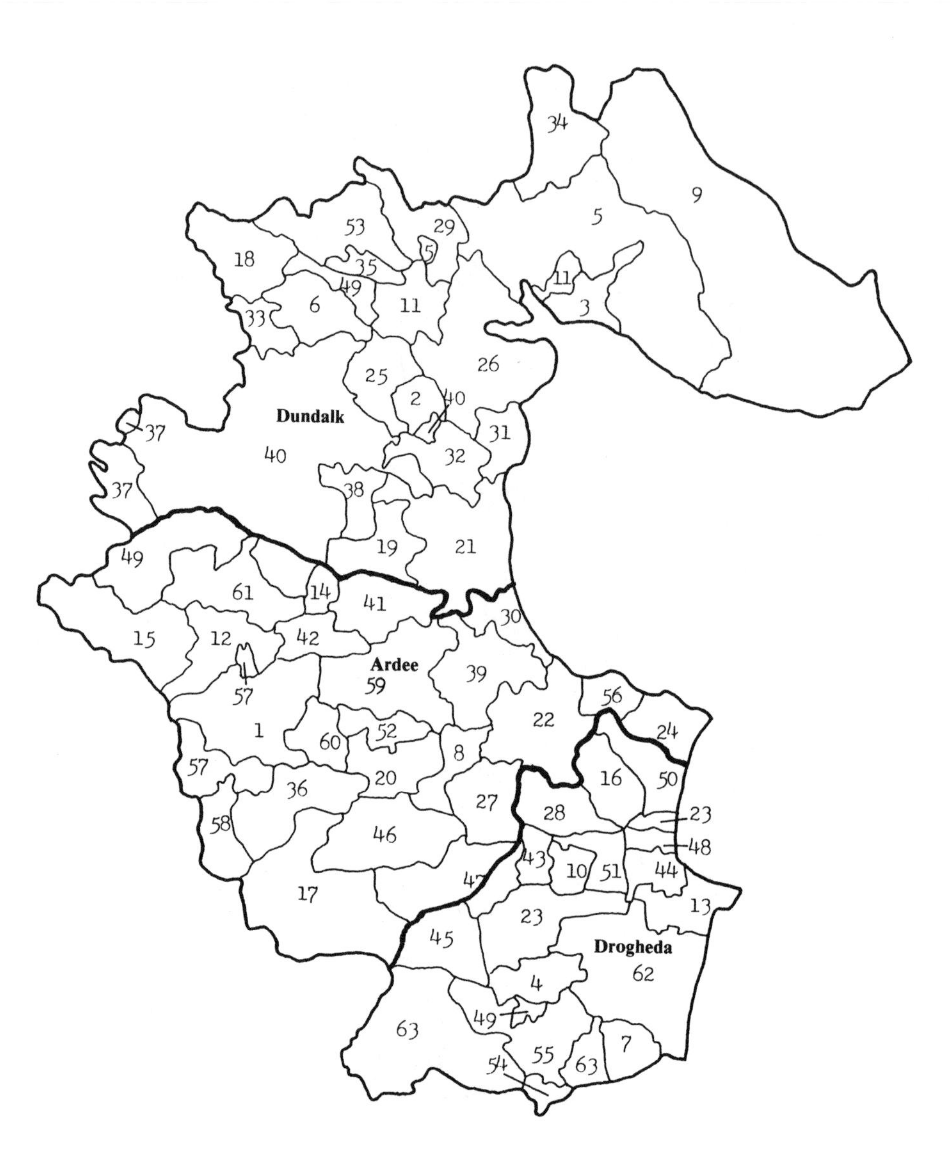

THE PROBATE DISTRICTS OF COUNTY LOUTH

ARMAGH: All parishes

THE PARISHES OF COUNTY MAYO

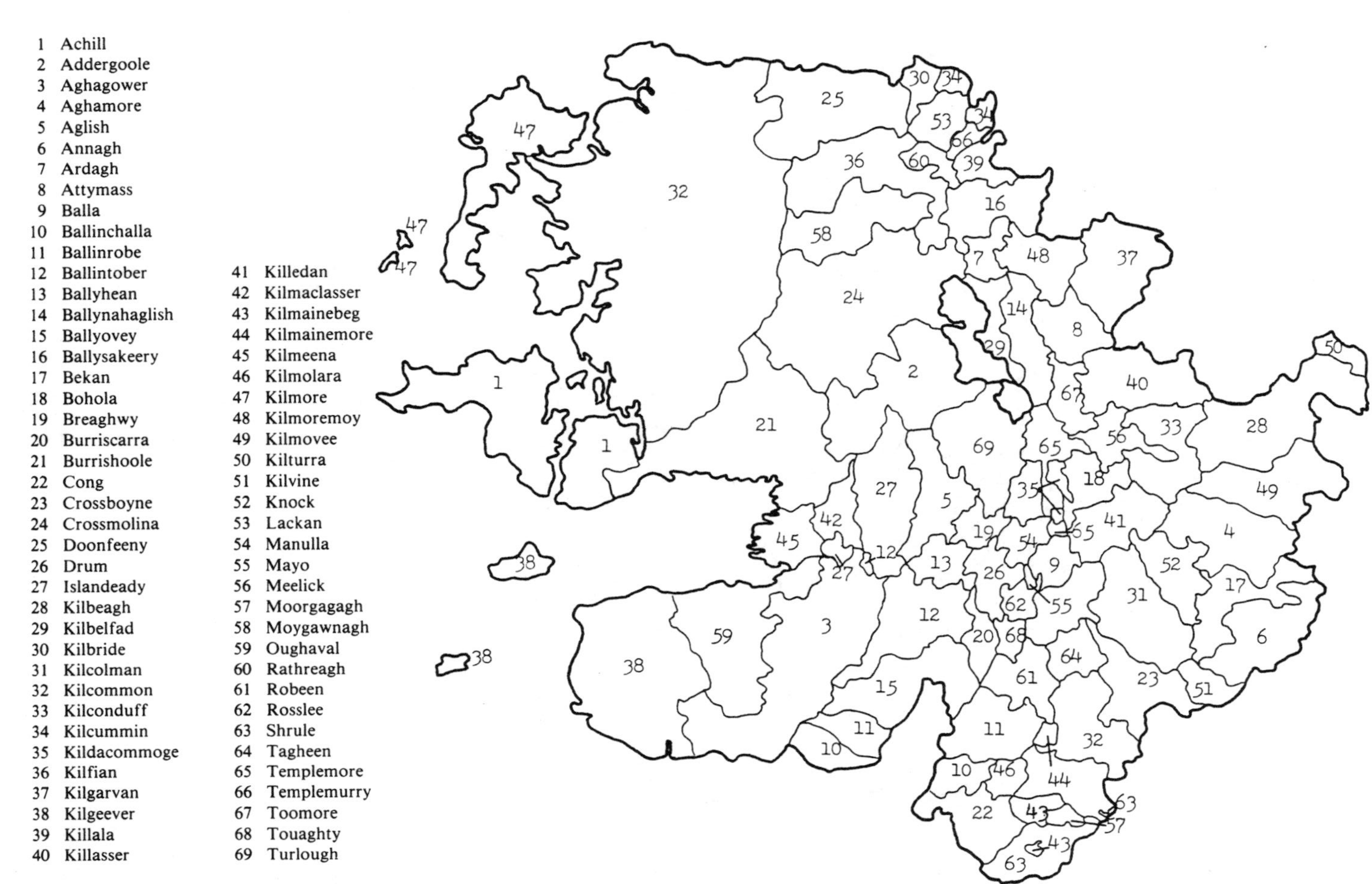

1 Achill
2 Addergoole
3 Aghagower
4 Aghamore
5 Aglish
6 Annagh
7 Ardagh
8 Attymass
9 Balla
10 Ballinchalla
11 Ballinrobe
12 Ballintober
13 Ballyhean
14 Ballynahaglish
15 Ballyovey
16 Ballysakeery
17 Bekan
18 Bohola
19 Breaghwy
20 Burriscarra
21 Burrishoole
22 Cong
23 Crossboyne
24 Crossmolina
25 Doonfeeny
26 Drum
27 Islandeady
28 Kilbeagh
29 Kilbelfad
30 Kilbride
31 Kilcolman
32 Kilcommon
33 Kilconduff
34 Kilcummin
35 Kildacommoge
36 Kilfian
37 Kilgarvan
38 Kilgeever
39 Killala
40 Killasser
41 Killedan
42 Kilmaclasser
43 Kilmainebeg
44 Kilmainemore
45 Kilmeena
46 Kilmolara
47 Kilmore
48 Kilmoremoy
49 Kilmovee
50 Kilturra
51 Kilvine
52 Knock
53 Lackan
54 Manulla
55 Mayo
56 Meelick
57 Moorgagagh
58 Moygawnagh
59 Oughaval
60 Rathreagh
61 Robeen
62 Rosslee
63 Shrule
64 Tagheen
65 Templemore
66 Templemurry
67 Toomore
68 Touaghty
69 Turlough

THE BARONIES OF COUNTY MAYO

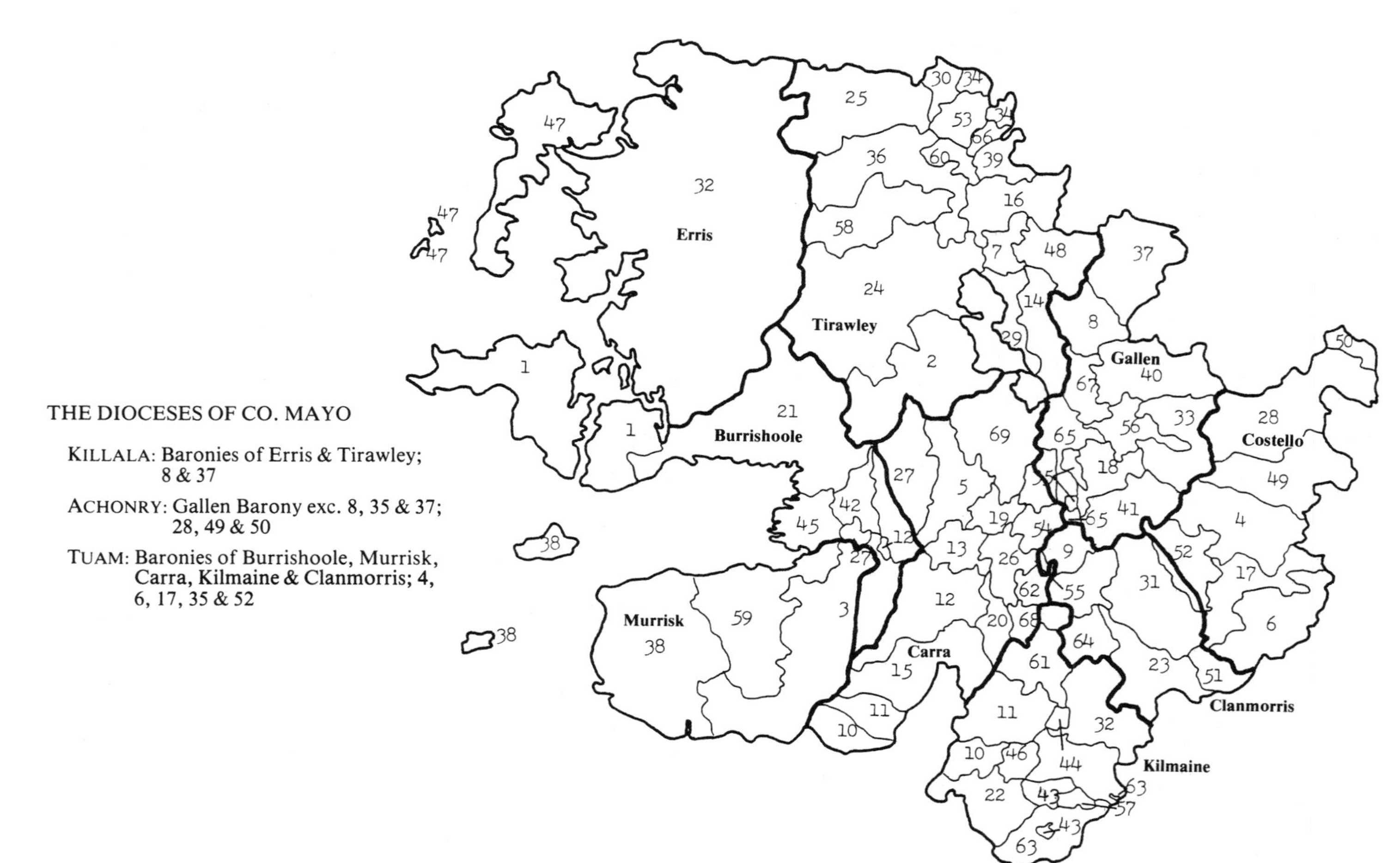

THE DIOCESES OF CO. MAYO

KILLALA: Baronies of Erris & Tirawley; 8 & 37

ACHONRY: Gallen Barony exc. 8, 35 & 37; 28, 49 & 50

TUAM: Baronies of Burrishoole, Murrisk, Carra, Kilmaine & Clanmorris; 4, 6, 17, 35 & 52

THE POOR LAW UNIONS OF COUNTY MAYO

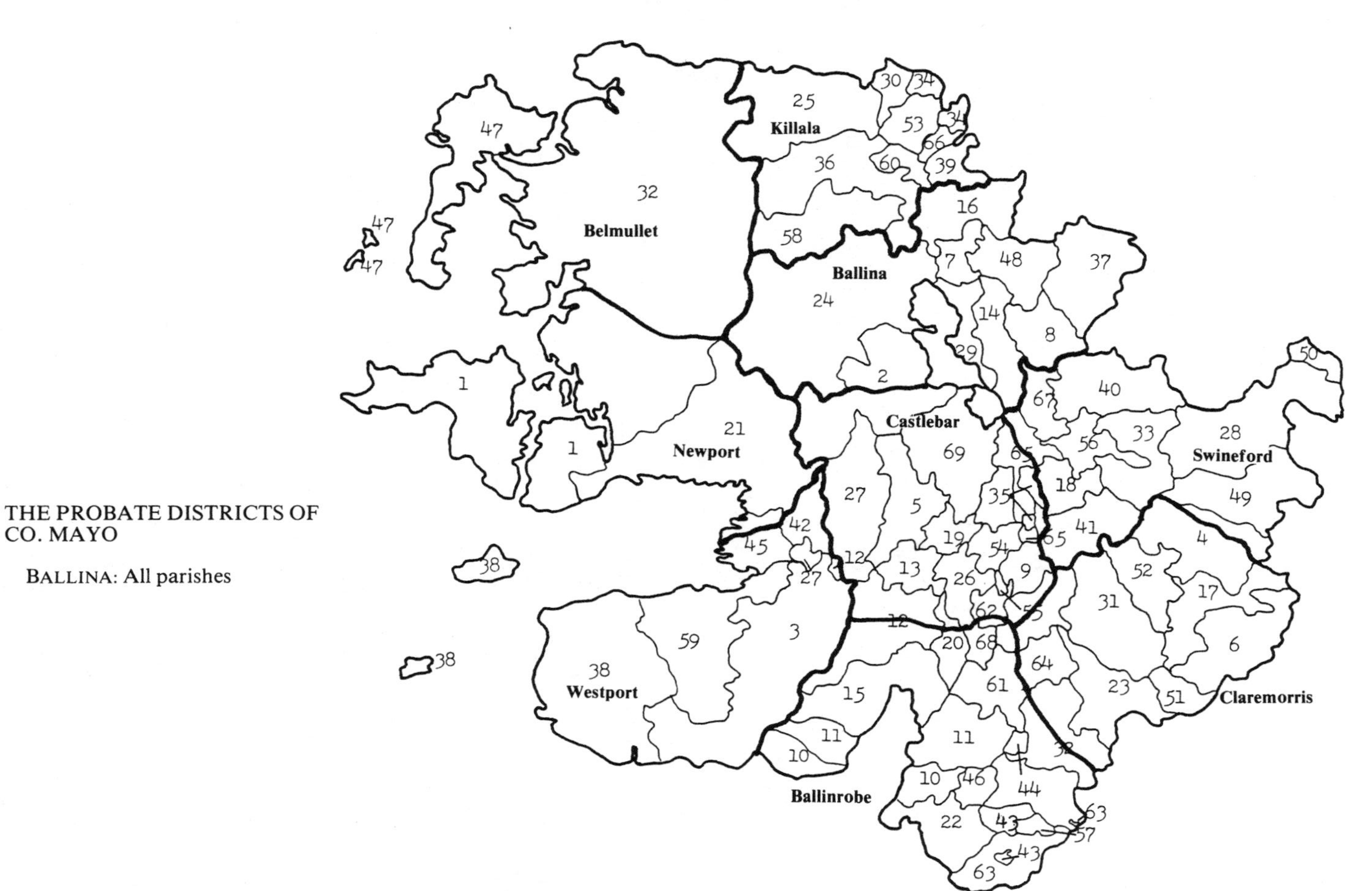

THE PROBATE DISTRICTS OF CO. MAYO

BALLINA: All parishes

THE PARISHES OF COUNTY MEATH

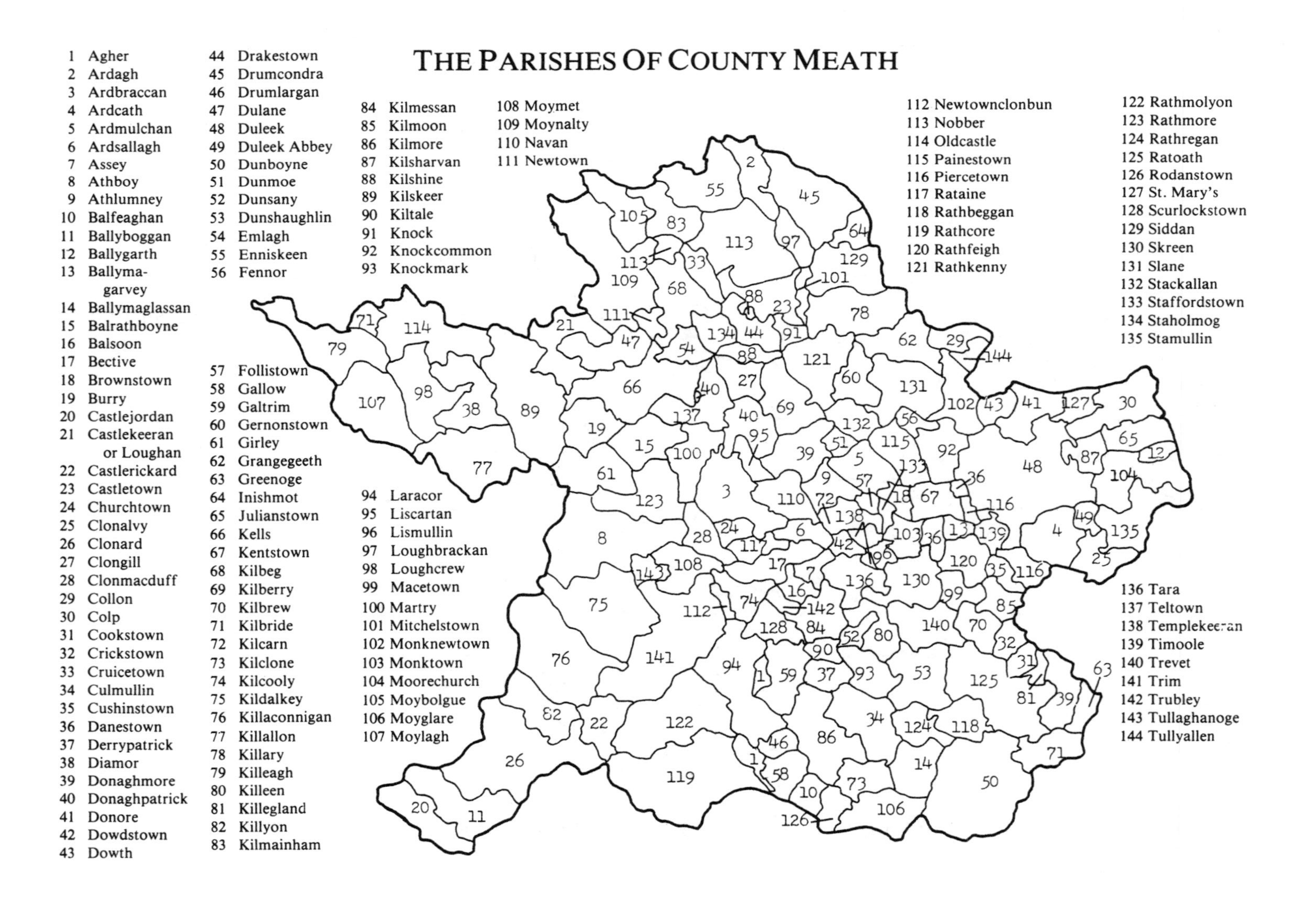

1 Agher
2 Ardagh
3 Ardbraccan
4 Ardcath
5 Ardmulchan
6 Ardsallagh
7 Assey
8 Athboy
9 Athlumney
10 Balfeaghan
11 Ballyboggan
12 Ballygarth
13 Ballyma-garvey
14 Ballymaglassan
15 Balrathboyne
16 Balsoon
17 Bective
18 Brownstown
19 Burry
20 Castlejordan
21 Castlekeeran or Loughan
22 Castlerickard
23 Castletown
24 Churchtown
25 Clonalvy
26 Clonard
27 Clongill
28 Clonmacduff
29 Collon
30 Colp
31 Cookstown
32 Crickstown
33 Cruicetown
34 Culmullin
35 Cushinstown
36 Danestown
37 Derrypatrick
38 Diamor
39 Donaghmore
40 Donaghpatrick
41 Donore
42 Dowdstown
43 Dowth
44 Drakestown
45 Drumcondra
46 Drumlargan
47 Dulane
48 Duleek
49 Duleek Abbey
50 Dunboyne
51 Dunmoe
52 Dunsany
53 Dunshaughlin
54 Emlagh
55 Enniskeen
56 Fennor
57 Follistown
58 Gallow
59 Galtrim
60 Gernonstown
61 Girley
62 Grangegeeth
63 Greenoge
64 Inishmot
65 Julianstown
66 Kells
67 Kentstown
68 Kilbeg
69 Kilberry
70 Kilbrew
71 Kilbride
72 Kilcarn
73 Kilclone
74 Kilcooly
75 Kildalkey
76 Killaconnigan
77 Killallon
78 Killary
79 Killeagh
80 Killeen
81 Killegland
82 Killyon
83 Kilmainham
84 Kilmessan
85 Kilmoon
86 Kilmore
87 Kilsharvan
88 Kilshine
89 Kilskeer
90 Kiltale
91 Knock
92 Knockcommon
93 Knockmark
94 Laracor
95 Liscartan
96 Lismullin
97 Loughbrackan
98 Loughcrew
99 Macetown
100 Martry
101 Mitchelstown
102 Monknewtown
103 Monktown
104 Moorechurch
105 Moybolgue
106 Moyglare
107 Moylagh
108 Moymet
109 Moynalty
110 Navan
111 Newtown
112 Newtownclonbun
113 Nobber
114 Oldcastle
115 Painestown
116 Piercetown
117 Rataine
118 Rathbeggan
119 Rathcore
120 Rathfeigh
121 Rathkenny
122 Rathmolyon
123 Rathmore
124 Rathregan
125 Ratoath
126 Rodanstown
127 St. Mary's
128 Scurlockstown
129 Siddan
130 Skreen
131 Slane
132 Stackallan
133 Staffordstown
134 Staholmog
135 Stamullin
136 Tara
137 Teltown
138 Templekeeran
139 Timoole
140 Trevet
141 Trim
142 Trubley
143 Tullaghanoge
144 Tullyallen

THE BARONIES OF COUNTY MEATH

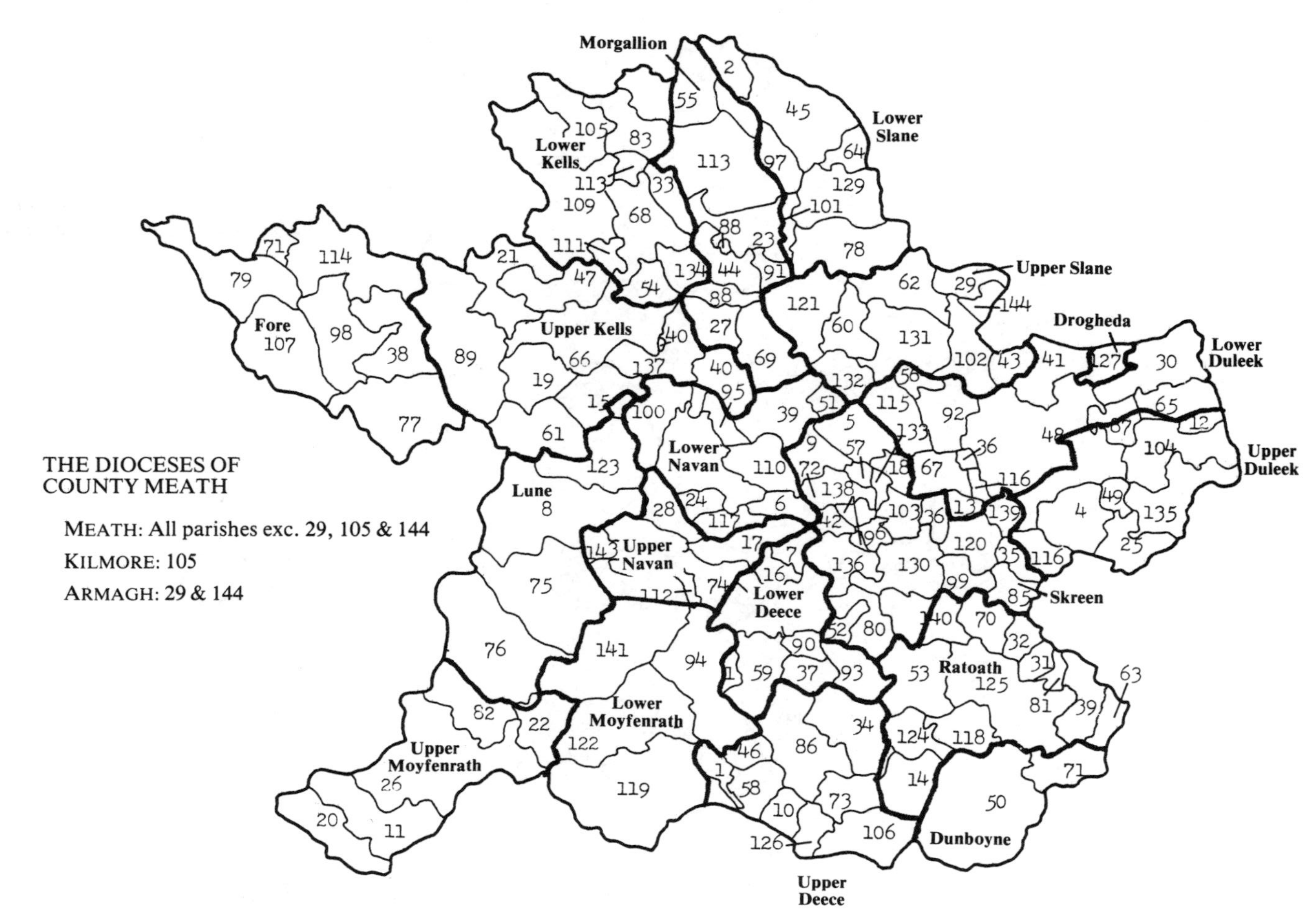

THE DIOCESES OF COUNTY MEATH

MEATH: All parishes exc. 29, 105 & 144

KILMORE: 105

ARMAGH: 29 & 144

THE POOR LAW UNIONS OF COUNTY MEATH

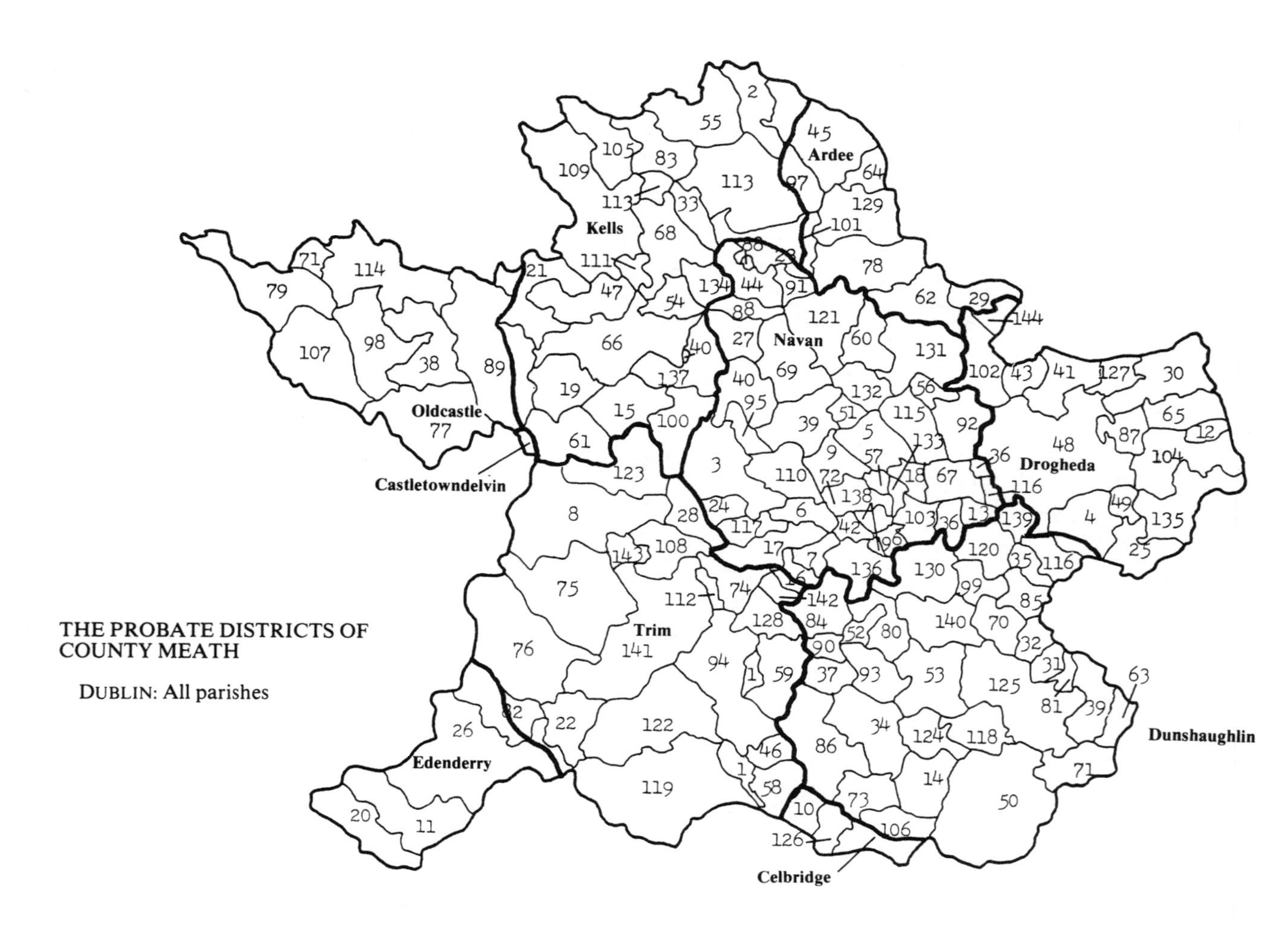

THE PROBATE DISTRICTS OF
COUNTY MEATH

DUBLIN: All parishes

THE PARISHES OF COUNTY MONAGHAN

THE BARONIES OF COUNTY MONAGHAN

THE DIOCESES OF CO. MONAGHAN

CLOGHER: All parishes

THE POOR LAW UNIONS OF COUNTY MONAGHAN

THE PROBATE DISTRICTS OF
CO. MONAGHAN

ARMAGH: All parishes

THE PARISHES OF COUNTY OFFALY (KING'S COUNTY)

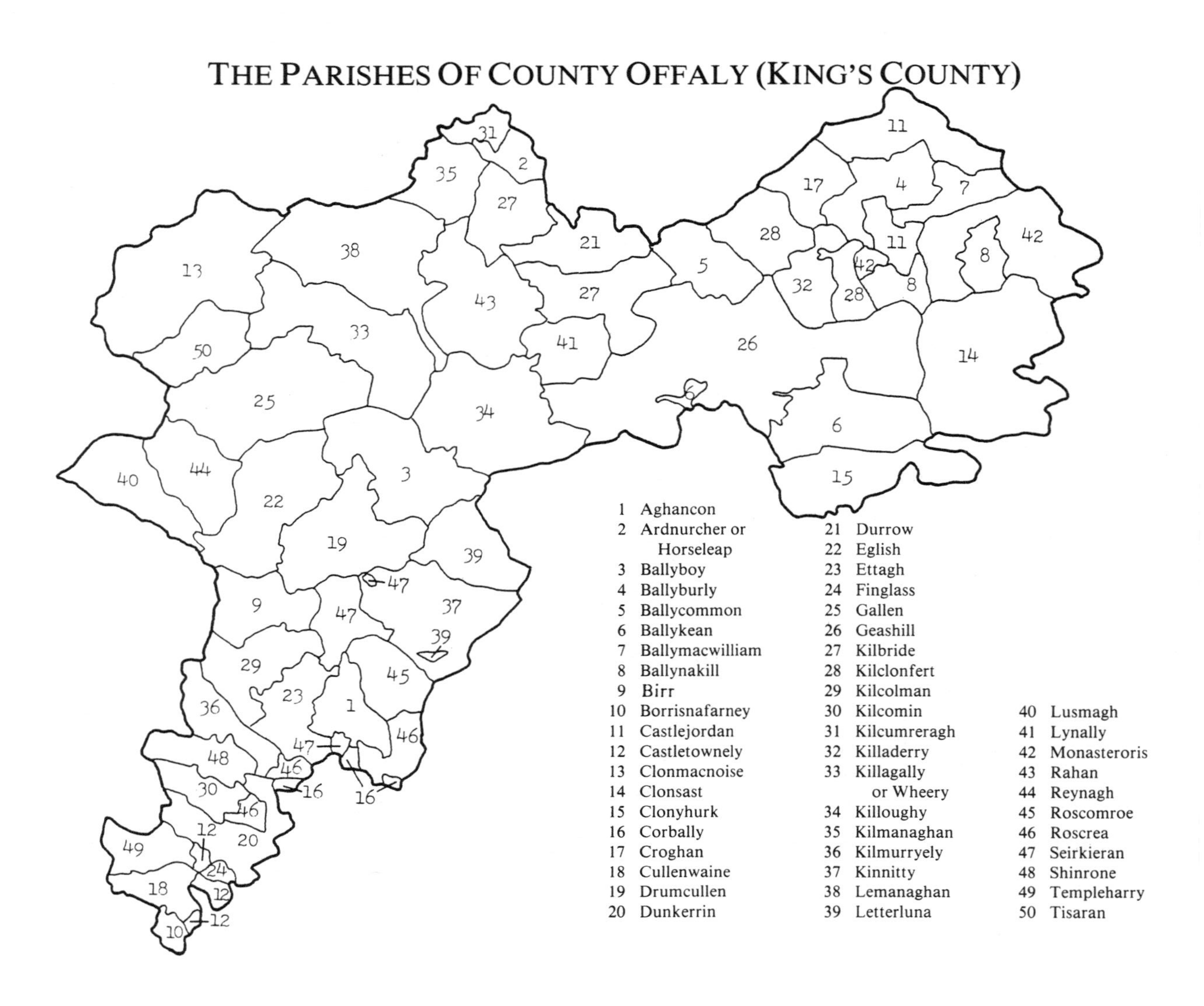

THE BARONIES OF COUNTY OFFALY (KING'S COUNTY)

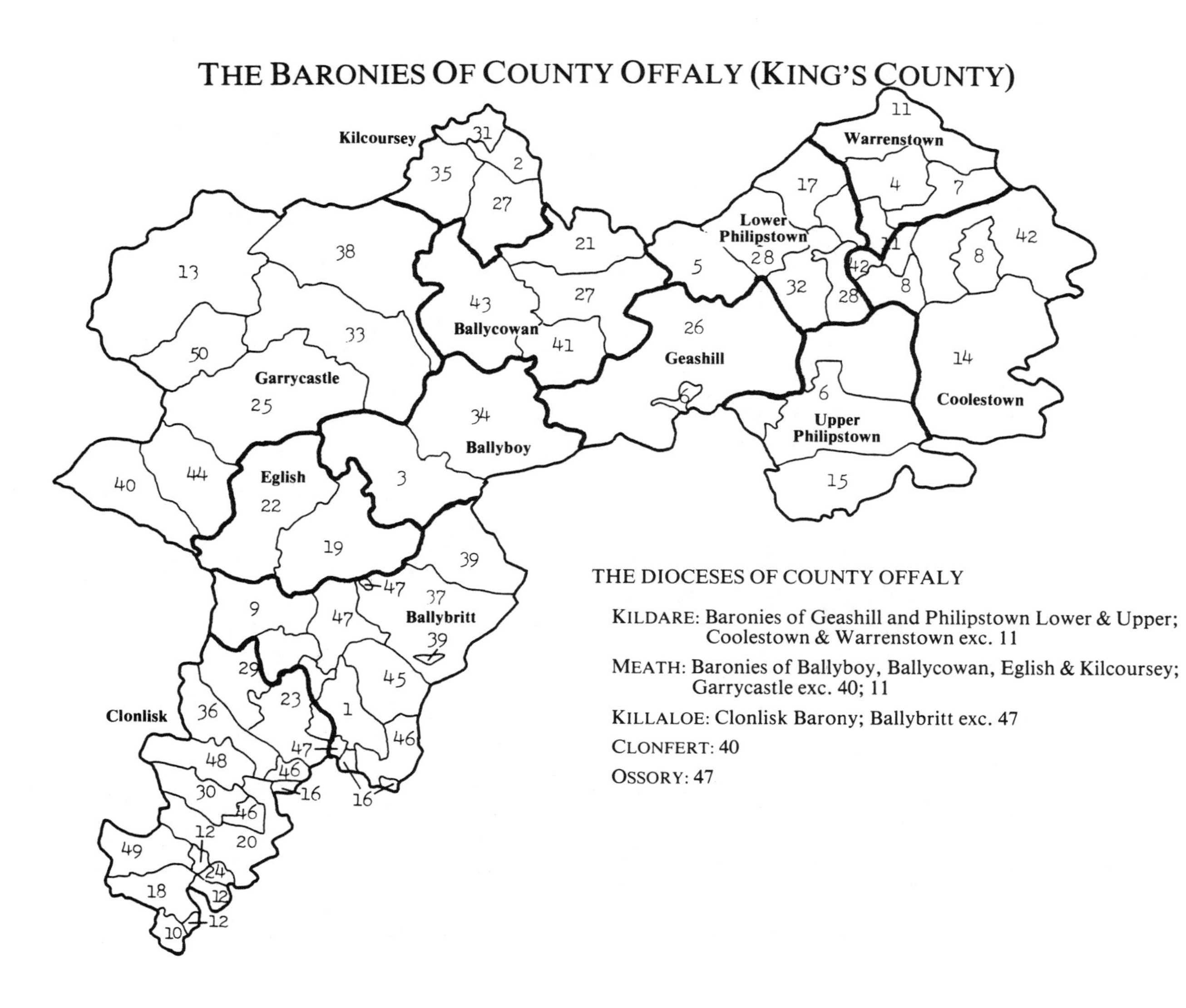

THE DIOCESES OF COUNTY OFFALY

KILDARE: Baronies of Geashill and Philipstown Lower & Upper; Coolestown & Warrenstown exc. 11

MEATH: Baronies of Ballyboy, Ballycowan, Eglish & Kilcoursey; Garrycastle exc. 40; 11

KILLALOE: Clonlisk Barony; Ballybritt exc. 47

CLONFERT: 40

OSSORY: 47

THE POOR LAW UNIONS OF COUNTY OFFALY (KING'S COUNTY)

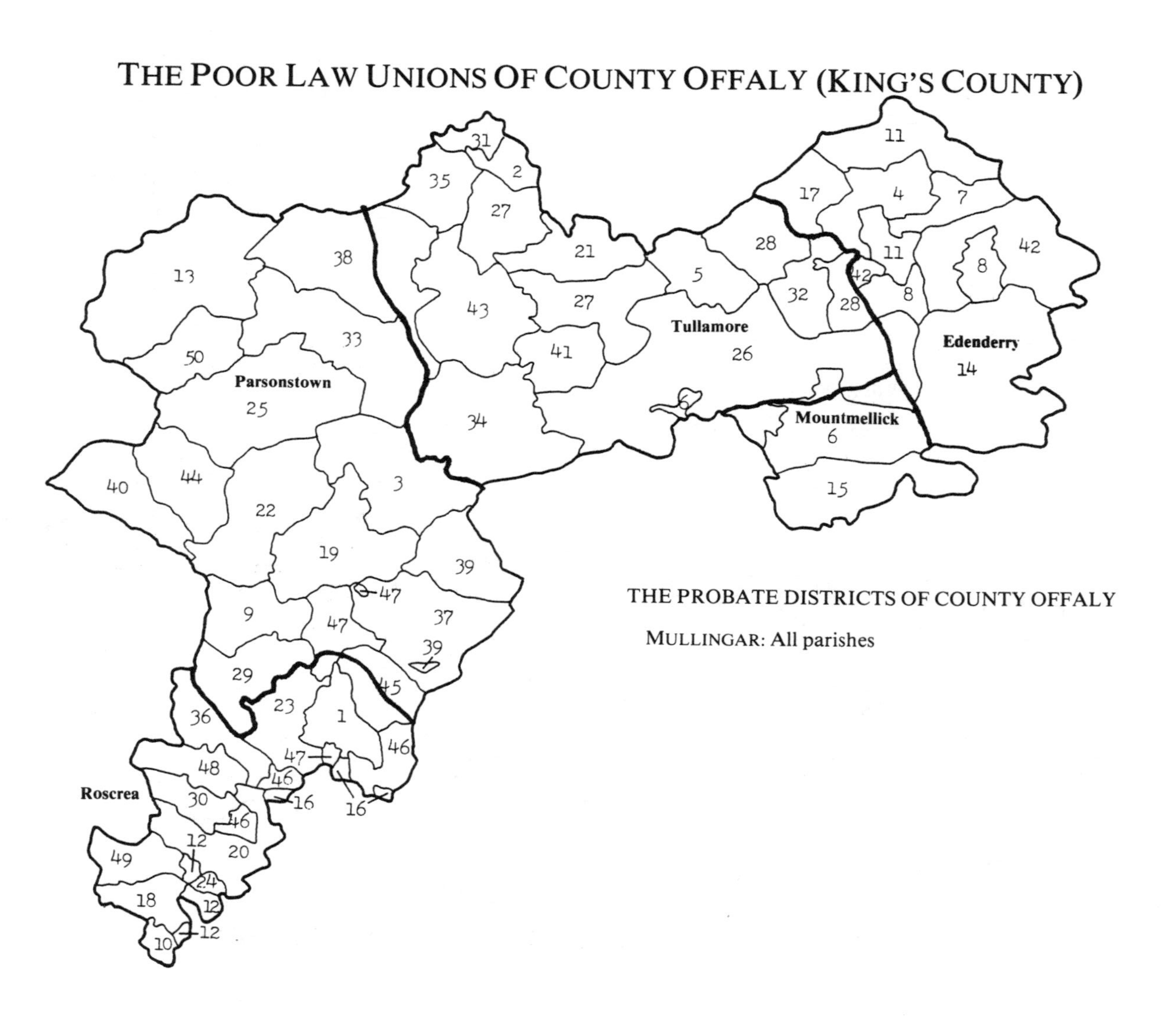

THE PROBATE DISTRICTS OF COUNTY OFFALY

MULLINGAR: All parishes

THE PARISHES OF COUNTY ROSCOMMON

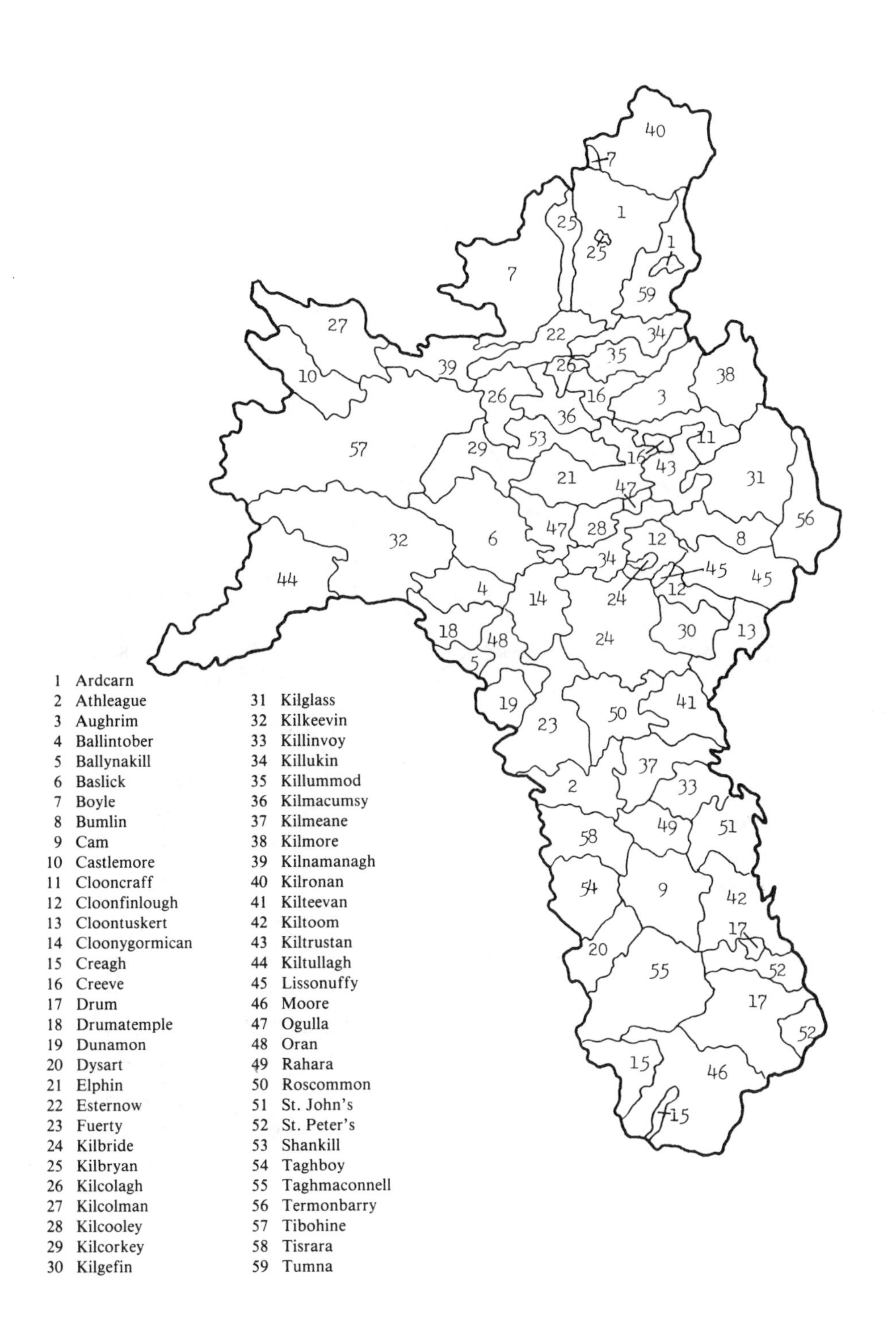

THE BARONIES OF COUNTY ROSCOMMON

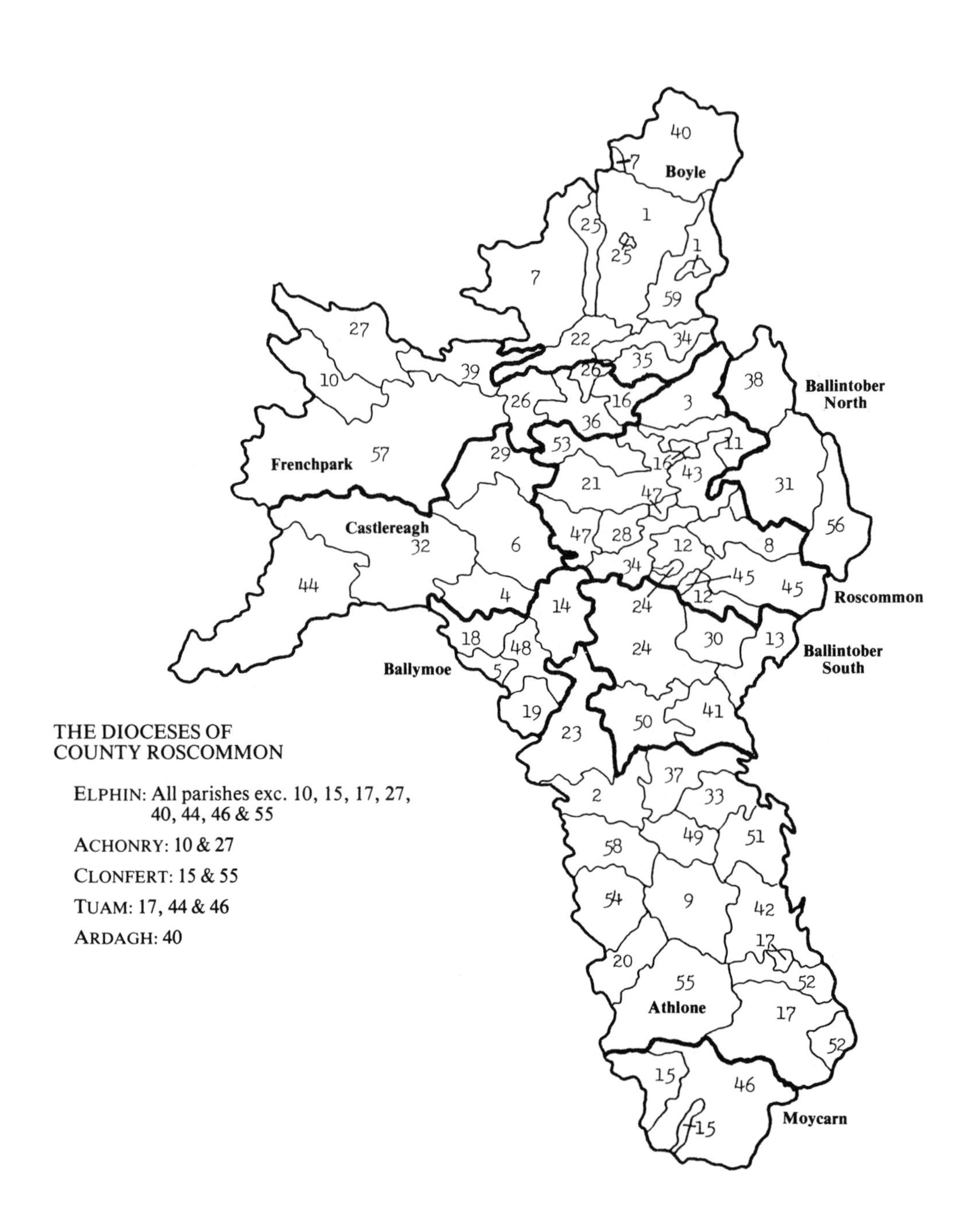

THE POOR LAW UNIONS OF COUNTY ROSCOMMON

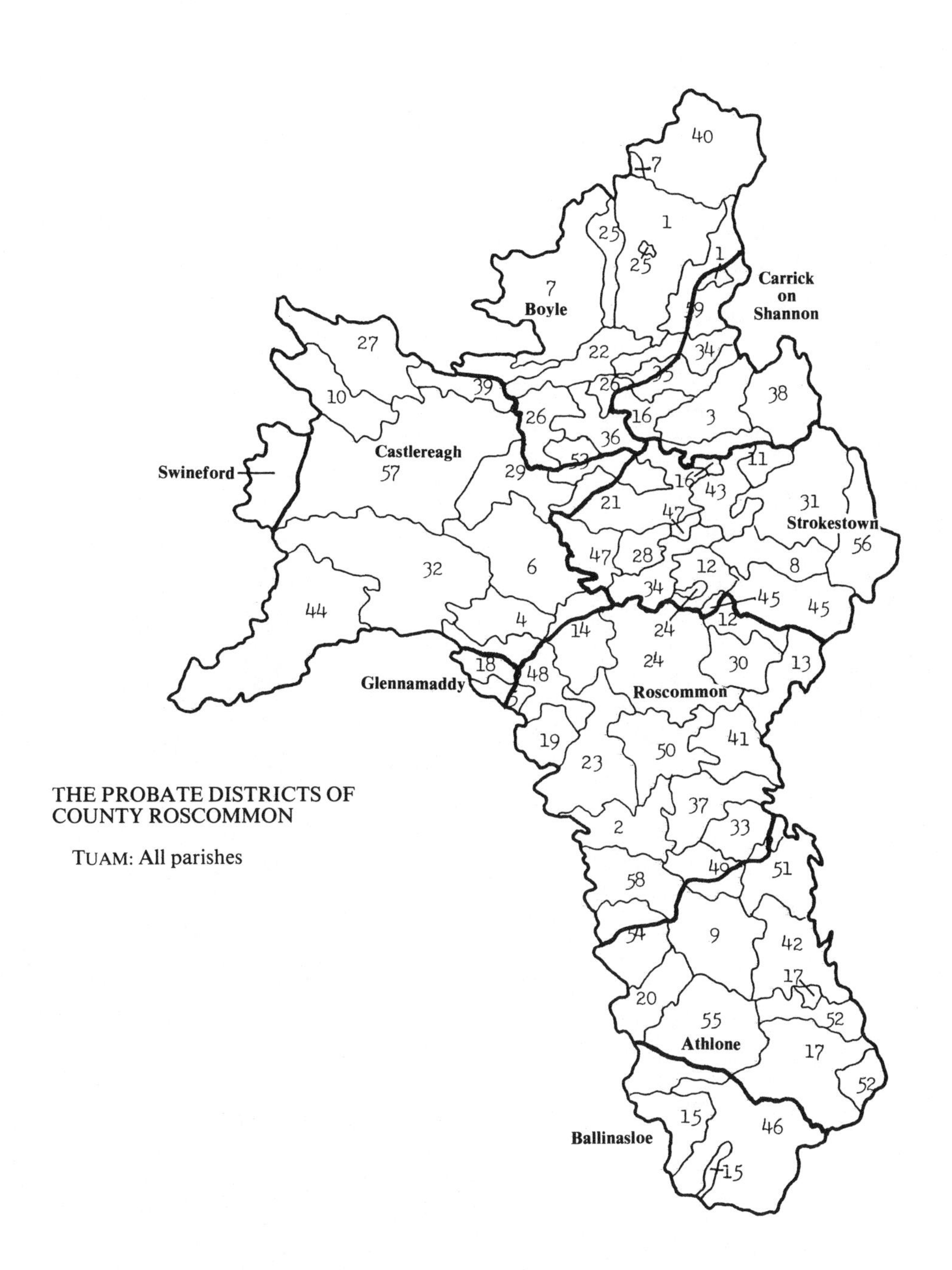

THE PROBATE DISTRICTS OF
COUNTY ROSCOMMON

TUAM: All parishes

THE PARISHES OF COUNTY SLIGO

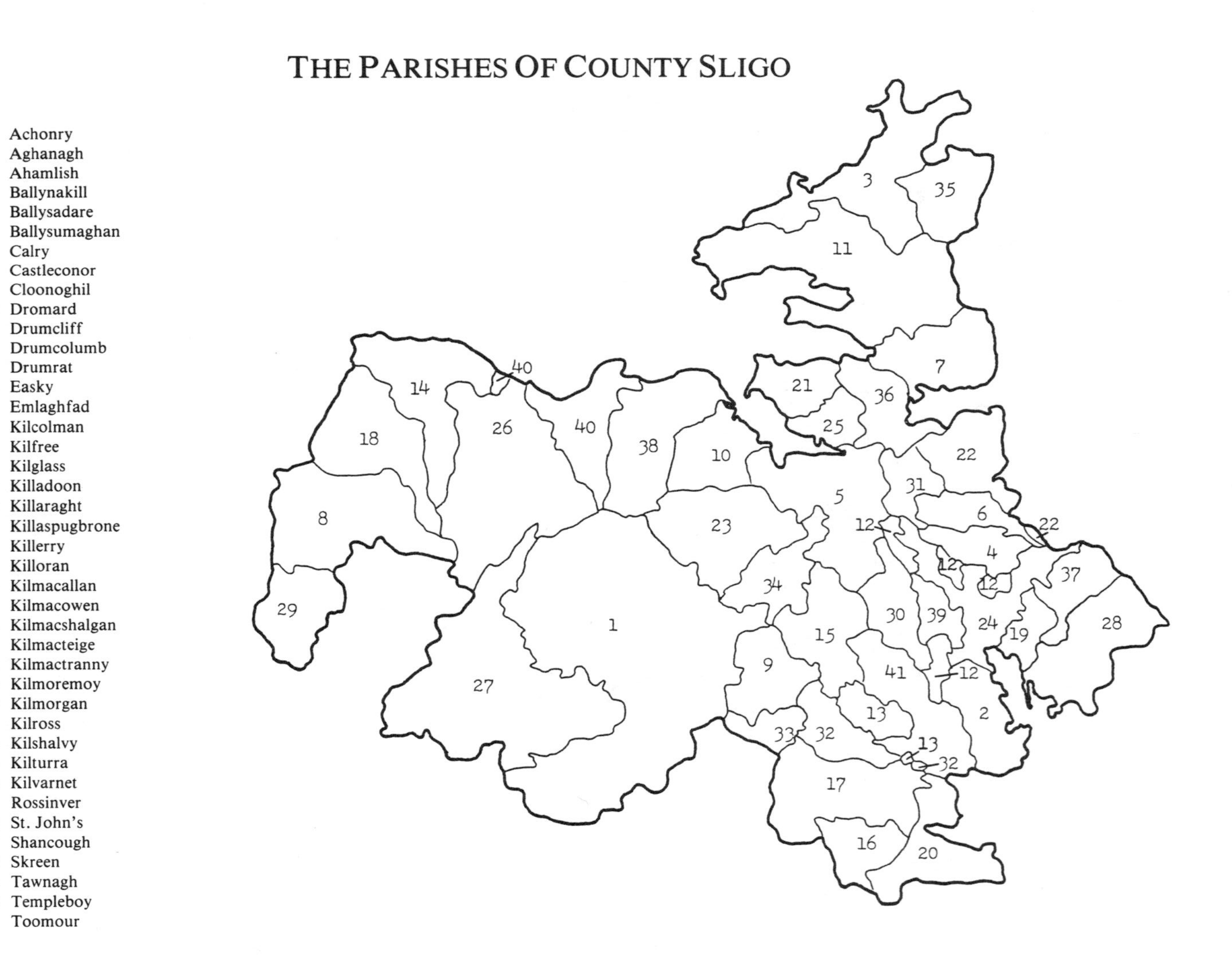

1 Achonry
2 Aghanagh
3 Ahamlish
4 Ballynakill
5 Ballysadare
6 Ballysumaghan
7 Calry
8 Castleconor
9 Cloonoghil
10 Dromard
11 Drumcliff
12 Drumcolumb
13 Drumrat
14 Easky
15 Emlaghfad
16 Kilcolman
17 Kilfree
18 Kilglass
19 Killadoon
20 Killaraght
21 Killaspugbrone
22 Killerry
23 Killoran
24 Kilmacallan
25 Kilmacowen
26 Kilmacshalgan
27 Kilmacteige
28 Kilmactranny
29 Kilmoremoy
30 Kilmorgan
31 Kilross
32 Kilshalvy
33 Kilturra
34 Kilvarnet
35 Rossinver
36 St. John's
37 Shancough
38 Skreen
39 Tawnagh
40 Templeboy
41 Toomour

THE BARONIES OF COUNTY SLIGO

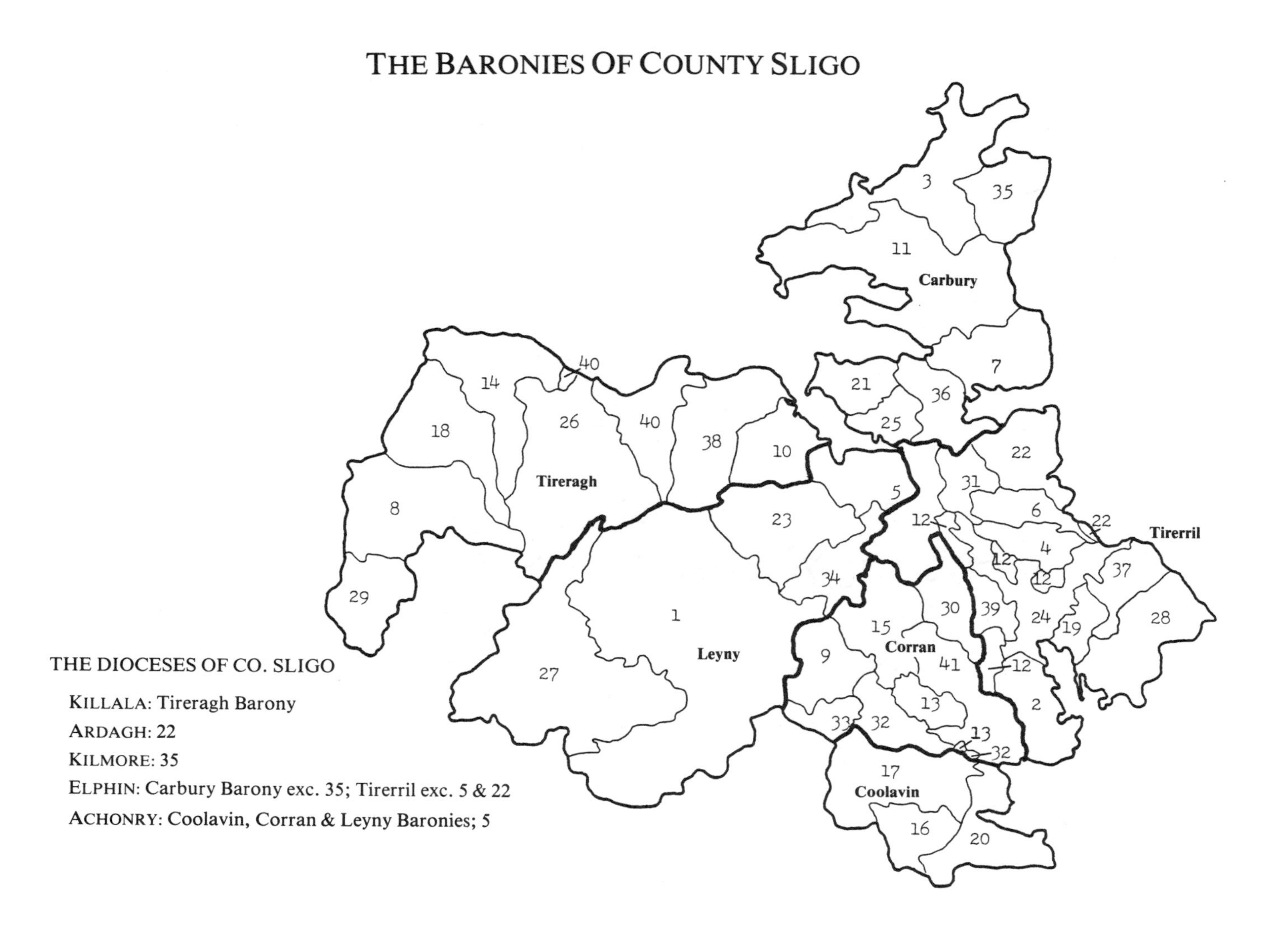

THE DIOCESES OF CO. SLIGO

KILLALA: Tireragh Barony

ARDAGH: 22

KILMORE: 35

ELPHIN: Carbury Barony exc. 35; Tirerril exc. 5 & 22

ACHONRY: Coolavin, Corran & Leyny Baronies; 5

THE POOR LAW UNIONS OF COUNTY SLIGO

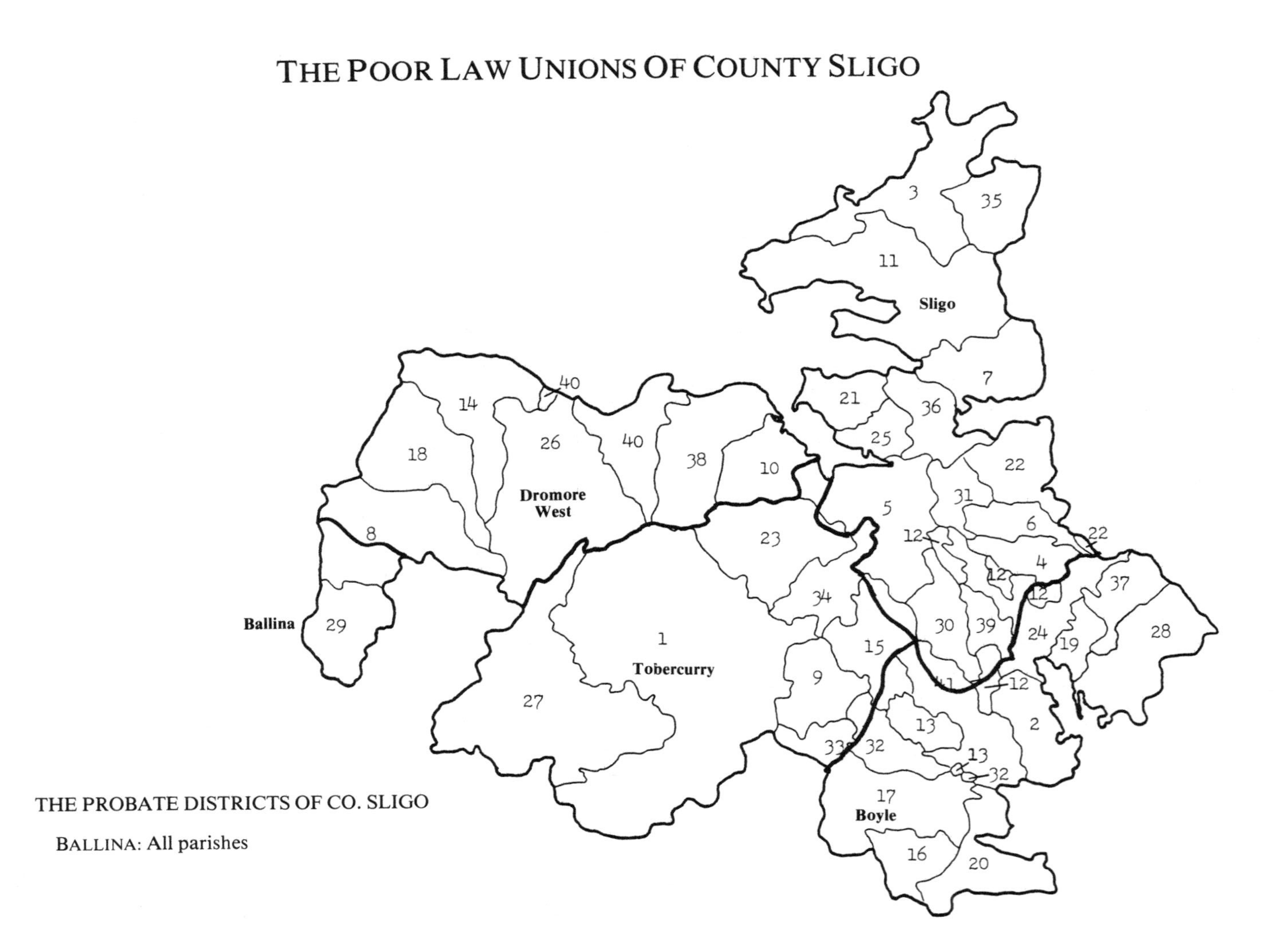

THE PROBATE DISTRICTS OF CO. SLIGO

BALLINA: All parishes

THE PARISHES OF COUNTY TIPPERARY NORTH

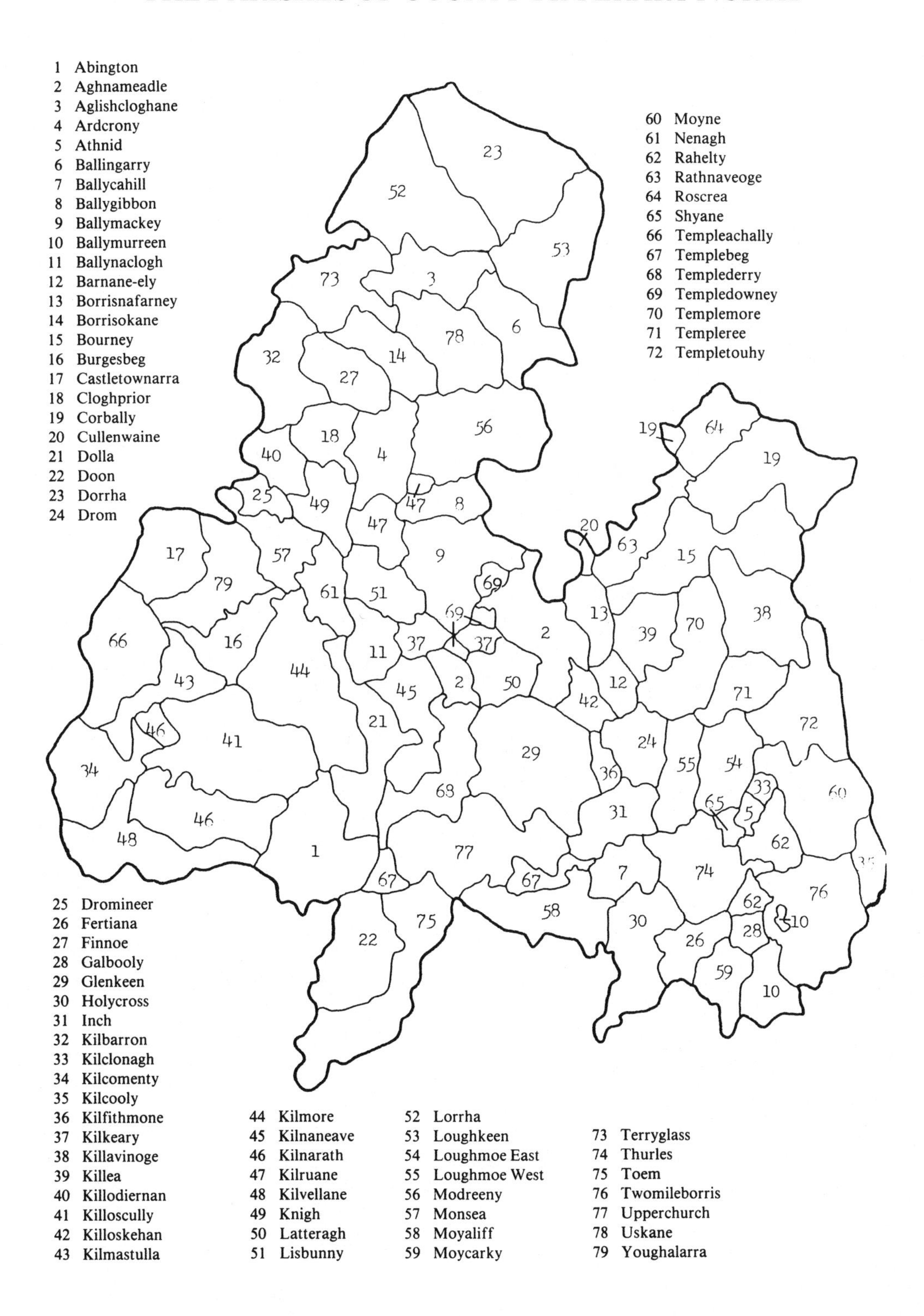

THE BARONIES OF COUNTY TIPPERARY NORTH

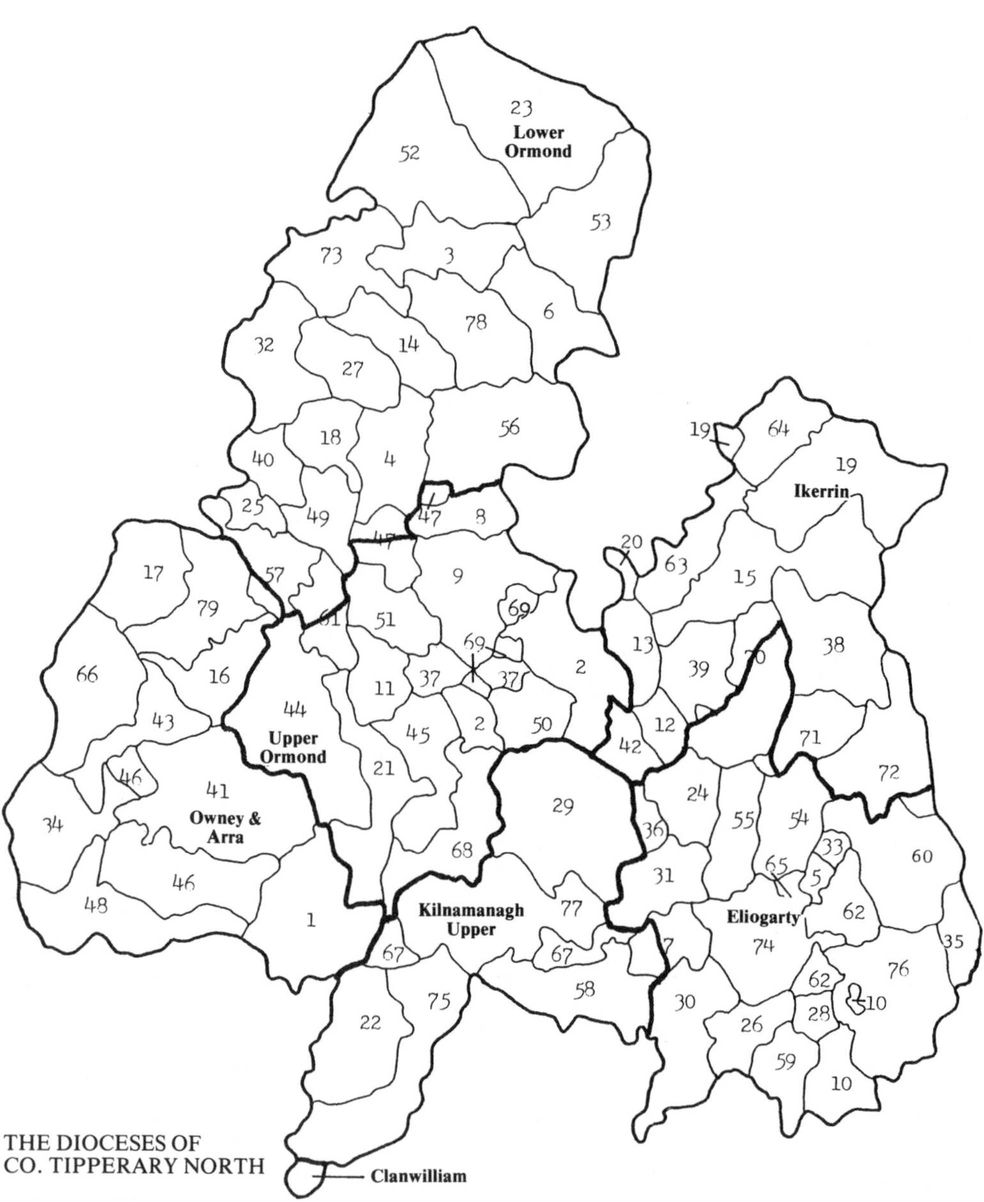

CASHEL: Eliogarty Barony; 7, 12, 29, 34, 38, 39, 41, 42, 46, 48, 58, 67, 70, 71, 72 & 77

EMLY: 1, 22, 43, 66 & 75

KILLALOE: Baronies of Ormond Lower & Upper; 13, 15, 16, 17, 19, 20, 57, 63, 64 & 79

THE POOR LAW UNIONS OF COUNTY TIPPERARY NORTH

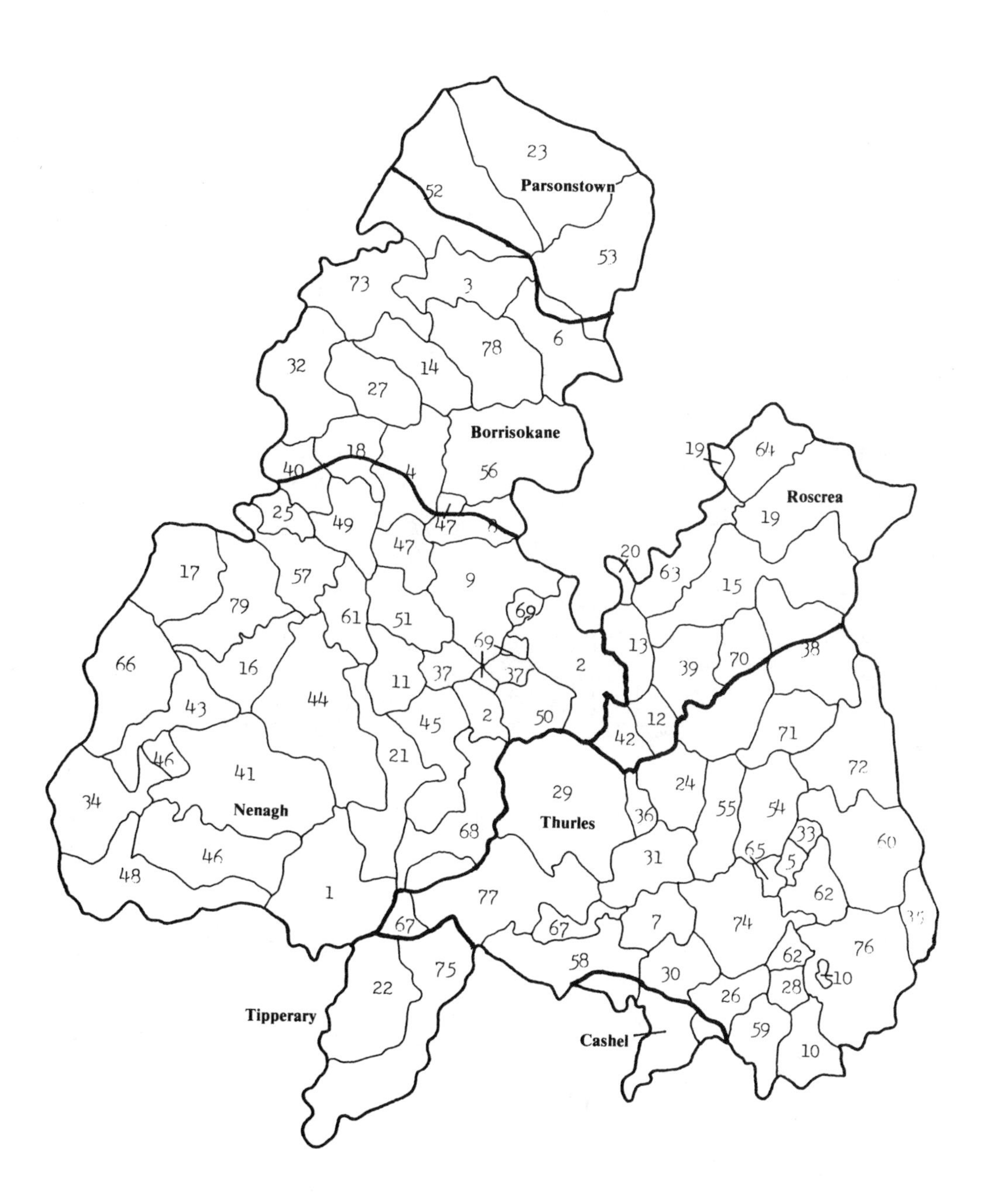

THE PROBATE DISTRICTS OF CO. TIPPERARY NORTH

LIMERICK: All parishes

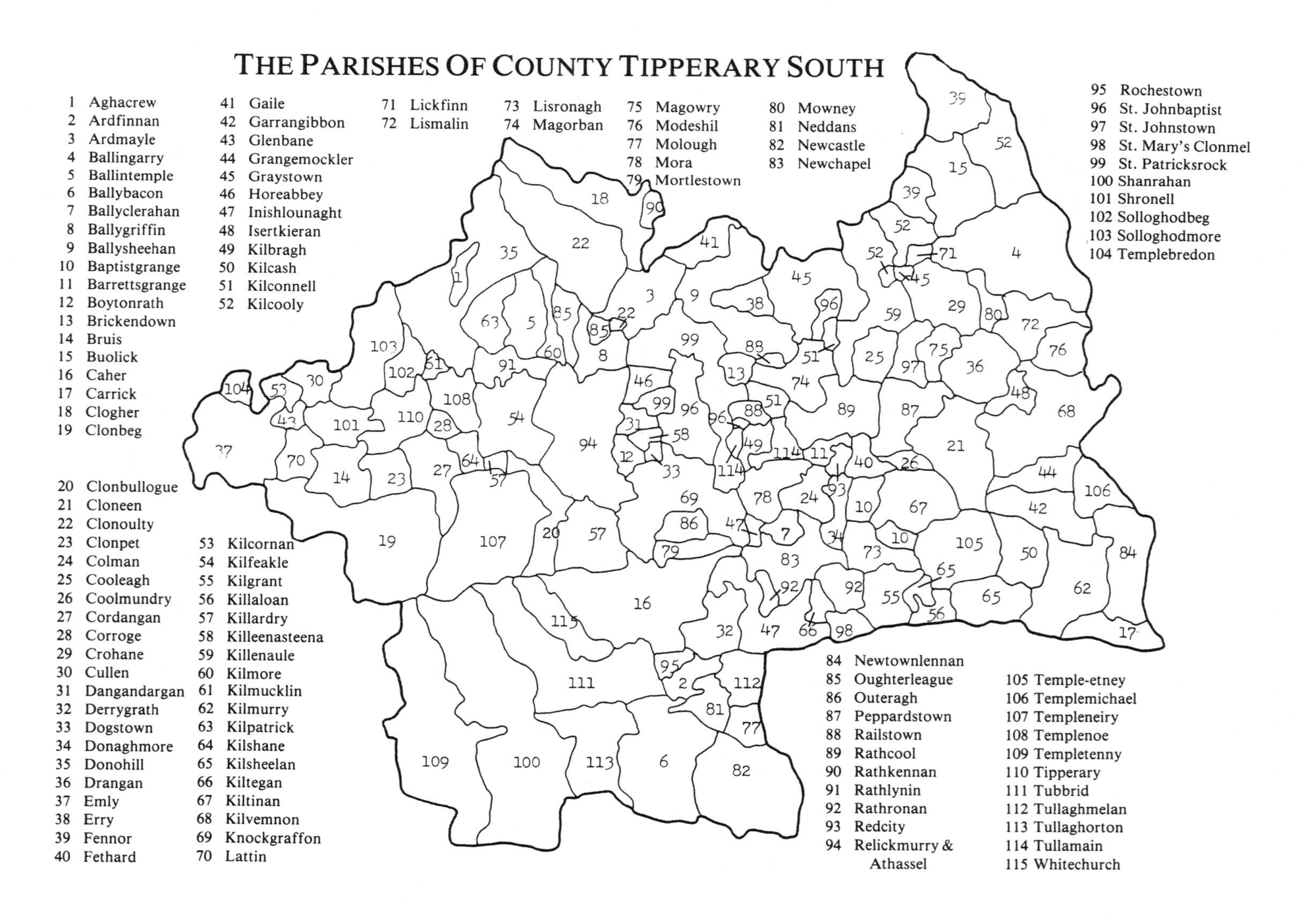
THE PARISHES OF COUNTY TIPPERARY SOUTH
1 Aghacrew
2 Ardfinnan
3 Ardmayle
4 Ballingarry
5 Ballintemple
6 Ballybacon
7 Ballyclerahan
8 Ballygriffin
9 Ballysheehan
10 Baptistgrange
11 Barrettsgrange
12 Boytonrath
13 Brickendown
14 Bruis
15 Buolick
16 Caher
17 Carrick
18 Clogher
19 Clonbeg
20 Clonbullogue
21 Cloneen
22 Clonoulty
23 Clonpet
24 Colman
25 Cooleagh
26 Coolmundry
27 Cordangan
28 Corroge
29 Crohane
30 Cullen
31 Dangandargan
32 Derrygrath
33 Dogstown
34 Donaghmore
35 Donohill
36 Drangan
37 Emly
38 Erry
39 Fennor
40 Fethard
41 Gaile
42 Garrangibbon
43 Glenbane
44 Grangemockler
45 Graystown
46 Horeabbey
47 Inishlounaght
48 Isertkieran
49 Kilbragh
50 Kilcash
51 Kilconnell
52 Kilcooly
53 Kilcornan
54 Kilfeakle
55 Kilgrant
56 Killaloan
57 Killardry
58 Killeenasteena
59 Killenaule
60 Kilmore
61 Kilmucklin
62 Kilmurry
63 Kilpatrick
64 Kilshane
65 Kilsheelan
66 Kiltegan
67 Kiltinan
68 Kilvemnon
69 Knockgraffon
70 Lattin
71 Lickfinn
72 Lismalin
73 Lisronagh
74 Magorban
75 Magowry
76 Modeshil
77 Molough
78 Mora
79 Mortlestown
80 Mowney
81 Neddans
82 Newcastle
83 Newchapel
84 Newtownlennan
85 Oughterleague
86 Outeragh
87 Peppardstown
88 Railstown
89 Rathcool
90 Rathkennan
91 Rathlynin
92 Rathronan
93 Redcity
94 Relickmurry & Athassel
95 Rochestown
96 St. Johnbaptist
97 St. Johnstown
98 St. Mary's Clonmel
99 St. Patricksrock
100 Shanrahan
101 Shronell
102 Sollohodbeg
103 Solloghodmore
104 Templebredon
105 Temple-etney
106 Templemichael
107 Templeneiry
108 Templenoe
109 Templetenny
110 Tipperary
111 Tubbrid
112 Tullaghmelan
113 Tullaghorton
114 Tullamain
115 Whitechurch

THE BARONIES OF COUNTY TIPPERARY SOUTH

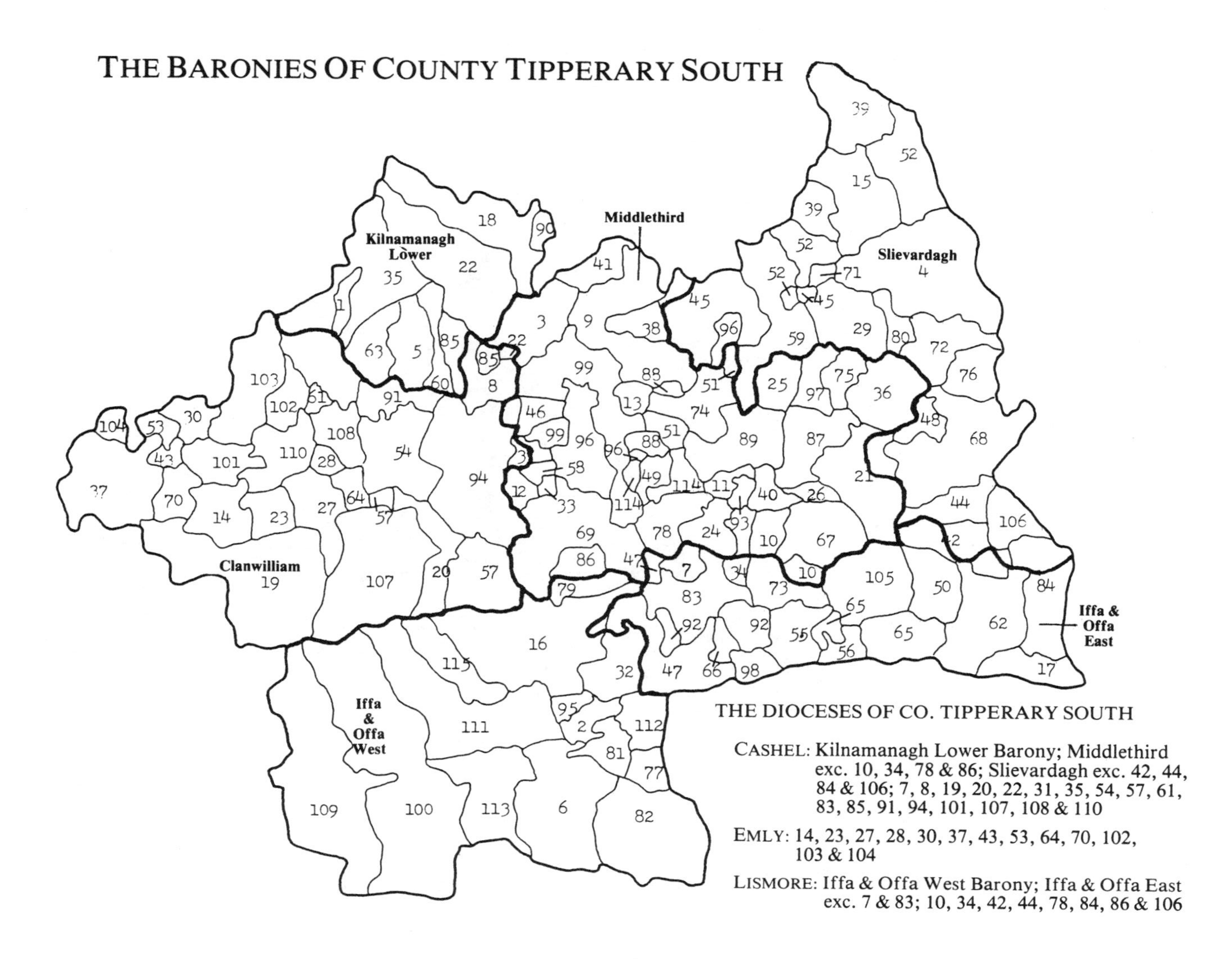

THE DIOCESES OF CO. TIPPERARY SOUTH

CASHEL: Kilnamanagh Lower Barony; Middlethird exc. 10, 34, 78 & 86; Slievardagh exc. 42, 44, 84 & 106; 7, 8, 19, 20, 22, 31, 35, 54, 57, 61, 83, 85, 91, 94, 101, 107, 108 & 110

EMLY: 14, 23, 27, 28, 30, 37, 43, 53, 64, 70, 102, 103 & 104

LISMORE: Iffa & Offa West Barony; Iffa & Offa East exc. 7 & 83; 10, 34, 42, 44, 78, 84, 86 & 106

THE POOR LAW UNIONS OF COUNTY TIPPERARY SOUTH

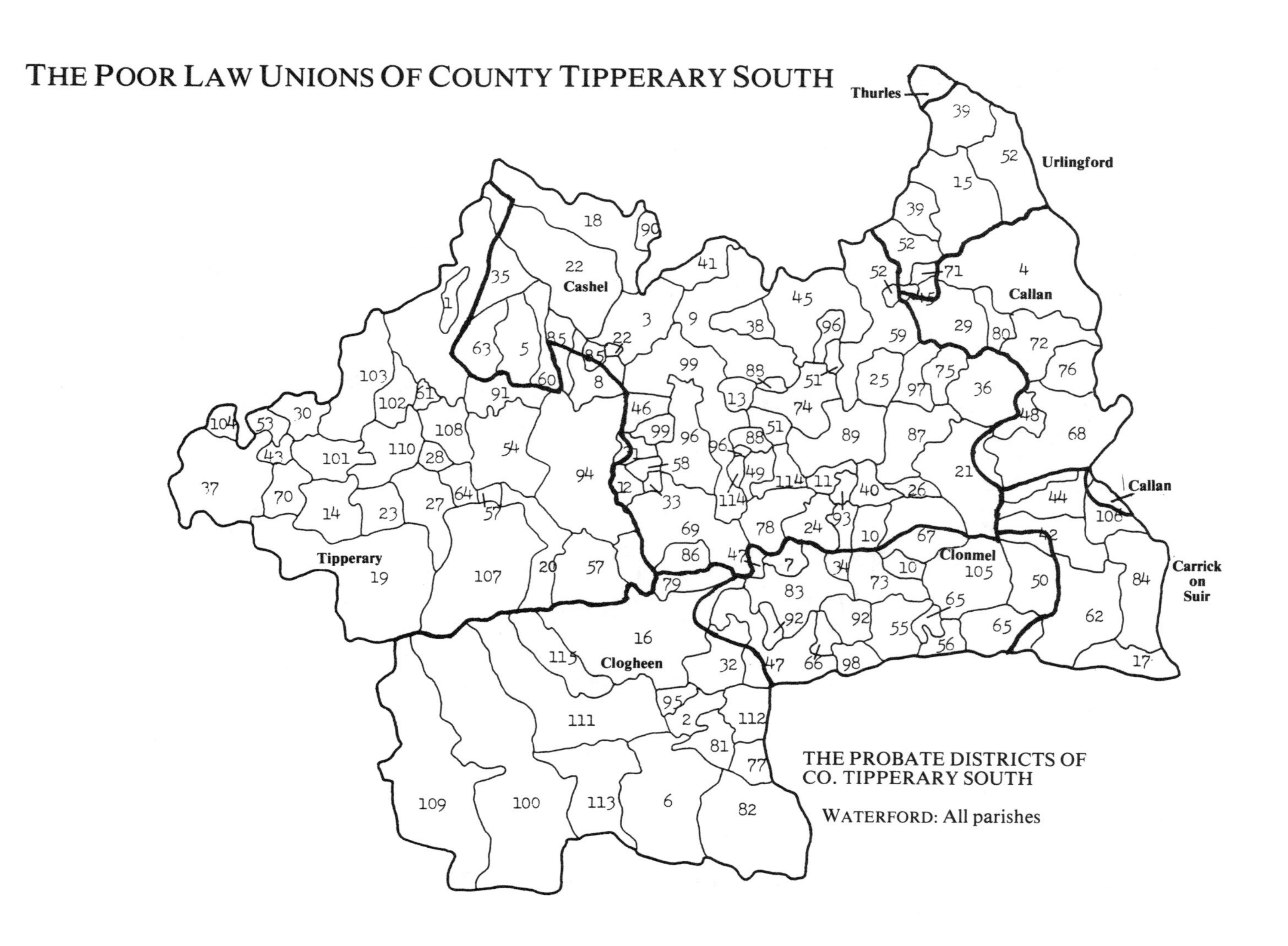

THE PROBATE DISTRICTS OF
CO. TIPPERARY SOUTH

WATERFORD: All parishes

THE PARISHES OF COUNTY TYRONE

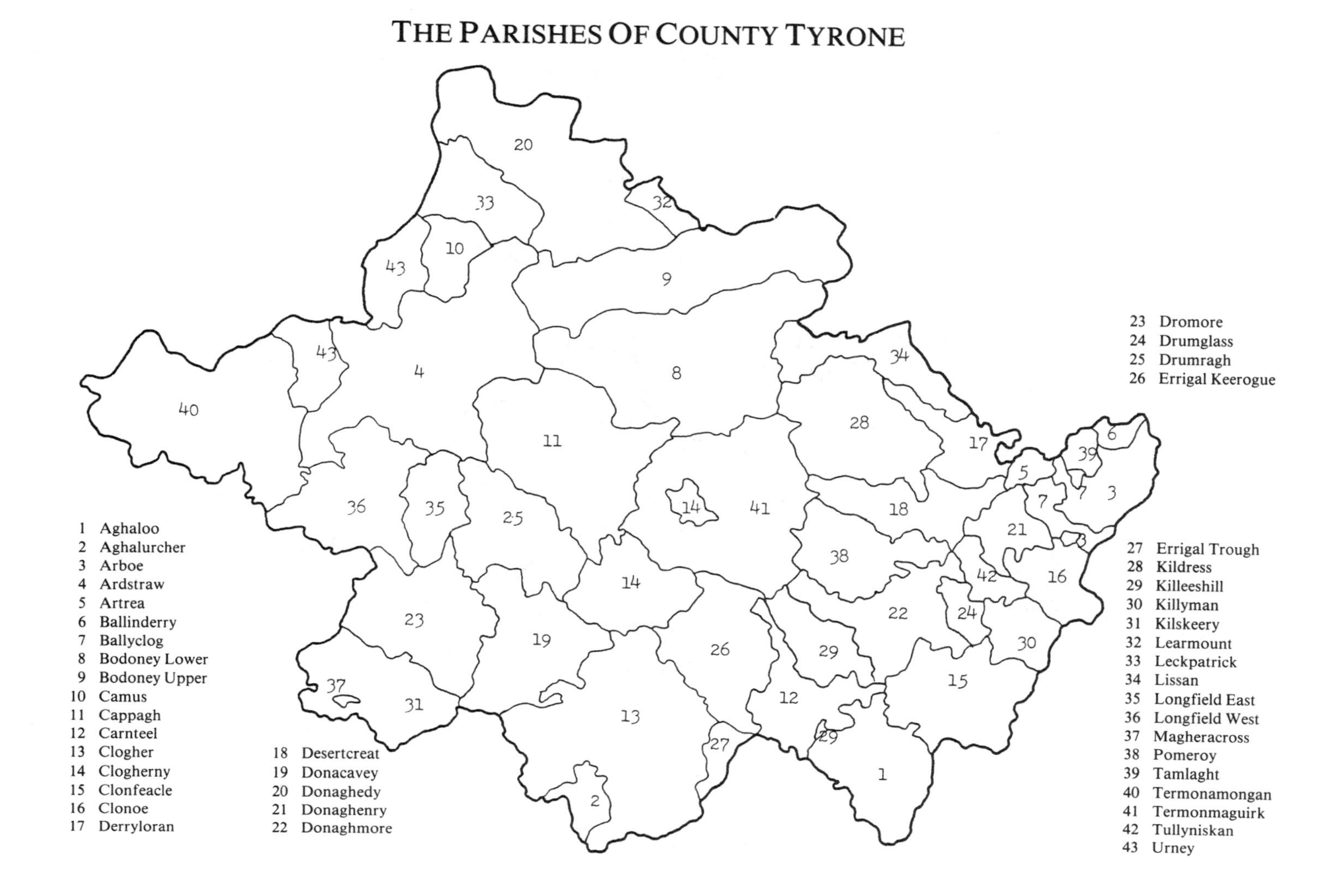

THE BARONIES OF COUNTY TYRONE

THE DIOCESES OF CO. TYRONE

ARMAGH: The Baronies of Dungannon Upper, Middle & Lower; 14, 26 & 41

DERRY: The Baronies of Strabane Lower & Omagh West; Strabane Upper exc. 41; 11 & 25

CLOGHER: 2, 13, 19, 23, 27, 31 & 37

The Poor Law Unions Of County Tyrone

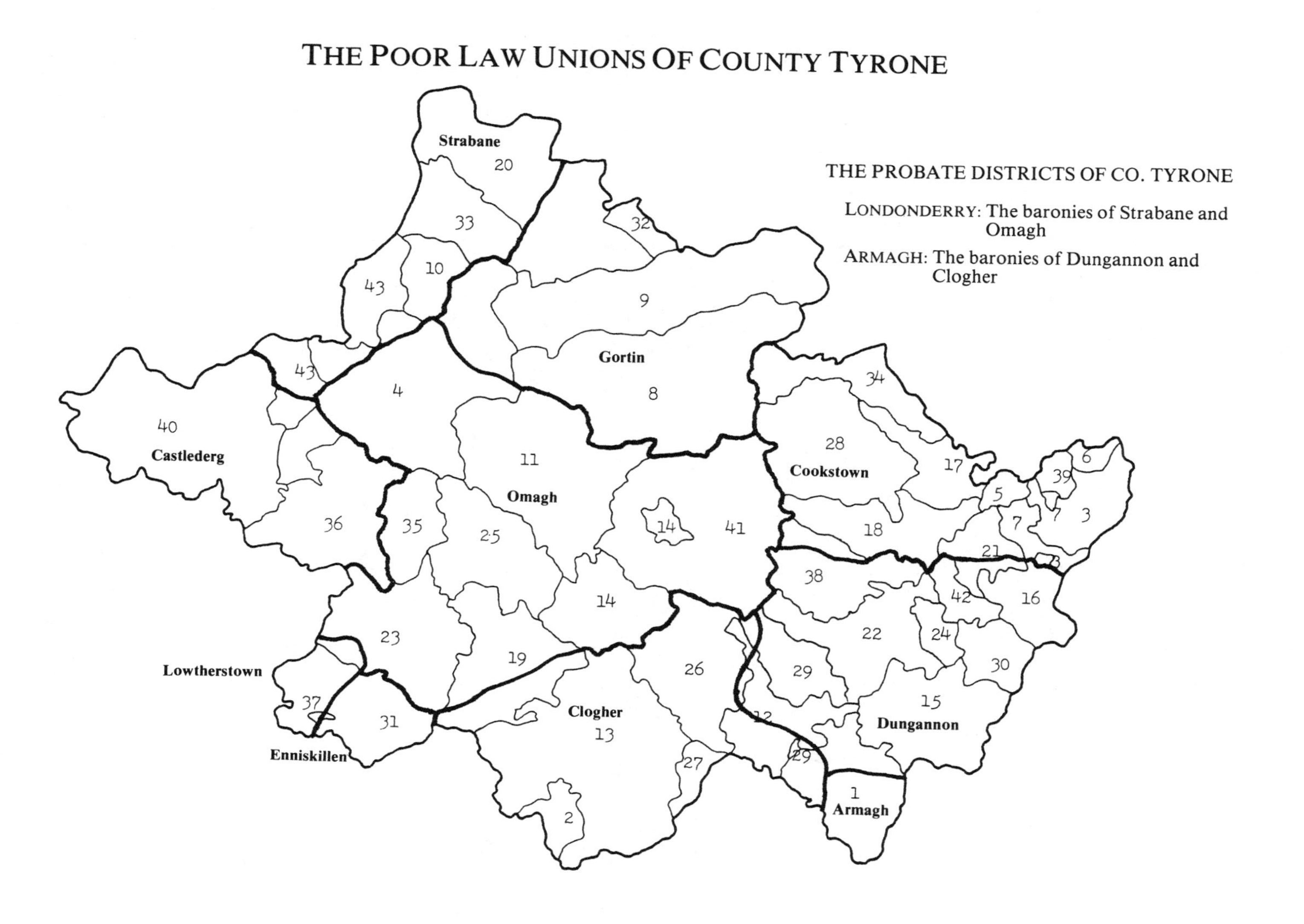

THE PROBATE DISTRICTS OF CO. TYRONE

LONDONDERRY: The baronies of Strabane and Omagh

ARMAGH: The baronies of Dungannon and Clogher

THE PARISHES OF COUNTY WATERFORD

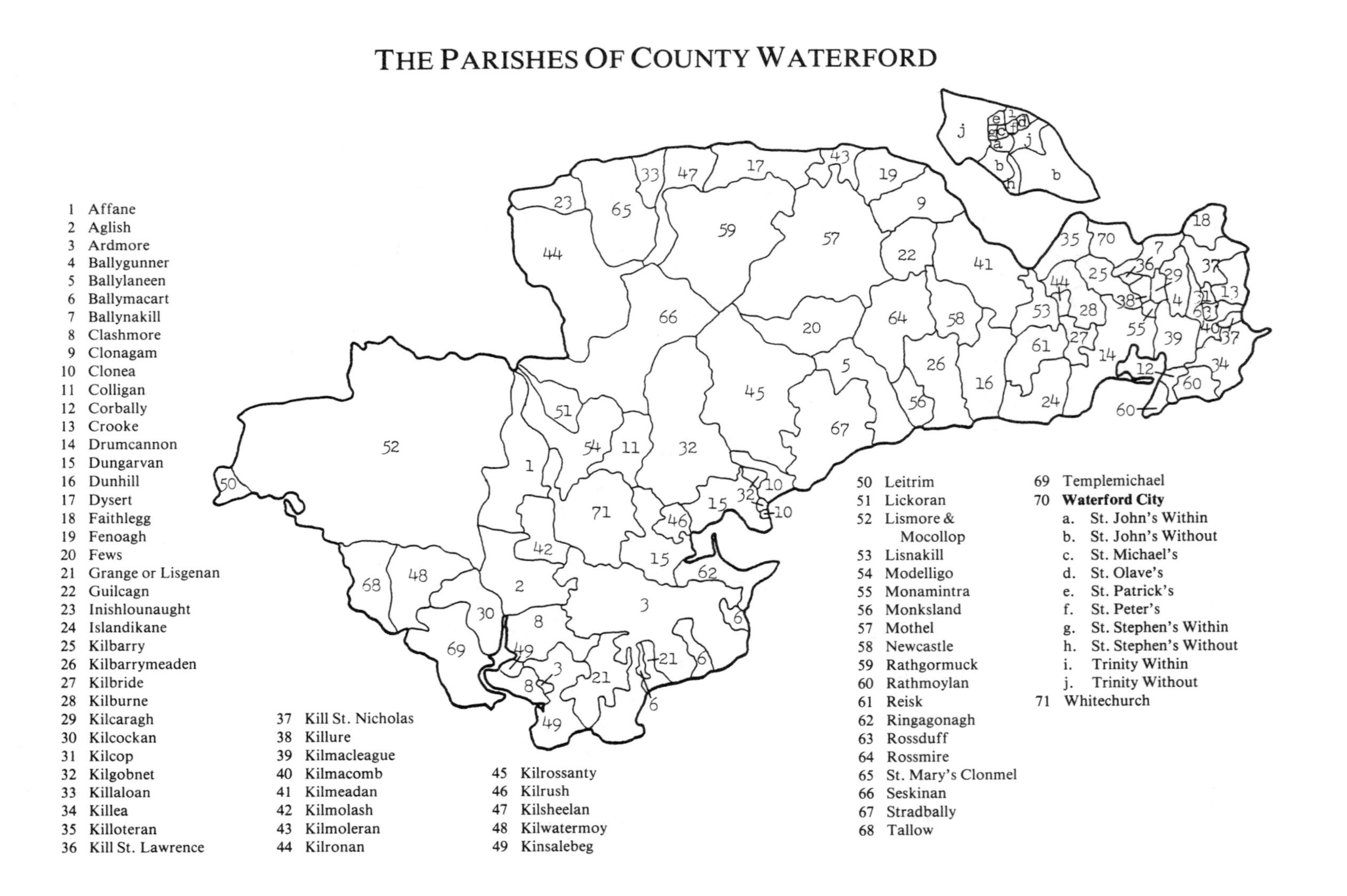

1 Affane
2 Aglish
3 Ardmore
4 Ballygunner
5 Ballylaneen
6 Ballymacart
7 Ballynakill
8 Clashmore
9 Clonagam
10 Clonea
11 Colligan
12 Corbally
13 Crooke
14 Drumcannon
15 Dungarvan
16 Dunhill
17 Dysert
18 Faithlegg
19 Fenoagh
20 Fews
21 Grange or Lisgenan
22 Guilcagn
23 Inishlounaught
24 Islandikane
25 Kilbarry
26 Kilbarrymeaden
27 Kilbride
28 Kilburne
29 Kilcaragh
30 Kilcockan
31 Kilcop
32 Kilgobnet
33 Killaloan
34 Killea
35 Killoteran
36 Kill St. Lawrence
37 Kill St. Nicholas
38 Killure
39 Kilmacleague
40 Kilmacomb
41 Kilmeadan
42 Kilmolash
43 Kilmoleran
44 Kilronan
45 Kilrossanty
46 Kilrush
47 Kilsheelan
48 Kilwatermoy
49 Kinsalebeg
50 Leitrim
51 Lickoran
52 Lismore & Mocollop
53 Lisnakill
54 Modelligo
55 Monamintra
56 Monksland
57 Mothel
58 Newcastle
59 Rathgormuck
60 Rathmoylan
61 Reisk
62 Ringagonagh
63 Rossduff
64 Rossmire
65 St. Mary's Clonmel
66 Seskinan
67 Stradbally
68 Tallow
69 Templemichael
70 **Waterford City**
a. St. John's Within
b. St. John's Without
c. St. Michael's
d. St. Olave's
e. St. Patrick's
f. St. Peter's
g. St. Stephen's Within
h. St. Stephen's Without
i. Trinity Within
j. Trinity Without
71 Whitechurch

THE BARONIES OF COUNTY WATERFORD

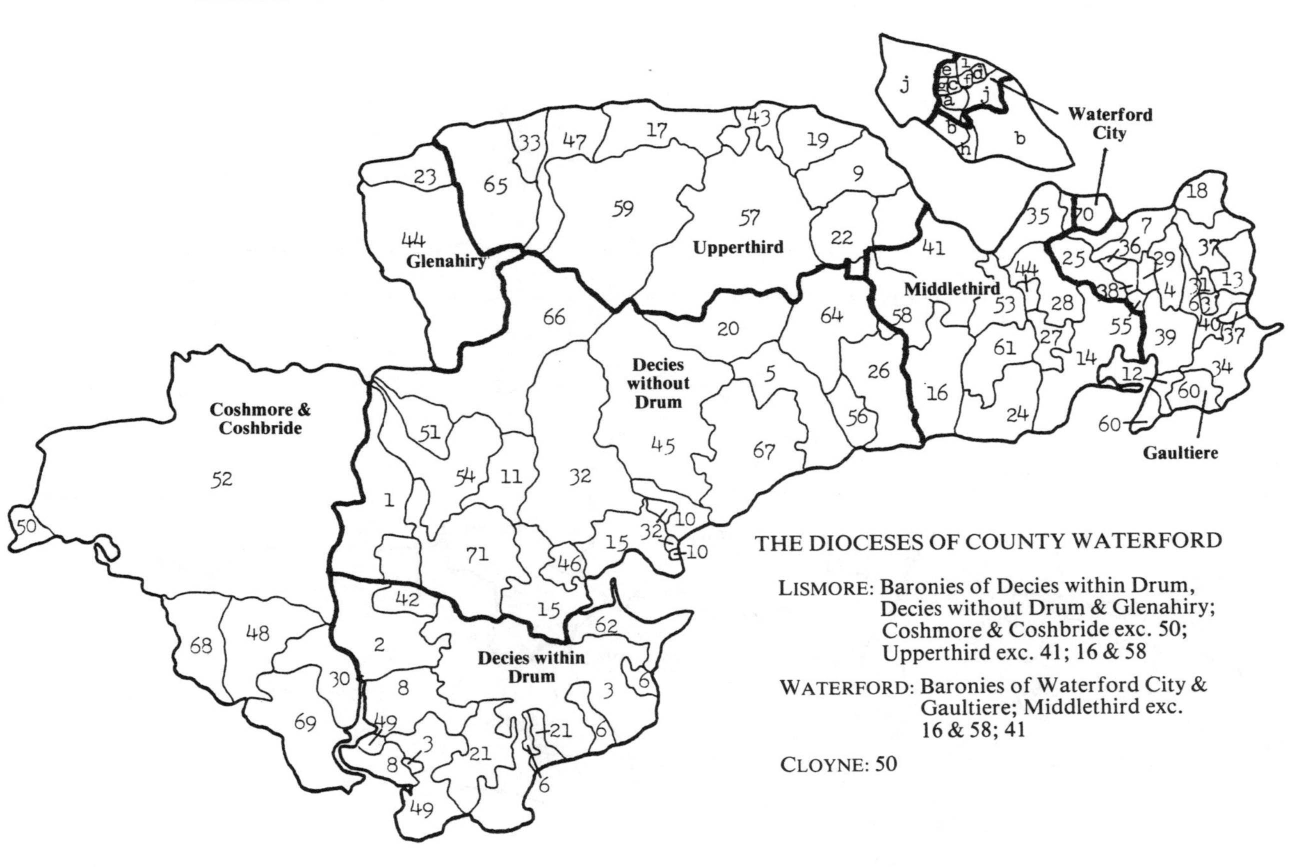

THE DIOCESES OF COUNTY WATERFORD

LISMORE: Baronies of Decies within Drum, Decies without Drum & Glenahiry; Coshmore & Coshbride exc. 50; Upperthird exc. 41; 16 & 58

WATERFORD: Baronies of Waterford City & Gaultiere; Middlethird exc. 16 & 58; 41

CLOYNE: 50

THE POOR LAW UNIONS OF COUNTY WATERFORD

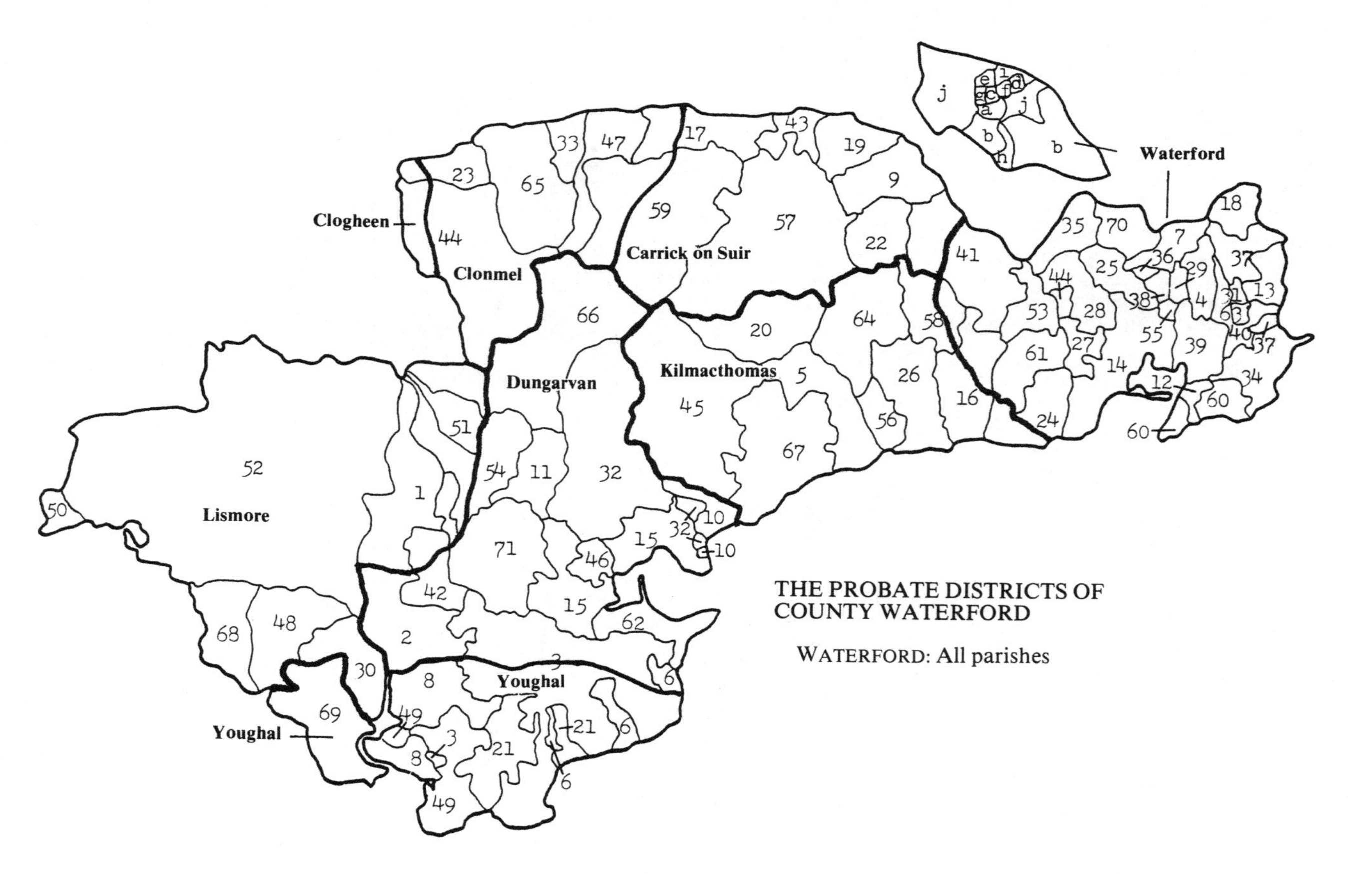

THE PROBATE DISTRICTS OF COUNTY WATERFORD

WATERFORD: All parishes

THE PARISHES OF COUNTY WESTMEATH

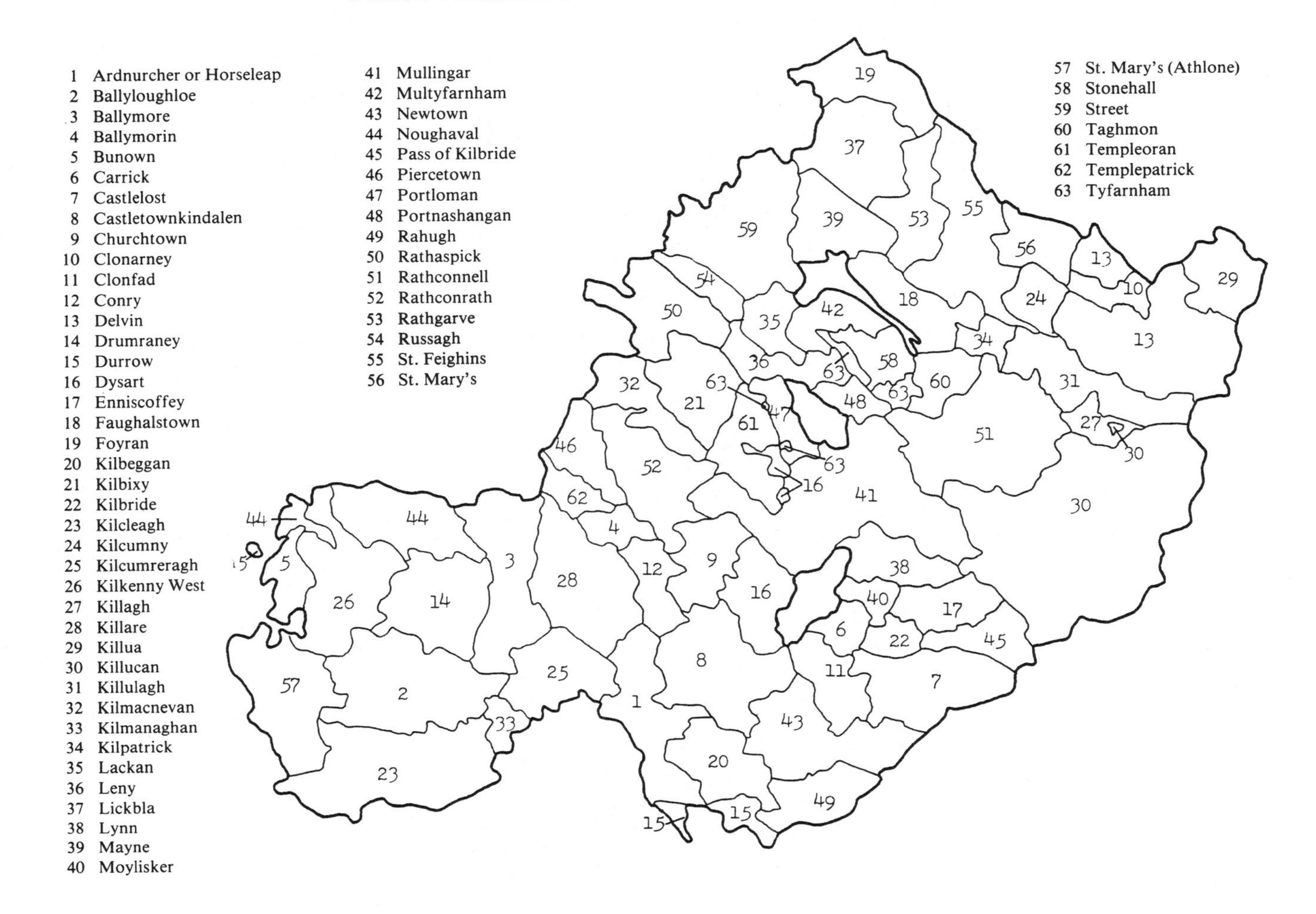

THE BARONIES OF COUNTY WESTMEATH

THE POOR LAW UNIONS OF COUNTY WESTMEATH

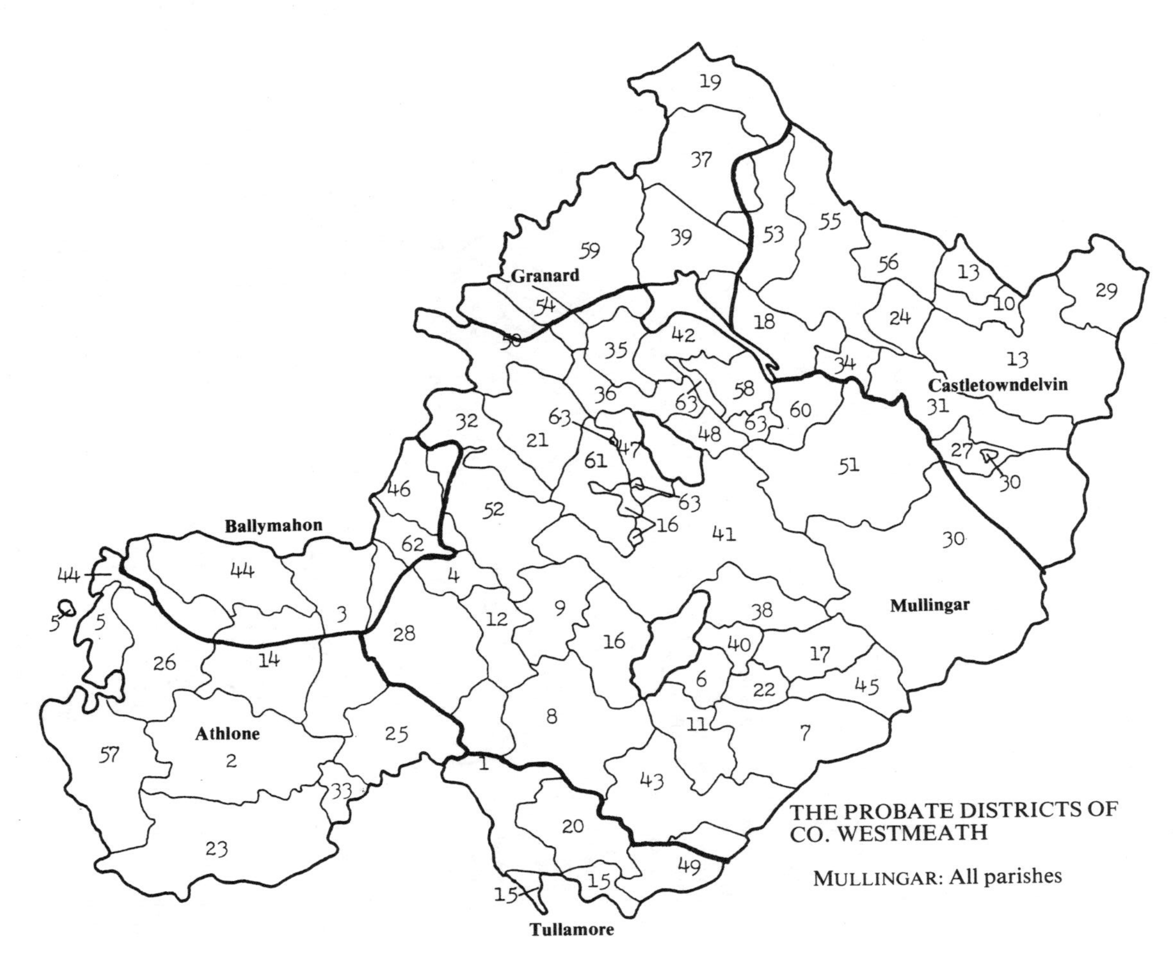

THE PROBATE DISTRICTS OF
CO. WESTMEATH

MULLINGAR: All parishes

THE PARISHES OF COUNTY WEXFORD

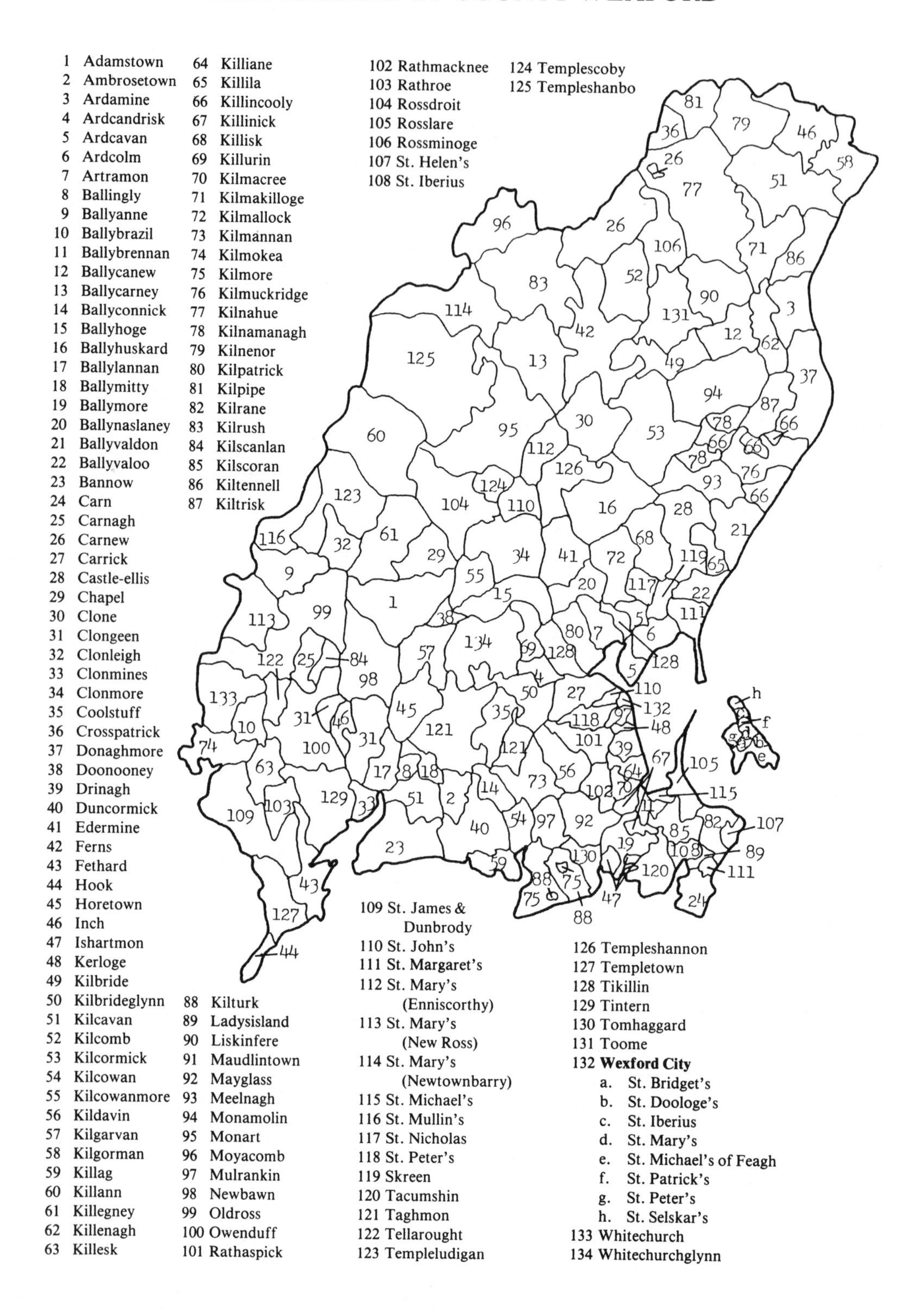

THE BARONIES OF COUNTY WEXFORD

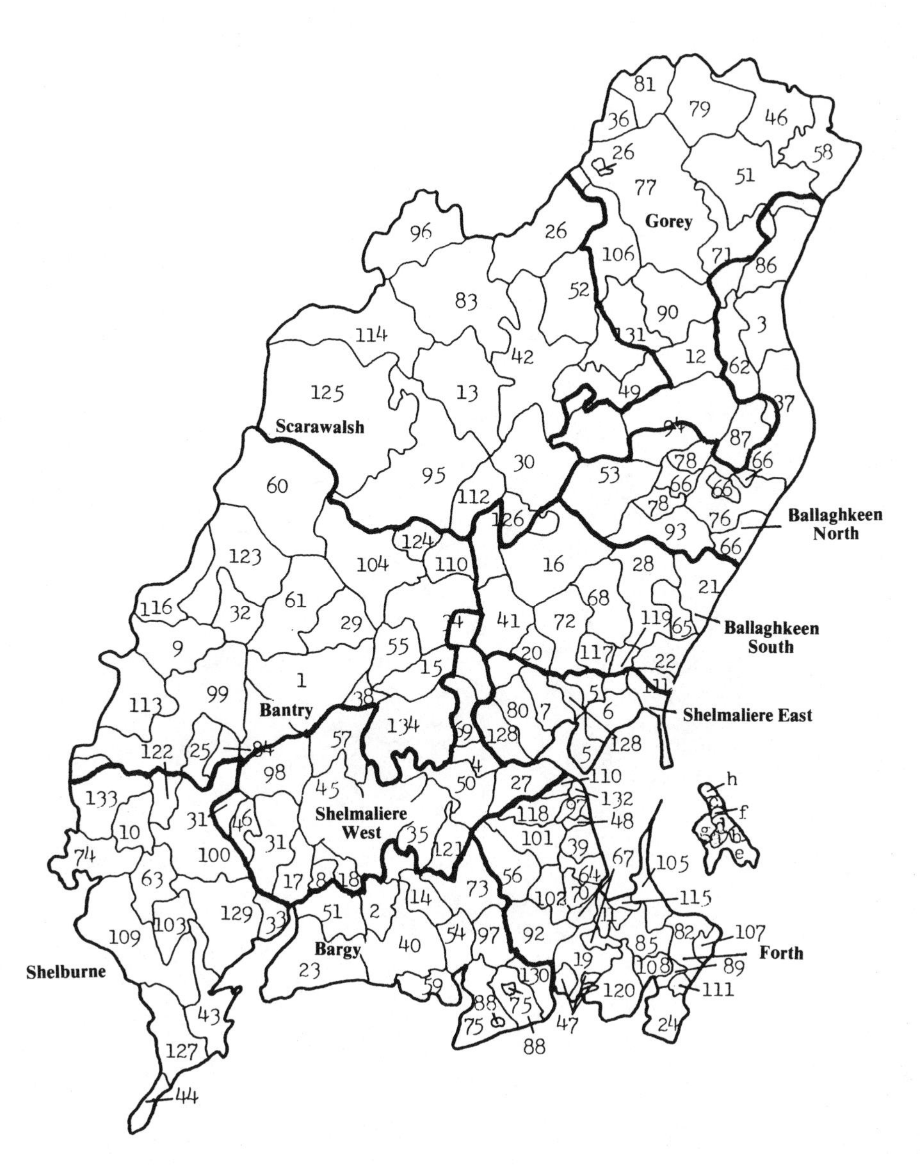

THE DIOCESES OF COUNTY WEXFORD

FERNS: All parishes exc. 46, 58 & 116

DUBLIN: 46 & 58

LEIGHLIN: 116

THE POOR LAW UNIONS OF COUNTY WEXFORD

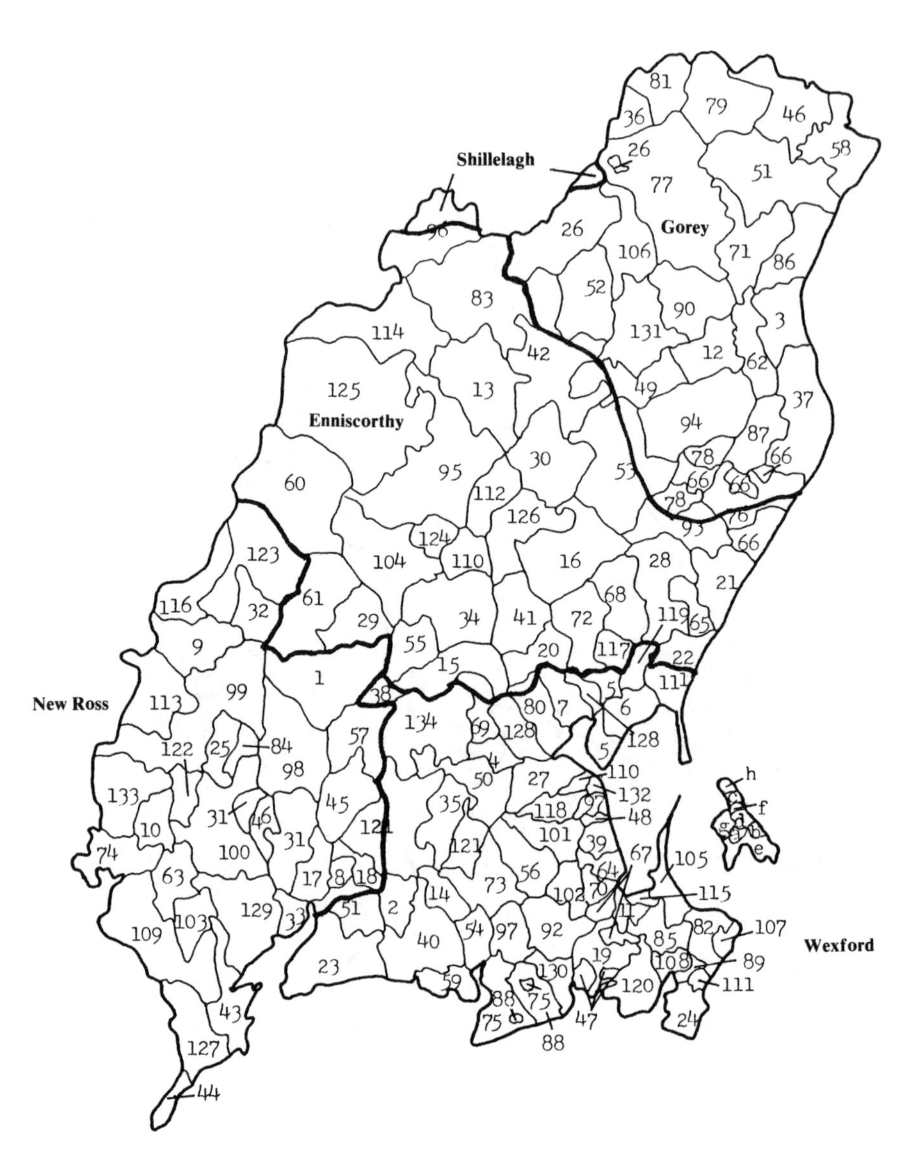

THE PROBATE DISTRICTS OF COUNTY WEXFORD

WATERFORD: All parishes

THE PARISHES OF COUNTY WICKLOW

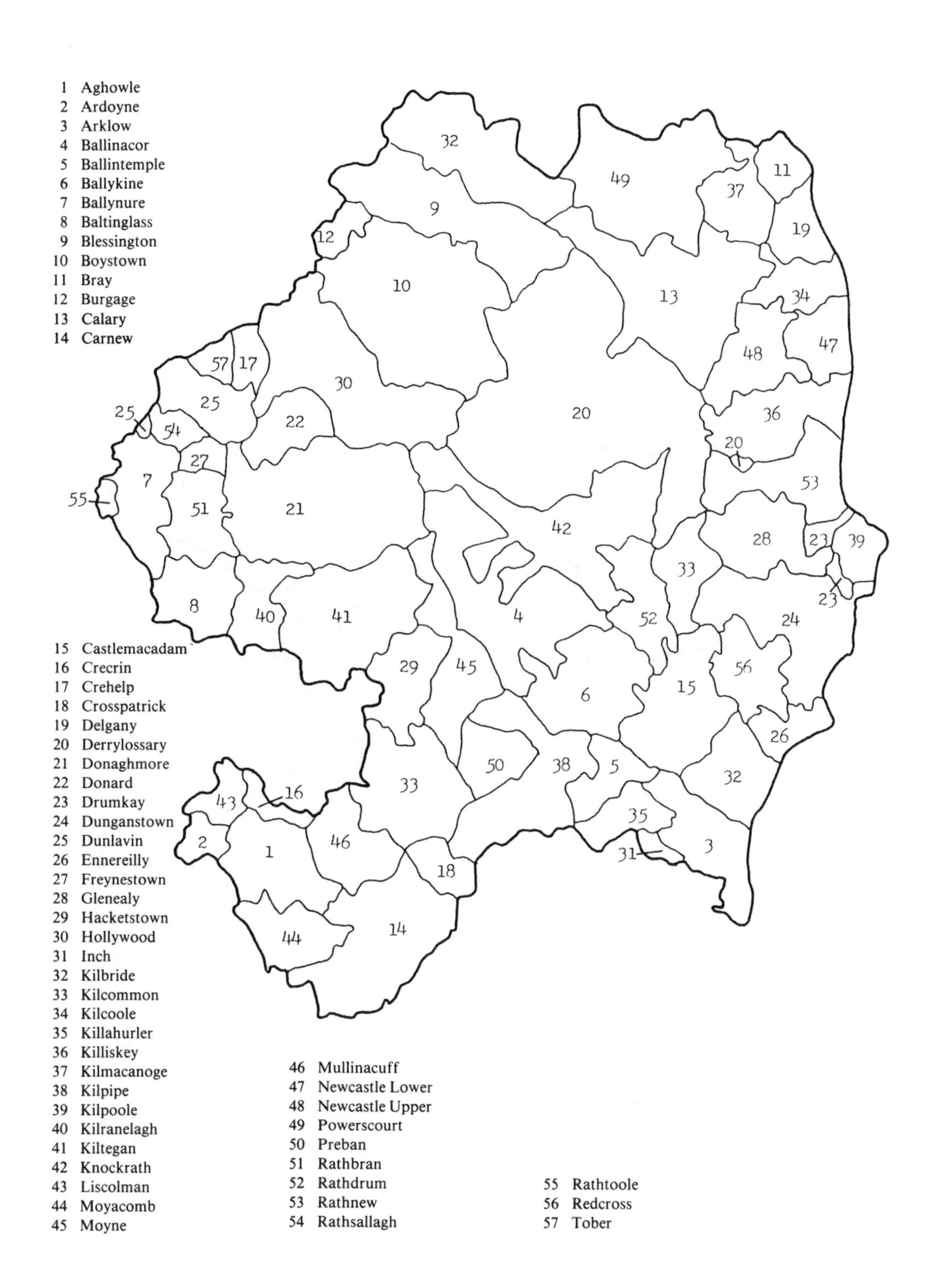

THE BARONIES OF COUNTY WICKLOW

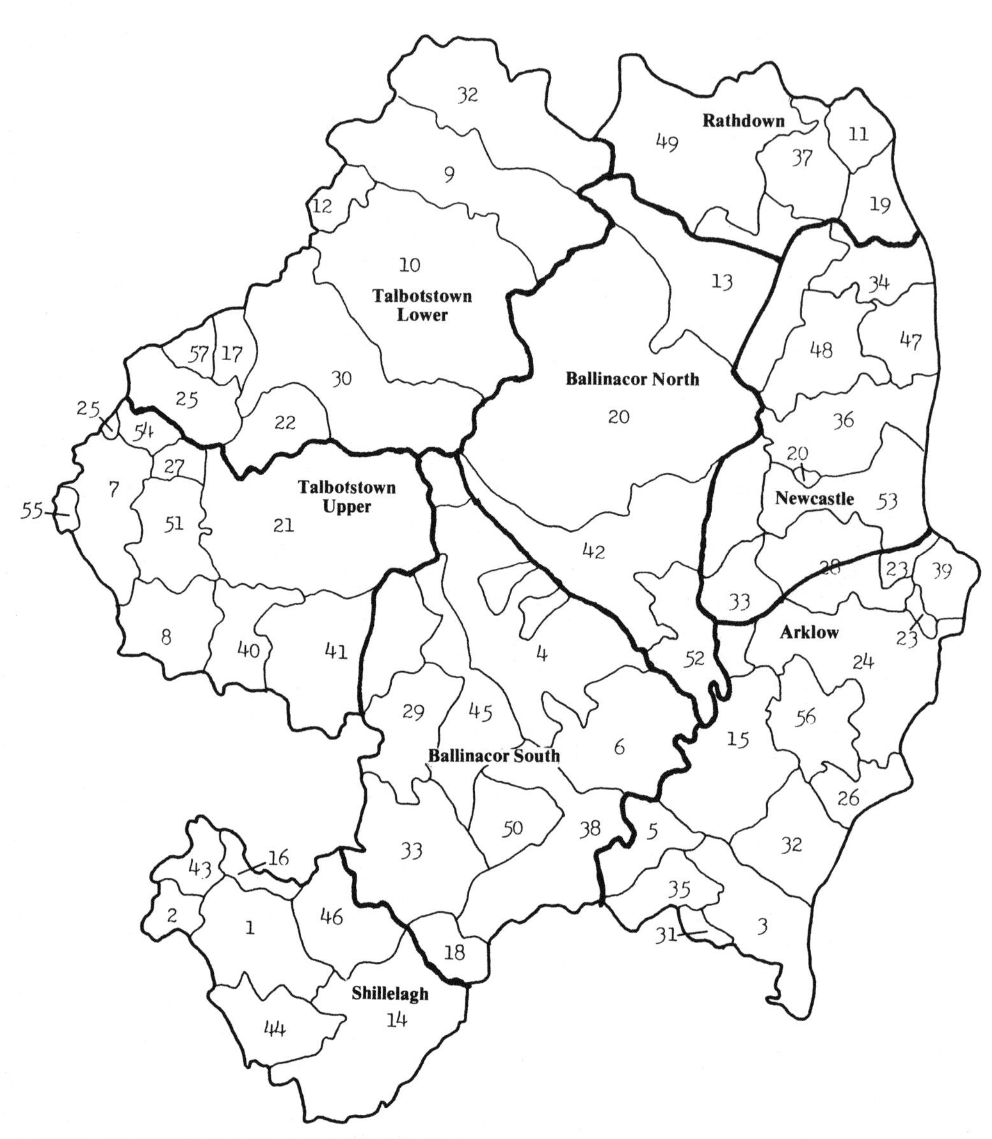

THE DIOCESES OF COUNTY WICKLOW

DUBLIN: Baronies of Arklow, Newcastle, Ballinacor North, Rathdown & Talbotstown Lower; 4, 6, 21, 25, 27 & 54

FERNS: 14, 18, 33, 38, 44 & 50

LEIGHLIN: 1, 2, 7, 8, 16, 29, 40, 41, 43, 45, 46 & 51

KILDARE: 55

THE POOR LAW UNIONS OF COUNTY WICKLOW

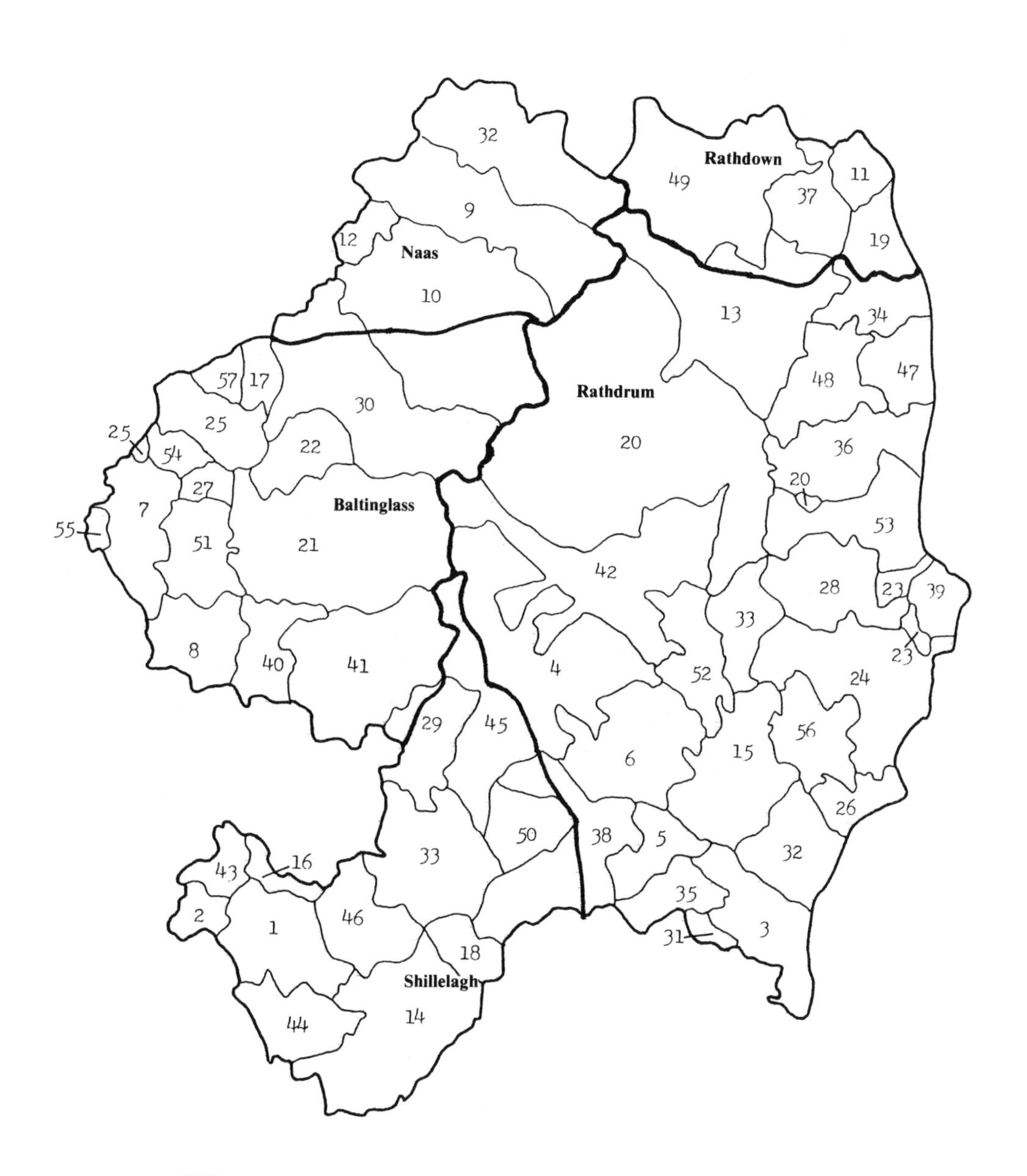

THE PROBATE DISTRICTS OF COUNTY WICKLOW

DUBLIN: All parishes